PENGUIN BOOKS

THE COURT AT WINDSOR

G000269475

Christopher Hibbert was born in Leicestershire in 1924 and educated at Radley and Oriel College, Oxford. He served as an infantry officer with the London Irish Rifles during the war, was twice wounded, and was awarded the M.C. in 1945. Described by Professor J.H. Plumb as 'a writer of the highest ability' and in the *New Statesman* as 'a pearl of biographers', he has established himself as a leading popular historian whose works reflect meticulous scholarship. His much acclaimed books include *The Destruction of Lord Raglan* (which won the Heinemann Award for Literature in 1962); *The Making of Charles Dickens*; *Benito Mussolini*; *London: The Biography of a City*; *George IV, Prince of Wales, 1762–1811*; *George IV, Regent and King, 1812–1830*; *The Rise and Fall of the House of Medici*; *The Great Mutiny: India 1857*; and, most recently, *The French Revolution*. Christopher Hibbert is married with three children, and lives at Henley-on-Thames.

Penguin Books

Christopher Hibbert

The Court at Windsor   *A Domestic History*

For Kate

Penguin Books Ltd, Harmondsworth, Middlesex, England
Penguin Books, 625 Madison Avenue, New York, New York 10022, U.S.A.
Penguin Books Australia Ltd, Ringwood, Victoria, Australia
Penguin Books Canada Ltd, 2801 John Street, Markham, Ontario, Canada L3R 1B4
Penguin Books (N.Z.) Ltd, 182–190 Wairau Road, Auckland 10, New Zealand

First published by Longmans Green & Co. Ltd 1964

This revised edition first published by Allen Lane 1977

Published in Penguin Books 1982

Copyright © Christopher Hibbert, 1964
All rights reserved

Made and printed in Great Britain by
The Fakenham Press Ltd, Norfolk
Composition in Monophoto Photina by
Filmtype Services Limited,
Scarborough, North Yorkshire

Designed by Gerald Cinamon

Author's Note 6

I. NORMANS AND PLANTAGENETS
1. Fortress and Feasting Hall 9
2. Knights of the Garter 15
3. Knights for the Body 25

II. TUDORS
1. The New Apollo and His Children 33
2. Queen Elizabeth I 42

III. STUARTS
1. James I 48
2. Charles I 55
3. Charles II 59
4. James II 77
5. William III and Mary II 79
6. Anne 82

IV. HANOVERIANS
1. George III — The Royal Farmer 89
2. George III — The Royal Patient 108
3. George IV — The *Cottage Orné* 124
4. George IV — The Gothic Castle 135
5. William IV — The Respectable Old Admiral 148

V. VICTORIANS
1. Victoria — The Young Queen 154
2. Victoria — The Widow at Windsor 180

VI. EDWARDIANS
1. Edward VII — 'A Very Bad Boy' 196
2. Edward VII — 'L'Oncle de l'Europe' 201

VII. WINDSORS
1. George V 213
2. Edward VIII 219
3. George VI 222
4. Elizabeth II 225

Bibliography 232
List of Illustrations and Acknowledgements 235
Index 237

AUTHOR'S NOTE

This is a book about private lives and the castle and lodges at Windsor in which they were led. No attempt has been made to examine constitutional or political problems; and very little space has been devoted either to architectural details or to the development of the Court. Every monarch from William I to Elizabeth II is mentioned in the book, but only those who have spent long periods at Windsor are discussed at length; and then it is with their personalities, interests, pleasures and with their daily routine that I have been principally concerned.

Most of the books from which I have quoted are by authors long since dead. Of more recent writers of memoirs, letters and diaries I am particularly grateful to Mabel, Countess of Airlie; Lady Diana Cooper; the Marchioness Curzon of Kedleston; Consuelo Vanderbilt Balsan; Georgiana, Baroness Bloomfield; the Duke of Windsor; Reginald, Viscount Esher; the third Baron Ormathwaite; Lord Ribblesdale; Mohamed Shah, Aga Khan and Sir Frederick Ponsonby whose books are listed in the bibliography.

The quotations from Fanny Burney's letters are from Charlotte Barrett's edition published in 1904; those from Mrs Papendiek's journal from Mrs Vernon Delves Broughton's edition published in 1887; those from Lady Lyttelton's letters from the Hon. Mrs Hugh Wyndham's edition published in 1912; those from the Hon. Eleanor Stanley from Mrs Steuart Erskine's edition published in 1916; and that from the diaries of Colonel the Hon. Fulke Greville from F. McKno Bladon's edition published in 1930. The edition of Charles Greville's diary which I have used is the one published by Macmillan in 1938 and edited by Roger Fulford and Lytton Strachey; and the edition of Miss Knight's autobiography that published by William Kimber in 1960, also edited by Roger Fulford.

Princess Lieven's letters to Prince Metternich are from *The Private Letters of Princess Lieven*, edited by Peter Quennell for John Murray (1948); and the letters to the Duchess of Manchester from *My Dear Duchess*, edited by A. L. Kennedy also for John Murray (1956). *The Journal of Mrs Arbuthnot* was edited by Francis Bamford and the Duke of Wellington and published by Macmillan (1950).

The description of George IV by Queen Victoria is from *The Letters of Queen Victoria* (1st Series) edited by A. C. Benson and Lord Esher (1908) and Lord Randolph Churchill's letter to his father about Edward VII and Queen Alexandra from *Lord Randolph Churchill* by Winston Churchill (1907).

What knowledge I have acquired and imparted about the architectural history of the castle comes almost entirely from W. H. St John Hope's monumental *Windsor Castle* (published in two volumes by

Country Life in 1913) and from Sir Owen Morshead's *Windsor Castle* (Phaidon Press, 1957).

I have to acknowledge the gracious permission of Her Majesty the Queen to reproduce prints, drawings and paintings in her private collections.

For their help in a variety of ways I also thank Mrs Joan St George Saunders of Writers' and Speakers' Research, Mrs Peter Crane, Mrs Stephen O'Malley, the Hon. Georgina Stonor, Mr Roger Fulford, Professor Arthur Aspinall, Miss Scott-Elliot and my wife. I am particularly grateful to Miss Olwen Hedley, on whose unrivalled knowledge of the castle's history I have been able to call, for her kindness in having read the manuscript.

C.H.

Eſtanglia hʒ in comitatꝰ vidm̄ · ʒ · north
folchia · ſouthfolchia · grāteb̄ · ʒ ꝯunidm̄
bedford · Et duos Epatꝰ · norwicenſem
ʒ Elyenſe.
Regnm̄ northhūb̄a hʒ archiepm̄
Eboracenſe · Epm̄ dunhalmenſe ·
ʒ ꝯдnliſem.

Eſſexia hʒ epm̄ london · comitatꝰ heu

oriens

Eſtanglia   Eſſex   Regni amae hʒ

I

NORMANS AND PLANTAGENETS

1

FORTRESS AND FEASTING HALL

The earliest known drawing of the Castle. A bird's-eye view across the river from the north drawn in the fifteenth century and forming part of a composition depicting a ceremony in connection with the recently begun Eton College Chapel. King Edward VI and Queen Margaret, accompanied by bishops, can be seen kneeling before the altar in the temporary chapel in the lower part of the picture. Perhaps the King is presenting the College with some of the relics of the saints which are known to have come into its possession in the 1440s. After Eton College Chapel was completed, the small chapel, which can be seen in the upper part of the picture in the Lower Ward, was replaced by St George's Chapel on the orders of Henry VI's rival, Edward IV.

He came from the Devil, it was said of him, and to the Devil he would return. There was a legend that the blood of Satan himself ran through his veins and his sons did not deny it. 'Do not deprive us of our heritage,' they protested when stopped from fighting each other. 'We cannot help acting like devils.'

When he was angry their father, Henry II, the first of the Angevin kings, would throw himself to the floor, and grind the rushes that covered it between his teeth; and once in his rage he fell screaming out of bed and crammed his mouth with the stuffing of his mattress.

He could never bear to be still; he sat down only in his horse's saddle or when he had to eat, and he always ate impatiently without apparent pleasure. All his business he transacted standing up, walking backwards and forwards on strong, bowed legs, cleaning or mending his hunting gear. Even during Mass, which he attended daily, he fidgeted and talked in a harsh, cracked voice, and scratched himself and scribbled orders, notes and messages. After a whole day spent riding or walking so hard that his legs and feet were covered in sores and blisters, he would stay up half the night talking and arguing. He had more learning than any other European king of his time and he was constantly increasing it. Yet he never seemed tired nor ever satisfied.

He was short and rather fat and a big hard round head, with reddish hair cropped very short, grew out of a neck like the neck of a bull. His grey eyes were prominent and occasionally bloodshot and his hands were large and coarse. He hunted with such ferocious energy, he said, to keep his weight down; but one of the chroniclers at his Court thought it was to dispel his erotic dreams. His sexual appetite surprised even his contemporaries.

His Court, though, was almost oriental in its complete seclusion from female influences. And it was, indeed, not a Court that held much appeal for most women, for it was so often and so uncomfortably on the move; while the food provided was apparently almost inedible. The bread, grumbled Peter of Blois, was 'not neaded, nor leavened, made of the dregs of beer; bread like lead, full of bran and unbaked'. The wine was 'thick, greasy and rancid' and tasted of pitch. 'I have sometimes seen wine so full of dregs put before noblemen,' he went on, 'that they were compelled rather to filter than to drink it, with their eyes shut and teeth closed. The beer at court is horrid to taste and filthy to look at. On account of the great demand, meat is sold whether it be fresh or not. The fish one buys is four days old, yet the fact that it stinks does not lessen the price.'

But to the King neither food nor comfort was important. He seemed to despise them both in his anxiety to keep moving and never to waste time. Impatient, energetic, industrious and wary, he was not a man to trust others to do things he could do himself. He had possessions abroad as well as in England and his marriage, two years before he became King in 1154, to Eleanor of Aquitaine, the divorced wife of Louis VII, greatly extended them. A strong taste as well as a real talent for legislation and administration urged on his restless nature to govern these possessions, as his son John was to try to govern them, by direct and personal rule. And so the long straggling lines of horses and pack animals, the wagons and carriages of the royal household became a familiar sight on the roads of England.

There were many animals and carts, for it was not only a household on the move but a government, not only the court of a king but of a man who had to prove himself a king. The most powerful officers of the Crown were also, when the King needed them to be, members of his peripatetic household, with household duties to perform and with stipulated allowances of food, wine and perquisites. The poulterers and fruiterers, the bakers, cooks and confectioners who prepared this food and the servitors who served it, the butlers who looked after the wine and the Keepers of the Cups who poured it out, the Usher of the Spithouse and the Keeper of the Dishes, the Master Steward of the Larder and the Workmen of the Buttery, all had to travel when the King travelled. Nor was it only the staffs of the kitchen, the buttery, the larder and the spithouse who had to do so. Chaplains, clerks, limners, ushers, lawyers, hornblowers, watchmen, guards, archers and huntsmen, Cat Hunters and Wolf Catchers, Keepers of Gazehounds and Keepers of Brachs, all had to follow the Court. There had to be a Keeper of the Tents and a Chamberlain of the Candles, a washerwoman to wash the King's clothes and a water-carrier to give him his bath. And rumbling along over the rough roads, in clouds of dust in summer, splashing through the mud in winter, were the wagons and pack animals, the horses and the oxen, with their bundled bags and leather pouches, their barrels of silver pennies, their boxes of jewels, their documents and kitchen utensils, hunting-spears and altar cloths, chalices, quills and parchment, tables and feather beds, chamber pots and scent bottles.

Riding along beside and behind this royal caravan were all sorts of scholars and artists as well as 'actors, singers, dicers, confectioners, huxters, gamblers, buffoons and barbers', and hurrying along ahead of it were express messengers whose duty it was to give warning of its approach and to advise the owners or tenants of estates on the route to collect provisions or to provide accommodation. In the week before Christmas 1184 these express messengers were riding to Windsor.

*

The castle was by then already a massive structure whose walls, built of immensely thick slabs of heath-stone, were commanded by a dominating tower in which the archers, looking through their high arrow-slits, could see for miles across the river valley to the south and west, and to the north as far as the hills of Buckinghamshire.

The site, covering about thirteen acres in the Manor of Clewer, had been chosen by Henry's great-grandfather, William I, who, attracted by a position at the top of a steep hill high above the river, from which a subject and unfriendly people could be constantly reminded of their

Probable arrangement of the Norman earthwork.

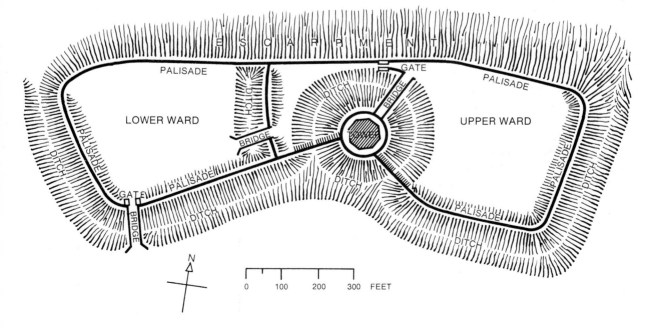

intimidating Norman conquerors, had built a fortress there to close a ring of other fortresses that secured the safety of his chosen capital in London.

Round the summit of this hill, except on the northern side where the sheer slope up from the river made it unnecessary, and from north to south across it, Norman soldiers and native labourers had dug a deep ditch; and the earth and chalk removed had been thrown up to make a high mound in the middle of the hill's crest. The quadrangular baileys or wards formed on either side of the mound were protected by the ditch on three sides and the escarpment on the fourth. Beyond the ditch a palisade of felled trees, whose branches had been lopped off and whose ends had been sharpened to points, followed the line of a rampart of earth and stones. The fortification was approached by means of the drawbridge in the south-western corner (in the position now occupied by King Henry VIII Gate) and the Upper Ward was approached from the Lower by means of another drawbridge across the ditch which divided them and through a gate placed between the bottom of the mound and the edge of the escarpment. The Upper Ward was, therefore, the safer and it was accordingly here that the King's houses developed.

The castle became for William I, though, as for most of his successors, a great deal more than a fortress. For around it, farther than the eye could stretch, lay a vast expanse of uncultivated country of heath and forest where wild oxen and boars, red and fallow deer, foxes, wolves and hares, roamed and ran, bred and multiplied beneath skies alive with the movement of birds. The Saxon kings had hunted there. And William I and his two sons, William II and Henry I, all followed their example, hunting by day and returning at night to their new castle on the hill. They enclosed tracts of woodland and appointed a parker; they instituted a system of fines for tenants on the royal demesne who failed to drive their deer for them; they built kennels for the royal hounds and mews for the royal falcons; and so Windsor became for the Norman kings a place of pleasure as well as of defence.

The new buildings that developed inside the palisade were for the most part still of wood. There were huts for the soldiers of the garrison and for the huntsmen and falconers; there were gatehouses by the drawbridges; there were stables; there were cages for prisoners; there were secret subterranean passages to provide outlets in time of siege; there was a great hall and a kitchen; there were houses for the king and his court; and there must have been — although nothing remains to indicate its position — a chapel, for the Bishop of Salisbury insisted that it was his right and not the Archbishop of Canterbury's to marry Henry I to his second Queen there in 1121. But there was very little masonry until Henry II, in the twelfth year of his reign, having rescued England from the chaos into which the civil war of Stephen's time had plunged it, began an ambitious building programme which was to last for six years.

Hard heath-stone blocks were brought up from quarries near Bagshot; lead for the roofs was brought down three hundred miles from Cumberland; workmen were brought from wherever they could be found. Soon large buildings developed in the Upper Ward, stone walls stretched for half a mile, and an immense stone tower was built on the artificial mound which had now settled firmly enough to bear its great weight.

By 1184 when the King came to Windsor for the Christmas holidays, the new castle was a home as well as one of the most powerful strongholds in England. Henry did not, of course, have either the time or the temperament to use it as a home. Nor did his son Richard I, a tall, commanding, gifted homosexual of savage and cruel temper, immense courage and churlish arrogance, who was preoccupied with plans to rescue the holy places from the infidel and to secure his Continental possessions from French attack. But Richard's youngest brother John who succeeded him in 1199 was a frequent visitor at Windsor.

A man with his father's restless energy and ruthless determination to govern his kingdom personally, John rarely stayed long and never for more than a week. His visits, though, were memorable events, for his tastes, unlike his father's, were far from frugal, while his love of hunting was quite as intense. When he came to the castle to enjoy the pleasures of hunting in the forest and hawking along the banks of the river, he took pains to ensure that his guests were lavishly entertained. At Christmas in 1213 the sheriffs of the surrounding counties were ordered to send to Windsor 2,000 capons, 15,000 herrings, 1,000 eels, 1,000 pounds of almonds and 6,000 gallons of wine, as well as quantities of spices, wagonloads of wood and coal, pitchers, cups and dishes, and rolls of cloth for his tailor to make up into towels and table-napkins and into new surcoats for his loyal knights.

The provision of clothes, as well as sport and entertainment, for these knights was, indeed, one of John's most regular expenses. And it was necessary that this should be so. For, having 'the mental abilities of a great King, but the inclinations of a petty tyrant', John had alienated most of those who might otherwise have supported him and was driving the feudal classes to revolt. In 1215 he was forced to open negotiations with the representatives of these classes at Runnymede, an island in the Thames four miles downstream from Windsor, and to approve a Great Charter renouncing his ambitions for a personal dictatorship. Each evening, after the long and aggravating discussions of the day, it is said that he rolled on the floor in his rage, in the characteristic Angevin manner, clawing at the air, gnawing sticks and straw, his face mottled with blue spots.

He signed the Charter, but only to deny its validity; and civil war broke out. The castle, however, defended by Engelard de Cicogné, its energetic constable, withstood all the onslaughts that were made upon it. The great tower and the high stone walls were pounded for nearly three months by the immense balls thrown at it by the besiegers' *perrière*, the beam of which was twice cut in half by Engelard's raiding parties, who crept out at night through the secret passages which led into the castle ditch. Several buildings were reduced to rubble, but the main defences held firm; and at the end of September 1216 the siege was abandoned.

Not until the Great Rebellion was the castle that John had 'loved above all others' attacked again. And for a hundred years, throughout the reigns of his son Henry III, of his grandson Edward I and of his great-grandson Edward II, Windsor Castle, growing and changing all the time, provided a background for the pleasures and business of a royal court and a setting for royal charity, rather than a stronghold for a threatened royal garrison. New towers, no longer square but D-shaped (since the experience of the Crusaders had revolutionized the science of military architecture) were built into the outer wall,

Edward III and the first Knights of the Garter. It is probable that the Garter was originally no more than a badge worn by two teams of twelve Knights, one team led by the King, the other by the Black Prince, during the tournament held at Windsor in the spring of 1348. This would explain why some of the earliest Knights were very young and almost unknown as soldiers, while other more distinguished Knights, who had fought in the recent war, were not at first elected.

for the castle, like all others, had still to have the strength and appearance of a fortress and had still to contain a strong garrison whose service to the Crown was accepted as an alternative to service in the field. But behind those towers and that faceless, threatening wall, a palace was taking shape — a palace with walls and towers gaily painted on the outside as well as within, with fine rooms overlooking fine gardens, and beyond the gardens a beautiful park where foreign visitors could be entertained with hunting parties and with tournaments. Windsor Castle was, in fact — so a chronicler said towards the end of the thirteenth century — the 'most magnificent palace that existed in all Europe'. And the entertainments that were given there were as renowned all over Europe as the buildings themselves.

No more splendid entertainment was given at Windsor than that in 1344 by Edward III who returned from his foreign wars with the intention of founding 'the greatest military Order in Christendom'.

2

KNIGHTS OF THE GARTER

Chivalry, Bishop Stubbs decided, was 'the gloss put by fine manners on vice and selfishness and contempt for the rights of man'. But for Edward III chivalry was far more than a gloss; it was an instrument of power. Handsome, brave, ambitious and self-indulgent, by turns revengeful and forgiving, flamboyantly pious without true religious feeling, of limitless energy and great physical strength, he was himself the epitome of the medieval knight. And it was by his successful appeal to the selfish instincts of the aristocratic classes that his triumphs were achieved. These classes did not want peace or retrenchment; they wanted the excitement and danger, the prestige and rewards of war. Edward, a fierce nationalism urging him to make France and Scotland dependent on England's will, was able to indulge them.

He gave them war and he shared with them the pleasures that followed war. They supported him because he was one of them; and no one knew better than he how strong are the bonds of friendship forged by pleasures shared. There is more than an element of propaganda in 'the most brilliant inspiration of the Age of Chivalry'.

This inspiration was not a sudden one. Towards the end of 1343, after defeating the Scots at Halidon Hill and destroying the French navy off Sluys, Edward went to his favourite castle at Windsor where he had been born thirty-one years before. Here he decided to hold a magnificent tournament, lasting four days, to which 'a great array of earls, barons, ladies and damoiselles' would be invited. The feast was to be 'most grand and noble with good cheer and good joustings'.

On 1 January 1344 letters of safe conduct were drawn up and sent out; and about three weeks later, from all over England as well as from 'parts beyond the seas', there came to Windsor 'an indescribable host of people to delight in so great a solemnity'. On the first evening the ladies were shown to their places in the great hall of the castle by the King himself, who arranged them according to their rank. His good and gentle wife Queen Philippa was there and his mother Queen Isabella and so many other 'countesses, baronesses, as well as ladies and gentlewomen' that they 'could not easily be counted'. There was, in fact, not enough room for the men to sit down with them and a tent had to be put up in the courtyard.

The meal was lavish, 'abounding in the most alluring of drinks', and as the guests ate and drank, minstrels wearing new tunics provided by the King specially for the occasion played music in the gallery. And afterwards, as a satisfied guest remembered, 'dances were not lacking, embraces and kissings alternately commingling'.

*

After the third day of the jousts at Windsor in 1344, the King, having himself won three of the six prizes, asked all his guests to remain in the castle until the following morning as he had an announcement to make. And when he came out of his chapel after Mass on Thursday morning nobody could doubt that the announcement would be an important one. He was wearing a cloak of 'very precious velvet and the royal crown was placed upon his head' and the royal sceptre was in his hand. The Earl of Derby, Seneschal of England, and the Earl of Salisbury, Marshal of England, went before him, and the Prince of Wales, later to be known as the Black Prince, and the Queen, stout and rather plain but 'most nobly adorned', followed him.

'At the place appointed for the assembly' the King solemnly placed his hand upon the Bible and 'took a corporeal oath that he would begin a Round Table in the same manner and conditions as the Lord

I

Edward IV
*A painting on panel by
an unknown artist,
probably done from life when
the King was about thirty years old.*

A choir stall with plates
of the Knights of the Garter
The oldest plates are enamel on gilt
or silvered copper and were brought
into St George's Chapel
from the previous chapel of the Order
in the reign of Richard III.
Between the seventeenth and early
twentieth centuries the coats of arms
were usually painted on copper.
Since 1908 enamel has been used
once more.

Arthur, formerly King of England, appointed it, namely to the number of 300 knights, a number always increasing, and he would cherish it and maintain it according to his power'.

The Round Table was one of chivalry's most treasured legends and purest ideals. By the time of Edward III it had admittedly come to mean little more than an association of knights who met from time to time, as Roger Mortimer's friends had done at Kenilworth, to joust during the day and to feast at night, sitting with their shields at their backs, at a table which set aside all distinctions of rank and quality, every place equally honourable. But as originally conceived by King Arthur — whose miraculous exploits in the sixth century were already the legends of a forgotten age — the Round Table was an expression of the eternal principles of knighthood. The knights of the first Round Table were bound, in the words of Sir Thomas Malory, 'never to do outrageousity, nor murder, and always to flee treason. Also by no means to be cruel, but to give mercy unto him that asketh mercy . . .; and always to do ladies, damsels, and gentlewomen succour upon pain of death.' This conception of the true knight's obligations to behave as a noble and gentle man was a real step forward into the light out of the shadows of the Dark Ages; and, although the knight did not in fact often live up to his high ideals, and although chivalry itself was dying in Edward III's time, in the face of the rising power of those outside the aristocratic class and in the choking smoke of gunpowder, the King's announcement at Windsor that January morning was an attempt to restore to the Round Table its early ideals and *mystique*.

It was also, of course, an excuse to bind his supporters more closely to his cause, and it was an excuse for further festivities.

Indeed, as soon as the oaths were taken, binding the knights to each other and to the service of the weak and the wronged, the trumpets and kettle drums sounded 'all together, and the guests hastened to a feast; which feast was complete with richness of fare, variety of dishes, and overflowing abundance of drinks: the delight was unutterable, the comfort inestimable, the enjoyment unalloyed, the hilarity without care'.

*

Within a few days, work began on a circular building in the great courtyard of the Upper Ward in which the feasts of the Round Table could, in future, regularly be held. The bridges over the castle ditch were covered with sand and heather to protect them from the wheels of the heavy wagons which were to come rumbling across with loads of stone and timber; and the King's carpenter and mason and their deputies were sent out as far afield as Kent and Norfolk with letters authorizing them to collect materials, to impress workmen and to 'arrest and take as often as there may be need' all punts on the Thames between Gravesend and Henley.

By the beginning of March over seven hundred men had been brought to Windsor where they were kept hard at work for five weeks. But then, as suddenly as it had begun, the activity ceased. A fortnight before Easter nearly all the men were sent away and by the autumn the building of the great feasting hall was abandoned altogether.

For the King was at war again. He had decided that 'much treasure must be got together for other affairs', and he could no longer afford the weekly wages bill and the cost of the materials still required at Windsor. On a hot August day in 1346, however, he defeated the French army of Philip VI at Crécy, and two months later various northern lords who were not serving with him in France routed the Scots at Neville's Cross and captured the young King David, afterwards sending him to Windsor Castle where so many other distinguished prisoners had been and were to be held. The following year, after a long siege, Calais was captured and Edward could return home once more in triumph to revel in his plunder.

He had never appeared more happy, more confident, or more successful. 'A new sun seemed to have risen in England' when he and his friends came back to Windsor, with clothes and furs and feather beds and the spoils of foreign cities, to abandon themselves to pleasure and to 'many deeds of love and nobleness, of pleasantry and of prowess'. The wild extravagance of their celebrations seemed, however, to some chroniclers wickedly wanton. Women paraded themselves in expensive dresses 'without thought of the French ladies' from whom they had been looted; and others 'of the most beautiful, but not of the best of the kingdom' appeared in 'divers and wonderful male apparel', with chequered tunics and tight belts and with their hair bound up in turbans, to 'vex their bodies with scurrilous wantonness'.

For the King himself, though, continuous pleasure was never enough. The unfinished feasting hall for the knights of the Round Table, its walls covered by tiles to protect them from the frost, still stood in the Upper Ward to remind him of his obligations as a knight and as a leader and sovereign of knights. And soon his restless ambition drove him to consider a far greater enterprise 'more particular and more select'.

*

The early statutes of the Order of the Garter have been lost, and for centuries men have speculated as to its origins. The most pleasant and romantic story is well known. It is that the King was dancing at a ball with Joane, Countess of Salisbury, when her garter fell off. Edward stooped down quickly and picked it up. Some of the other dancers saw him do so and began to tease him. He replied sharply, *'Honi soit qui mal y pense'* and added, when they continued laughing and snatching the garter out of each other's hands, that in a short time they should 'see the garter advanced to so high honour and estimation, as to account themselves happy to wear it'.

Edward III from the effigy at Westminster Abbey, c. 1378, probably cast by John Orchard.

The earliest authority for this traditional story is Polydore Vergil, who did not arrive in England until the next century. The chronicles of Jean Froissart, the Flemish courtier who came to Edward III's Court with a letter of introduction from the Court of Hainault, Queen Philippa's uncle, do not mention it.

The story, in fact, came to be dismissed as a 'vain and idle romance derogatory both to the founder and to the Order'. And Elias Ashmole, the seventeenth-century antiquary, whose history of the Order remains the most authoritative, thought it a 'vulgar' invention. Ashmole recorded another legend – although he thought it equally unfounded – which suggested that it was the Queen's garter which slipped from her leg as she was going to her room and that the King, after telling an attendant to pick it up, said to him, 'You make but small account of this garter, but within a few months I will cause the best of you all to reverence the like.' The motto, according to this legend, was the Queen's answer to the King's question as to what men would think of her losing a garter so indecorously.

There was a legend, too, that Richard I had once inspired some of his fellow Crusaders, worn out by days of fighting in the burning sun, to further efforts by tying round their legs, with his own hands, a leather thong to remind them that he relied upon them for the 'successful conclusion of his noble enterprise'. Ashmole concluded, however, that it was not Richard I in the Holy Land but Edward III himself at Crécy who had used the symbol of the Garter, as being one of 'unity and society', to encourage his knights on the battlefield and afterwards to reward them for their victory. The motto, Ashmole believed, was intended as a reflection of shame upon those who did not think well of his determination to gain the French crown by force of arms, and a later historian of the Order has supported this view.

In more recent years, however, Dr Margaret Murray put forward a quite different and startlingly original theory. It was her belief that in Edward III's time Christianity had not yet overthrown the old religion of witches and devil-worshippers and that the garter was a symbol of deep significance in that old religion. 'The confusion of the Countess,' she wrote, 'was not from the shock to her modesty – it took more than a dropped garter to shock a lady of the fourteenth century – but the possession of that garter proved that she was not only a member of the Old Religion but that she held the highest place in it.' Edward III's words on picking it up, Dr Murray thought, were to indicate to his guests that he understood the garter's significance and that he, too, was a devotee of the old religion.

While this view of the Order's origin has not found wide acceptance, it does not seem necessary to turn back to a specifically military origin. A garter certainly represented, as Ashmole said, a 'badge of unity and concord'; but it was also the sort of favour which was not only worn by knights at a tournament as a compliment to their ladies – and was constantly used by Edward III himself for this romantic purpose – but which frequently became the device of medieval orders of chivalry.

The most recent research suggests that Edward III's dancing partner did drop her garter. She has been satisfactorily identified as Joane, Countess of Salisbury, in Froissart's opinion, *'la plus belle dame de tout la roiaulme d'Engleterre, et la plus amoureuse'*. She was probably Chaucer's model for the heroine of *Troilus and Criseyde*, and she married Edward III's son, the Black Prince, in 1361.

Recent research also supports Sir Harris Nicolas's argument that the garter was originally no more than a badge worn by two teams of twelve knights, one team led by the King, the other by the Black Prince, during the tournament held at Windsor in the spring of 1348. And certainly the men chosen to be the first members of the Order lend weight to this theory, for some of them were very young and almost unknown as soldiers, while more distinguished knights, who had fought well in the recent war, were not at first elected.

There were never to be more than twenty-five knights in all, with the King as Sovereign of the Order, for its exclusiveness, Edward decided, would be its guarantee of worth and nobility – a nobility to be enhanced by the splendour of its robes. The colour of these robes was to be blue, the colour of the arms of France, and they were all to

The Regalia of the Garter. The collar was gold, of thirty ounces troy weight, with a bejewelled image of St George, the martyred hero of the early Christian Church who (with the Holy Trinity, the Blessed Virgin Mary and Edward the Confessor) was one of the Order's patrons. The Lesser George (depicted beneath the Sovereign's Mantle) was worn on a silk ribbon on the breast or, after this position was altered by Charles II, under the right arm. The Garter itself was worn on the left leg a little below the knee.

be alike, for the equality of the Round Table was to be faithfully observed. The Sovereign's mantle, made of fine woollen cloth, 'to give a reputation to that homebred and native Commodity', was, however, unlike the others, to have a long train; and his surcoat, as well as being lined with miniver, as were those of the other knights, was to be bordered with ermine.

In time the style of the robes changed and became more elaborate than ever, and the materials from which they were made became richer and more rare. Mantles in the fifteenth century were made of velvet and lined with white damask. Surcoats were powdered all over with little garters of silk and gold plate, carrying the Order's motto delicately embroidered in each. It became customary to embroider a larger garter on the left shoulder and to attach long silk cords to the collar. The hood was replaced by a cap of black velvet which later became a high crowned hat with a brim tacked up with immense jewels and a plume of white feathers, 'a stately Heron's feather rising in the middle' and then it returned once more to its present shape of a sixteenth-century cap. Eventually a collar of gold, of thirty ounces troy weight, with a bejewelled image of St George, the martyred hero of the early Christian Church who was one of the Order's patrons, was added to the robes; and another image, known as the Lesser George, was worn on a silk ribbon before the breast and, after this position was altered by Charles II, under the right arm. The garter itself, worn on the left leg a little below the knee, also became more elaborate as the years passed.

Although it was originally the Sovereign himself who bore much of the heavy costs incurred by English as well as foreign knights, paying for their surcoats as well as for the robes of those of their ladies who were received into the Order as *Dames de la Fraternité de St George*, the more elaborate the robes and insignia grew and the less the Sovereign contributed towards them, the more expensive it became to be elected to the Order. Nor did the expense end with these cloaks of silk and fur and velvet, these lavishly jewelled images and garters, these plumed hats with their cascades of rubies and pearls and diamonds; for each knight had to provide a helm, crest and sword to be hung up over his stall in the chapel of the Order. The helm, larger than the real one upon which it was modelled, was to be of steel 'parcel gilt with fine Gold in Oyle, wrought with Rabeskys and other works, and burnished with fine Gold'. The mantlings were to be cloth of gold lined with sarcenet, and beneath them gilt knobs had to be placed on which could hang tassels of gold and silver intertwined with silk of the main colour of the knight's arms. The pommel, cross and chape of his sword had to be gilded and the scabbard had to be of cloth of gold. Embroidered banners became obligatory later.

*

For the first century and a half of the Order's history, the Knights' banners were displayed in the chapel which was built in 1240 by Henry III, who had personally supervised the painting of it, and which was later repaired by Edward III who also provided for the maintenance of twenty-four Poor Knights, 'impotent of themselves or inclining to poverty', who would daily attend Mass and pray for the souls of the Knights of the Garter.

Although excused by these poor proxies from daily attendance to pray for their own souls, the Knights of the Garter were, however, required to celebrate a set number of Masses whenever one of their number died. The number laid down for the King, as Sovereign of the Order, was one thousand, and the rule was, it seems, constantly observed until the reign of Henry VIII, when the Masses were compounded for a money compensation, ranging from £8 6s. 8d. for the Sovereign to 16s. 8d. for a Bachelor Knight. It was intended that the money handed over by the Knights should be devoted to charity and public works, but there was apparently always difficulty in collecting it. In the reign of Charles I, however, a considerable sum was collected. It was spent, though, not in the way originally intended but on the provision of new plate for the chapel altar.

By then the College of St George was not nearly so rich as it once had been and could not perhaps otherwise have afforded the large sum involved. From its foundation the College had been endowed with lands and advowsons and freed from the payment of many taxes; and as the years passed many private grants had been made to it. But some of these grants were no more profitable than that made by the Corporation of Yarmouth which, on consideration that the Corporation were 'taken into their prayers', allowed the Canons every year 'a last of red herrings, well dried and cleansed'. Also, since the Reformation, the College's most profitable source of income had ceased; for pilgrims no longer came to give offerings to its relics.

At one time these treasures had been numerous. In the fourteenth century, when faith in the power of relics of the earthly lives of Christ and his saints was still almost universal, they had included a thorn of Christ's crown, parts of his supper table, some of his mother's milk, and a piece of the Holy Cross which Edward I had been given by a former Crusader while campaigning in Wales.

In 1414 the collection was augmented by the Emperor Sigismund, brother-in-law to Richard II, who generously presented the very heart of St George together with his fingers. By the end of the century the body of the holy king, Henry VI, was also in the chapel having been sent there with some of his armour, clothes and other possessions by Richard III in 1484.

Badges commemorating pilgrimages to St George's Chapel. These badges, which were fixed by pilgrims to their hats, date from the end of the fifteenth and the beginning of the sixteenth century. They both show the figure of a king; the one below stands on an antelope.

These relics of Henry VI were amongst the chapel's most treasured possessions, and pilgrims came from as far away as Cornwall to worship at the tomb on which they were placed. 'Seely betwitched People' – so a contemptuous writer said, looking back with horrified disdain upon the 'late Tyme of general Darkness when no place was free from one Sorte of superstitious Mawmetrie or other' – flocked to 'this Churche of Wyndsore' being 'persuaded that a small Chippe of his Bedsteade (which was kept heare) was a precious Relique, and that to put upon a Man's Heade an olde red Velvet Hatte of his (that lay heare also) was a Sovereign Medicine against the Headache'.

Nor were the remains of Henry VI, although the most distinguished that the chapel possessed, the only ones that were revered by ailing pilgrims. For on the south side of the altar, opposite the tomb of Edward IV, who was buried in the chapel at his own request, lay the bones of John Schorne, a parish priest who, in addition to a remarkable ability to cure the ague, had also possessed the even more remarkable power of forcing the devil into a boot.

Strong iron money-boxes received the offerings of the pilgrims who came to worship at John Schorne's tomb. These boxes, still to be seen in St George's Chapel, were provided not only with numerous coin slots, but also with four different locks, a precaution which seemed justified. For, according to the Poor Knights, the behaviour of the Canons was outrageous. They misappropriated the donations and, having collected fines from the Poor Knights whenever they missed a Mass, they misappropriated the fines as well. Adorned in their gor-

The Gilbertus Door in St George's Chapel. Formerly the entrance to King Henry III's Chapel of 1240. The woodwork was originally covered with scarlet gesso. The wrought iron scroll work is signed by the smith, Gilbertus.

geous vestments and surrounded by the most lavish assortment of silver images, candlesticks, illuminated books, bells, jewelled chalices, staves, crosses, morses and paxes, they gabbled through their offices, and as soon as they had collected enough money, they went home. One of them spent the time of Mass gossiping with his neighbour, another was out most of the day hunting and fishing, a third was often to be found in bed with another man's wife.

The Poor Knights' charges were investigated by the Chancellor, who found there was much justice in them. He also found, though, that some of the Knights themselves were far from blameless and one at least, when he did attend Mass, was nearly always late, went to sleep immediately he got into the chapel, and could only with difficulty be aroused to receive the sacrament. Whether or not either side in the dispute was as lax or unscrupulous as the other suggested, it is at least certain that this fourteenth-century quarrel was the first of many and that until recent years the Poor Knights were frequently regarded as a troublesome and somewhat sordid appendage to an otherwise glorious Order.

Henry VIII did what he could to raise their standing and self-respect and in his will provided for thirteen additional Poor Knights who were to be given a shilling a day for ever and, once a year, 'a long gown of white cloth, with the Garter upon the breast, imbrothered with a shield and cross of St George within the Garter, and a mantle of red cloth'. By 1720, however, their total number had fallen to eighteen, and these forlorn old men as they walked to chapel twice a day, each from 'a little cell round the square', under the shadow of crumbling, ivy-covered and rook-infested walls, seemed to a visitor a sad reminder of those more splendid days when Edward III first chose the Garter as the symbol of his Most Noble Order.

3

KNIGHTS FOR THE BODY

As Edward III, senile at sixty-four, lay helpless in the room in which he was soon to die, talking of hunting and hawking, deserted by opportunist courtiers and in the end by his mistress, Alice Perrers, who waited only long enough to take the rings from his fingers before leaving him with a priest, the structure of society which he had so much admired and tried so hard to preserve was already crumbling.

The Black Death had carried off almost half his country's five million people, most of them poor labourers and their families; and the survivors soon learned the value of their labour. They demanded higher wages and were met by a statute which made it illegal for them to receive the increases. The braver amongst them marched on London and, having executed the King's Chancellor and his Treasurer and carried their heads through the streets on pikes, were met by promises which were immediately broken.

Quarrels between employer and employed, master and servant, landlord and tenant, had for long been exacerbated by statutes which, whatever the official reason for their enactment and however impossible it proved to enforce them, proclaimed the difference between the rich courtier and the ordinary man. Men were told what they might not eat and what they might not wear; but the regulations were openly ignored by the rich and in many cases were not even intended to apply to them, being directed against men who wore clothes unsuitable to their estate and against 'common lewd women' who presumed to dress like 'good noble dames and damsels'.

And yet the courtier in Edward III's time, and even more extravagantly in the time of his successor Richard II, dressed in a fashion as outrageously provocative as that of the early twelfth-century Norman courtier, who, according to William of Malmesbury, 'put on false tresses' and attempted 'to rival women in delicacy of person and to mince their gait'. The coat sleeves of the courtier at Windsor in Richard II's reign were tipped with fur and worn so long that they trailed on the ground; the points of his shoes were usually far longer than the feet themselves and had to be held up by gold chains stretched from the end of the toes to the knees; golden ribbons with wide bows were tied round his legs which were clothed in stockings of vividly contrasting colours; velvet bands were tied round hair that grew thick and long upon his shoulders; precious stones sparkled all over him and upon the rings which he wore round the fingers of his scented gloves. Even the clergy curled and powdered their hair, wore caps with tippets of a wonderful length, furred cloaks, chequered shoes, and knives in scabbards so long that they looked like the scabbards of swords.

The Queen, Anne of Bohemia, and her ladies wore horned and pearl-studded head-dresses of an astonishing size. And on Anne's death, the governess of Richard's second Queen, the nine-year-old Isabella of Valois, kept several goldsmiths and furriers constantly at work making her own dresses as lavish as her pupil's.

The meals at Court — ten thousand of which were served every day — were quite as sumptuous as the clothes. And so were the entertainments provided by the King's musicians, jugglers and comedians. The travelling players with their bawdy songs and comic or lascivious acts, were gradually replacing in the favour of the rich those reciting minstrels whose principal stocks in trade were a loud voice and a good memory. The versatile minstrels who could juggle and walk on a tight-rope, who were prepared to 'distort their bodies by lewd dance and gesture or strip themselves and put on horrible masks' were the ones most welcome in fourteenth-century households. Dwarfs and simpletons were always welcome, too; although most noble households had resident freaks and fools of their own.

These poor creatures, dressed in absurd particoloured clothes, sat at table with their owners, whose digestion was helped by the laughter evoked by their appearance and antics, by their inhuman sounds and uncoordinated, spastic movements. Freaks and simpletons also provided a butt for the coarse humour of the jester whose repertoire seems usually to have been limited to preposterous insults and practical jokes.

The wasteful extravagance of the royal household was prodigious. It continued long after the abdication of Richard II, until, in the next century, Edward IV, although well aware that splendour not only bolstered the royal authority but was 'an essential attribute of kingship itself', felt constrained to regulate the numbers of attendants at Court, which had grown to many hundreds, to limit their allowances, which had become a matter of dispute, and to establish rules for the observance of their duties, which had frequently been unperformed. He decided, in fact, as he put it himself, that he would have his goods 'dispended but not wasted'.

Ordinances, of course, had been issued before to regulate the conduct and ceremonial of the royal household; but they had never been strictly observed. The courts of Henry IV and Henry V were less lavish than those of their immediate predecessors, while that of Henry VI, a kind and studious man, who had been born at Windsor in 1421, was comparatively modest. Henry VI, founder of King's College, Cambridge, and of Eton, was a man preoccupied with religious observances and education. He loved to send for the scholars of Eton when he was at Windsor and, when still sane enough to do so, to give them his advice, to tell them to be 'good boys, gentle and teachable', and to forbid them to come to his Court lest 'the young lambs should come to relish the corrupt deeds and habits of his courtiers'. He himself certainly never came to relish the habits of his courtiers, and the story is told that 'at Christmas time a certain great lord brought before him a Dance or show of young ladies with bared bosoms who were to dance in that guise before the King . . . who very angrily averted his eyes, turned his back upon them, and went out to his chamber, saying "Fy, fy, for shame".'

Edward IV, a man of voracious sexual appetite, would never have objected to such performances. He did, however, object to the waste that Henry's weakness had allowed to continue in the royal household, a waste that was at least partly responsible for an increase in expenditure from £13,000 in 1433 to £24,000 in 1449. And so *The Black Book of the Household* was issued. In this book the rights and duties of all those who attended upon the King at Windsor and at his other royal palaces, from the Knights of the Body to the Servants of the Kitchen, were carefully stipulated. It was, though, far more than a measure to enforce an economy which the Crown's increasing financial problems had rendered necessary. In an age when the worth and power of men was judged by the grace and splendour of their hospitality, a king could not allow a subject to outdo him. A nobleman who entered London as the Earl of Warwick did, accompanied by six hundred attendants all wearing his livery and badge, was a real threat to the King's prestige. And foreign visitors – such as those who came over with the Queen of Bohemia's brother in 1466 and were entertained by the King at a dinner with fifty courses, and on subsequent days by two Earls who each provided them with sixty courses – were likely to remember and discuss this sort of evidence of the superior standards of seigniorial munificence. Nor was it only magnificence which was recognized as an important political instrument and social ideal. Courtly manners and etiquette, raised by symbolism and allegory to an esoteric art, were also regarded as essential to the preservation of order and respect in a competitive and ever-changing society.

Books on etiquette prescribed rules of behaviour which turned a meeting between two noblemen into a sort of ritualistic dance. The number of steps which hosts of varying ranks should take to greet their guests, for instance, and the number of times places of precedence should be offered to inferiors before their refusal of them was finally accepted, were laid down with as much elaboration as the rules for polite eating prescribed for princes and noble pages. These young men were advised – and clearly they needed some advice – that wine must not be drunk while the mouth was full of food; that the upper part of the body must not lean forward over the table with the head hanging over the dish; that neither the nose nor the teeth nor the nails must be picked at table; that salt should be put on the plate and not taken out of the cellar whenever required with a knife; that dirty soup spoons should not be put down on the tablecloth; that the knife must never be used to carry food to the mouth; and that when the meal was finished the guest must 'ryse uppe withoute lauhtere, japynge, or boystrous worde'.

The rules laid down by the *Black Book*, and the Ordinances which preceded and followed it, dealt with all this and more. They had to be extensive for the household was still an extensive one, the King's Chamber at Windsor alone, for example, being served by the attendance of more than four hundred men of varying rank presided over by the Lord Chamberlain. At the top of the hierarchy of attendants upon the King in his Chamber were the Knights for the Body who had tours of duty lasting eight weeks. These were followed by the King's Knights and the Squires for the Body. Then there were Squires for the Household, twenty of whom were required to serve each day at table, and Gentlemen Ushers who enforced the protocol and supervised the activities of the Yeomen of the Crown and the Yeomen of the Chamber, the message carriers and torch-bearers. Lastly came the Grooms of the Chamber and the Pages, young sons of noble families who combined

The choir stall plate of Ralph de Bassett. This, the earliest surviving plate in St George's Chapel, dates from the middle of the fourteenth century. Ralph de Bassett, 4th Lord Bassett of Drayton, fought under the Black Prince at the battle of Poitiers.

lessons in horsemanship and languages with more menial tasks, which included making sure that the dogs did not dirty the floors.

In the morning the King was dressed by the Squires for the Body, who had slept on truckle-beds in his room, and he was attended when eating breakfast, as at all meals, by twenty Squires for the Household and at least one Gentleman Usher. A Server, who was required to be 'ful cunyng' in the ceremonial of presenting the dishes, went to fetch the meat from the kitchen, accompanied by the Squires, and on his return asked the Ewer for a towel and a basin of water so that the King could wash when he had eaten. A 'Doctoure of Physyque' stood nearby to advise the King as to 'wich dyet is best according, and to the nature and operacion of all the metes'. And throughout the meal thirteen minstrels played in the gallery.

The regulations governing the making of the King's bed were even more elaborate than those laid down for feeding him. Two Squires for the Body stood at the head and two Grooms of the Chamber at the foot while a Yeoman of the Chamber carried in the bedclothes and a Gentleman Usher held back the curtains. The manner of putting on, shaking out and striking down the lower sheet was as minutely described as the way in which the fustian upper sheets and ermine counterpane were to be laid above it and then rolled down 'the space of an ell'. When the Yeomen had beaten the pillows well and thrown them to the Squires to place in position, the bed was to be sprinkled with holy water.

There was inevitably, of course, a wide difference between practice and precept, for Edward, intelligent and wonderfully energetic, was not a man to allow restricting codes of behaviour to interfere with his pleasures. Handsome, extremely tall, autocratic, and exuberantly sensual, he had married Elizabeth Woodville, universally considered of too humble an origin for a queen-consort, when he had failed to overcome her strong will and force her to accept him as her lover — by threatening her, so it was said, as he held a dagger to her throat — and he filled his Court with her relations. After his marriage he had countless mistresses, many of them from far humbler homes than his wife's, including Jane Shore, the wife of a London mercer, who was to lend her name to some of London's most squalid eighteenth-century brothels and flash-houses. When he and his Court went hunting at Windsor, no tiresome rules of precedence were allowed to spoil the atmosphere of gay abandon. 'Tables heavy with roasted meats and sugared dainties were stretched in the shade of the trees, and silken tents grew like gargantuan flowers on the lawns. The King and his courtiers glided on the Thames in gilded barges,' jousted and feasted, 'made love by moonlight and torchlight, rose at dawn to hear Mass, broke their fast with a mess of meat and ale, and quickly took horse to be beforehand of the sun in their pursuit of royal disports.' Edward's infectious enthusiasm and affable manner made him a delightful companion; and he made good use of these attributes not only in flattering courtiers and citizens whose wives he intended to seduce, but also in the entertainment of foreign visitors whose good opinion of him might help his cause. Louis de la Gruthuyse, Governor of Holland, for instance, who came to England in September 1472 and was entertained at Windsor Castle in the lavish manner which the opulent standards of the Court of Burgundy had made *de rigueur* in Europe, found Edward an entrancing host. One of the King's heralds, Bluemantle Pursuivant, wrote an account of the visit.

Louis was met inside the castle gate by Lord Hastings, the Chamberlain, who showed him to a set of chambers, hung with arras, where he and his servants had supper. When he had finished his meal, Lord Hastings took him to the King, who greeted him warmly and led him to Queen Elizabeth's rooms where he found her and her ladies-in-waiting playing *marteaux* — a game like bowls — and throwing balls at ivory ninepins. There were minstrels there and some of the ladies were dancing and the King took his eldest daughter in his arms and swung her round the room. She was seven then, and thirteen years later, after her two little brothers had been murdered in the Tower, she was to marry Henry, the first of the Tudor kings.

The following morning after Mass, which was 'melodyousely songe', the King gave Louis a present. It was a gold cup encrusted with pearls and with a big sapphire on the lid. Inside was a 'great Pece of an Vnicorne's horne', an antidote to poison. When breakfast was over Edward brought his baby son out into the courtyard to introduce him to the distinguished visitor and then the two men went out to hunt together in the Little Park. In the Park the King gave Louis another present, a crossbow, with a velvet-covered case bearing the royal arms, together with a set of gilt-headed arrows. They had little luck hunting, and before their midday meal, which was served in the lodge, they succeeded in killing only a single doe. But in the afternoon several deer were killed and half a dozen bucks which Edward gave to his guest. 'By that tyme yt was nere night, yett the Kinge shewed him his garden, and Vineyard of Pleasour, and so turned to the Castell ageyne, where they herde evensonge in their chambres.'

That night the Queen gave a banquet in her dining-room. At her table, with the King and Louis and her daughter Elizabeth, sat her sister the Duchess of Buckingham and her husband, her sister-in-law, Lady Rivers, and the King's sister, the Duchess of Exeter. Lower down the table were 'divers ladyes and certeyn nobles of the Kinges owen courte' including Lord Hastings and Lord Berners, Constable of the Castle. At a separate table, all sitting down the same side of it, was a 'great Vue' of other ladies; and in an outer room sat a long row of the Queen's gentlemen facing the servants of the foreign visitor. After dinner there was dancing and at 'aboute six of the clocke, the Kinge and the quene, wᵗ her ladies and gentlewomen, brought the sayde Lord Grautehuse to iii chaumbres of Pleasance, all hanged wᵗ Whyte Sylke and lynnen clothe, and alle the Floures covered wᵗ Carpettes'. Here, in the first silk-lined chamber, was a gorgeous bed with a soft down mattress, a cloth of gold canopy and curtains of white sarcenet; in the second chamber was a feather-stuffed sofa inside a tent; and in the third chamber were two baths each enclosed in tents of white cloth. When the King and Queen had shown him these chambers and provided him with dishes of green ginger and sugared sweets, with bottles of liqueurs and spice-flavoured wine, they left him to enjoy the pleasures of the bath, and of the bed.

The castle, in which these gracious and exciting entertainments were provided, had altered much since Edward III had died a hundred years before. In Edward's lifetime William of Wykeham, the founder of Winchester College and of New College, Oxford, who was appointed Surveyor of the King's Works in 1356, had organized the construction and completion of many 'fair and sumptuous' buildings, work on some of which had been abandoned during the time of the Black Death. And after William left Windsor, his work was continued by William of Mulsho, and by Adam of Hartington, who by the time of Edward III's death had supervised the entire rebuilding of the royal apartments in the Upper Ward. In the following reign, Geoffrey Chaucer, clerk of the King's works in the Palace of Westminster, and already the author of his century's most celebrated poems, was instructed to repair the Chapel of St George, which was 'threatened with ruin and on the point of falling to the ground'. Considerable works of repair were carried out, under the supervision of Chaucer (who was paid two shillings a day), but not enough to prevent its being again in decay in 1478 when Edward IV decided to pull it down and 'replace it by another and altogether more glorious building'. If this should outshine the chapel lately built just across the river at Eton by his rival and victim, King Henry VI, so much the better. The new chapel which was finished in about 1525 was, indeed, altogether more glorious, and now remains

A misericord in St George's Chapel.

as one of the most beautiful examples of the Gothic perpendicular taste in the world.

Here, after the smoke and fury of the Wars of the Roses had brought the Middle Ages to a close, the body of Elizabeth, the widow of Edward

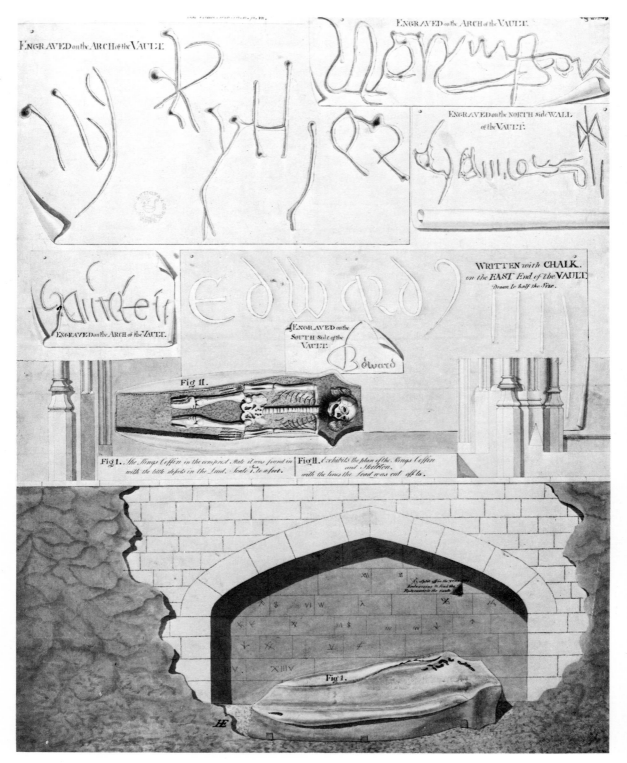

The Grave of Edward IV
The grave of the King who was buried in 1483
was opened in 1789 when this drawing was made by the Chapter's architect, Henry Emlyn.
The King's skeleton was found to measure no less than 6 ft 3 ins in length.

3

The castle from the north in the reign of James I
The meadows below the north terrace were then used as a bowling ground.

4

The castle from the north in the reign of Charles II
A painting by Henry Danckerts who came to England in about 1668.

IV, was buried in her husband's vault in accordance with her last request. Accompanied only by her chaplain and one of her long-dead husband's numerous bastard daughters, she was buried at 'ix o'clocke at night w'oute any solempne dirge or the ringing of any bell'.

Not for more than a hundred and fifty years was there to be another funeral in the chapel so quiet and restrained. For when Elizabeth Woodville died, her son-in-law, Henry VII, had already secured the success of a dynasty for which so modest a ceremony was to hold little appeal.

II

TUDORS

1

THE NEW APOLLO
AND HIS CHILDREN

In the winter of 1547 when Elizabeth Woodville's grandson died, the funeral ceremony was far less restrained. The King's body was taken to Windsor from Westminster along roads specially cleared and swept and in some places widened, on a carriage drawn by eight black-trapped horses, on each of which a page sat carrying the royal banner.

The effigy which it was customary to place on top of the coffin was clothed in crimson velvet, trimmed with miniver and powdered with ermine. There was a crown on its head placed over a 'night-cap of black satin, set full of precious stones'. There were precious stones, too, in the gold bracelets which encircled the wrists, and in the numerous rings on the fingers of the velvet-gloved hands. As the *cortège*, four miles long, approached the castle hill and entered between the barriers, draped with black cloth and studded with escutcheons, the choir began to sing. Three bishops in pontificals approached the coffin, which was carried into the chapel by sixteen yeomen bearing long black staves. The senior officers of the royal household carried white staves which they broke into three pieces and threw down upon the coffin when it had been lowered into the vault.

It was a final act of homage to a magnificent and cataclysmic career. Forty years before, this dead king, Henry VIII, whose immense corpse and coarsened face now lay in St George's Chapel next to his 'true and loving wife Queen Jane', was a boy of great intelligence, excessive self-confidence and numerous accomplishments. Despite a large and ugly high-bridged nose he was also considered extremely good-looking. He had the fair skin, faint eyebrows, and auburn hair which his contemporaries so much admired and his 'round face' was so 'very beautiful', a Venetian thought, that it would have become a 'pretty woman'. He was lazy and inclined to be frivolous, but he brought to physical pursuits a seemingly tireless energy. Every day he was up early, hunting, shooting, hawking, riding, jousting, or wrestling. He was a most agile dancer, leaping about like a stag in the energetic style which southern Europeans found so astonishing an oddity; he loved singing; he could play recorder, flute and virginals with equal grace and facility; he composed music; he wrote anthems. He was at once dashing, strong and charming, and his shrewd and clever Welsh father, who within five months of his defeat of Richard III at Bosworth Field in 1485 had united the houses of Lancaster and York by marrying Elizabeth, eldest daughter of Edward IV, was determined to make good use of this tall, virile son, this 'new Apollo'.

One day at the beginning of 1505 a ship on its way from the Netherlands to Spain was forced by bad weather to take shelter in a Dorset harbour, and Henry, Prince of Wales, was given an early lesson in the art of hospitality.

On board the damaged ship were Juana, the new Queen of Castile — *La Loca*, the mad one — and her husband Philip the Handsome, Archduke of Austria and heir to the Holy Roman Empire. Juana was the daughter of Isabella of Castile and Ferdinand of Aragon, and her youngest sister Catherine had been married to Prince Arthur, Henry VII's elder son, who had died at the age of sixteen three years before. King Henry had originally wanted the young widow Catherine to marry his other son, the new Prince of Wales, but now that Isabella, her mother, was dead the match was not so favourable a one. The King decided instead that a marriage between Prince Henry and the

The roof of St George's Chapel. The heraldic beasts were originally placed on the pinnacles in the reign of Henry VII. They were decayed two centuries later, and Christopher Wren, who was appointed Comptroller of the Works at Windsor in 1684, suggested that they should be replaced by representations of pineapples, a fashionable motif since Charles II's gardener had succeeded in growing one. The suggestion was not adopted, however. The present beasts were placed on the pinnacles during the restoration of the chapel in 1921–30. During a previous restoration in Queen Victoria's reign quantities of broken skeletons were found secreted in holes in the pinnacles. The Canons believed they must be saintly relics until, sent to London for analysis, they were proved to be the bones of stags picked up in the Park by jackdaws who dropped them into the crevices.

Archduke Philip's daughter Eleanor and, perhaps, a second marriage between his daughter Mary and Philip's son Charles would be far more useful. The fortuitous arrival of Philip in England gave him an opportunity to further these ambitions.

As soon as he heard of Philip's landing, he sent the Earl of Arundel to ask him and Juana to come to Windsor, which was, as it had been and would remain for centuries, 'an ideal settynge' for the arrangement of the treaties and alliances that the English King had in mind. Philip said that he would come at once and that his wife would come later. He was met, five miles from the castle, by 'five hundred persons all gorgeously apparelled' led by the Prince of Wales, who, although not yet fourteen, 'received him after the most honourable fashion'.

Prince Henry watched his father greet the Archduke inside the castle gate. The minstrels were playing beneath the grey walls in the cold winter air; and to the sound of trombones the two men went through the extravagant rites which court etiquette demanded.

Philip made as if to dismount first but Henry refused to accept the gesture; and so they stepped to the ground together. Henry, noticing that Philip had taken his hat off, quickly took off his own and declined to put it on again until Philip was ready to do the same. Once more they acted in unison.

When Philip said that the King need not accompany him to his lodgings, Henry insisted on doing so. The Archduke said that he would agree only if he were allowed to accompany his host back to the royal apartments afterwards. This was at last agreed, but, having completed the two journeys, Henry made as if to go back with Philip to the rooms which he had just showed him. Philip, however, 'wolde not suffere it, and so they saluted the one the other and departed; the Kynge remained in his Chamber, and the Kynge of Casteele wente to his and so they both wente to dynner every eiche in his own Chambre for it was ffastynday and our Lady's evene'.

On Sunday morning the King went to Mass at his chapel and then went to Philip's room where a private Mass had been said by the chaplain. 'And at the meetynge the Kynge of Casteele Tooke off his Bonnete and made a Lowe Curtesye and bade the Kinge god morrowe, and the Kynge said to him that he could not have welle dined that day unlese that he had seene him and bade him good morowe. The Kinge of Casteele thanked the Kinge of his greate Curtesye and payne, and so with diveres other goode words they both proceeded together to the Kynge of Casteel's dininge Chambere, and both stood by the fyere together.'

After dinner that day Henry asked Philip if, as it was Sunday and they could not go hunting, he would like to see the ladies dancing and he took him to a room next to his dining-room where Catherine danced with another Spanish girl, both in their national costumes; and Princess Mary danced with an English girl. Catherine asked her brother-in-law, Philip, to dance with her but he said he was too clumsy and preferred to watch. His eyes were fixed on Mary, performing with such liveliness and grace. She was only nine but she could play the lute and clarabel as skilfully as she could dance, and although he had previously declined to consider the proposed marriage between her and his son Charles, he was induced during this visit to Windsor to change his mind.

Philip stayed twelve days in the castle and everything possible was done to impress him. The chapel, where he and Henry attended Mass daily, was hung with cloth of gold and lit by hundreds of beautifully moulded tapers. In the tennis-court he and his host sat on cloth of gold cushions while they watched the players below, and Philip was persuaded to believe that he was better than any of them and he challenged the Marquess of Dorset to a match, giving himself a handicap of fifteen points. Henry created him a Knight of the Garter and presented him with robes of exceptional splendour. He was entertained with the spectacle of a fine horse being baited to death beneath the windows of the delicately painted towers in which his lodgings were; and whenever the weather was fine he was taken out into the Park to hunt deer with a crossbow.

*

A day's hunting in the Park, always one of the most exciting pleasures that Windsor had to offer, was also usually an occasion for the King to demonstrate the lavish excellence of English food. At the banquets held in the castle the meals were sumptuous, of course, but the atmosphere of formality, the effort to make polite conversation, the necessary observances of etiquette, took some of the pleasure out of eating, whereas at the hunting lodge in the Little Park hungry men and women could eat without restraint.

Henry VIII brought to eating, as he brought to everything he did, a wonderful zest and lustiness. His father, by discipline and a calculating policy, by forcing men to fear a scarcely human King whom he dared not let them like or even understand, had restored the ravaged fortunes of the Crown. He had spent no more than the traditional necessity for occasional displays of lavish entertainment and ostentation demanded; he had kept profitable appointments in royal hands

Henry VIII and the Knights of the Garter in 1534. An illustration from the *Black Book of the Order of the Garter* by either Richard Lydenor or Robert Aldridge and clearly influenced by Holbein.

and employed cheap professional deputies; he had hoarded treasure and money, cut court expenses to a minimum while keeping a necessarily 'sumptuous table', and had left his son a fortune of £1,250,000.

Such parsimony was not for Henry VIII, nor was it necessary. The Court at Windsor became, and could afford to become, as splendid a place as it had been at the beginning of the previous century. The number of servants and attendants grew each year. There were constant entertainments, dances, tournaments, games and banquets. But if it was a rowdy place, extrovert and uninhibited, it was also a place of learning. Erasmus found it more like a home of the Muses than a court.

Catherine of Aragon, now married to the King, shared her husband's interests and pleasures. She too enjoyed riding and hunting, jousting, dancing, conversation and music. And he himself, so far as respect for the Queen allowed, delighted not only in the company of scholars and sportsmen but also in that of her lively ladies-in-waiting. He had a son by one of them, Elizabeth Blount, and he fell in love with another, Anne Boleyn, and having divorced Catherine to whom he was, according to Francis Bacon, 'no indulgent husband', he married Anne on a winter's morning when she was pregnant with his child.

Anne Boleyn, swarthy and flat-chested but exciting and excitable, witty, provocative and calculating, had come to Windsor from the Court of Francis I where she had been a lady-in-waiting to Queen Claude, and the King was captivated by her dark, flashing eyes, her long, loose black hair, and her vivacity. She refused to become his mistress until she was certain that he would marry her; but not long after she was crowned, the King was excited by someone else. Charged with having committed adultery with five different men, one of whom was her brother, Anne Boleyn, who had failed to provide her husband with a male heir, was convicted of high treason and beheaded on Tower Green on 19 May 1536. The King, who was out hunting, reined in his horse to listen to the sound of the guns and married one of her ladies-in-waiting, Jane Seymour, the next morning. The following year the new Queen, having given birth to a son, died of puerperal fever and for the first time in his life the King knew the grief of losing someone he loved. He left Hampton Court immediately for Windsor, 'too broken to be able to consider the arrangements for the lying-in-state or the funeral'.

He had aged much since his coronation. He danced and hunted and jousted as energetically as ever, but men believed he did so no longer because he enjoyed these activities but because he wanted to show that he was still as strong and jovial as he had been in his youth. In fact he had become grimly masterful and inordinately selfish. He suffered increasingly from feverish headaches and depression; he had an ulcer on his thigh which broke out spasmodically, giving him such pain that at times he was speechless and his face grew black; he had, also, perhaps through some glandular maladjustment, become immensely fat. 'He had a body and a half, very abdominous and un-

HENRICVS DEI GRA REX ANGLIE

Henry VIII in middle age. 'He had a body and a half,' according to Thomas Fuller, 'very abdominous and unwieldy with fat'.

wieldy with fat. It was death to him to be dieted, so great his appetite, and death to him not to be dieted, so great his corpulency.' In five years, if his armour provides an accurate guide, he added seventeen inches to his waist measurement. At Windsor and his other royal palaces, machines with ropes and pulleys had to be provided for him as he could no longer get up the stairs.

His Court, though, remained the glittering place that he had made it. And so it had to be, for like the Court of his daughter Elizabeth, it was the world, the power and the glory, 'the fountain of power and influence, the source of fortune, magnet of all eyes . . . a centre of education, in the arts of culture and manners, in worldliness and sophistication, intrigue and treachery'. It was still the seat of government as well as the royal setting. Its splendour and liveliness were

necessary both as a means of impressing foreign visitors and of attract-
ing young men of energy and talent into the service of the Crown,
and of keeping them out of mischievous employment elsewhere. It
had to provide a home not only for many high officials of state but also
for boys and girls of good birth finishing their education there. It had
to open its doors to important ambassadors as well as to the hundreds
of lesser functionaries who came there to eat at the tables of their
masters. And consequently it had, of course, to be prepared to supply
prodigious quantities of food.

While they were eating, the members of the Court watched the
antics of the various entertainers in the household who included Jane,
a female fool, and Will Somers, one of the most famous jesters of his
time.

Somers could send guests in the hall at dinner time into paroxysms
of laughter by grinning through a gap in the arras and then making
his way to the tables 'in such a rolling and antic posture, holding his
hands and setting his eyes that was past describing unless one saw
him'. Usually attended by a monkey which sat on his shoulder and did
funny tricks, he told joke after joke, laughing helplessly and infectiously
at each one and screwing his cheerful, malicious face into cruel caricatures of the people he was deriding.

The King himself, despite an increasing insistence on the rights
and pleasures of privacy, was still also expected to be part of the show
at Court. He was rarely alone even in his Withdrawing Chambers.
Access to his Privy Chamber was supposedly limited, but it was
frequently full of people who had no business there, merely wishing
to see what the King looked like. And the Presence Chamber was, in
effect, a stage.

The King's children, too, were expected to spend most of their lives
in public, so that a naturally reserved and introspective boy like Jane
Seymour's son and Henry's successor, Edward VI, could live and die in
loneliness without ever having known what it was like to be left alone.

Edward succeeded his father at the age of nine and died three
months before his sixteenth birthday. Extremely pale and very fair,
solemn and precociously learned, potentially, perhaps, the ablest of
the Tudors but potentially, too, the least attractive, he grew up in the
shadow of a father held up to him as 'the greatest man in the world',
and in the company of men whose struggles for power drew out of an
essentially generous nature characteristics both equivocal and un-
appealing. He did not like Windsor. 'Methinks I am in prison,' he said
of it when he was twelve. 'Here be no galleries, nor no gardens to walk
in.' And it was not only at Windsor that he felt this burden of restraint.
Energetic, yet so solemn he is reported to have laughed only once,
capable of a disarming responsiveness yet remaining warily cold and
withdrawn, at once priggish and introspective, he had neither the
temperament nor the physique to lead the life expected of him. Finally,
in June 1553, poisoned by the medicine that had at first so stimulated
him, with swollen legs and arms and darkened skin, with fingers and

toes touched by gangrene, his hair and nails began to fall out, and on 6 July he died, too weak to cough, murmuring a prayer.

Convinced of the 'divine right of Protestantism', he had agreed to exclude from the accession in his will his Catholic half-sister Mary, the daughter of Catherine of Aragon, in favour of Lady Jane Grey. It was, however, as Queen that Mary came to Windsor in the summer of 1554, after Lady Jane Grey had been beheaded, to prepare herself for her marriage with Philip II, King of Spain, grandson of Philip the Handsome who had been entertained at Windsor by her grandfather Henry VII half a century before.

Philip II came to Windsor in August and was installed as a Knight of the Garter and afterwards he and his wife went hunting in the Forest. Mary was obviously in love with him, or at least 'in love with what he represented — the prospect of a Catholic heir, reunion with Rome, her martyred mother's Spanish dynasty, the Spain that stood for centuries of knight-errantry against the infidel'. 'All the affection, all the passion that her starved and thwarted youth had been unable to spend, she now threw at the feet of this restrained, courteous young husband.' She was eleven years older than he was, and Philip's friend, Ruy Gomez, thought she looked older even than that. She was a 'dear thing' and perhaps if she had dressed in the Spanish fashion she might not have looked 'so old and flabby'; but as another young Spaniard said, she was 'not at all beautiful, small . . . of white complexion, and fair, and has no eyebrows'. She had tight, thin lips and a somewhat spatulate nose and few remaining teeth; and she spoke in a deep, loud voice 'almost like a man's'. Her eyes were 'greyish and pale and so short-sighted that to read she must hold the page close to her face'; and she was quick-tempered and imperious, obstinate, unworldly and narrow-minded. Her husband — who went home to Spain as soon as he could — apparently found her unattractive and lacking 'all sensibility of the flesh'.

Yet she was, beneath that unprepossessing exterior and despite her many faults, much more the 'dear thing' that the young Spaniard had called her than the 'Bloody Mary' that new generations were to decry. The Venetian ambassador while noting that she was of 'low stature, with a red and white complexion and very thin', thought that the 'great benignity and clemency' that illumined her face made her almost *'bella'*. 'She is of very spare diet,' he continued, 'and never eats until one or two o'clock, although she rises at daybreak when, after saying her prayers and hearing Mass in private, she transacts business incessantly until after midnight, when she retires to rest.'

She was not cruel. She knew her way to God and could not conceive that there was any other way. Men suffered for their refusal to accept it, not to be punished but to be saved. It was not that she had no sensibility, but that she had no judgement. Courageous, unshakably loyal to those she loved and to the religion which was the mainstay of her life, capable of passionate affection, yet virtuous, conscientious and devout, she appeared more like a practical housewife or even a nun than a queen. She loved jewels and gay clothes, but her principal pre-occupations were people, babies and religion. During her visits to Windsor as a young woman, she had gone out almost every day visiting the old and sick with her ladies, dressed as they were dressed so as not to be recognized; she had enjoyed riding and long walks which she felt were good for the amenorrhoea that troubled her intermittently throughout her life; she had stood as godmother to numerous babies, had attended Mass with unfailing regularity, had played cards and listened to music. She had lived, in fact, the life of quiet innocence for which her character and capacities suited her. It was fortunate for her country that, after her brief sad reign was over, there was waiting to follow her a half-sister whose temperament and talents were so different from hers.

2

QUEEN ELIZABETH I

'She readeth here now at Windsore,' Roger Ascham, her tutor, said of the young Elizabeth, 'more Greek every day than some Prebendaries of this Church do read in a whole week.' She could read Latin as well, and she could speak it without stopping for a word. She spoke French, Spanish and Italian, too, and even Welsh. Ascham had never known a woman with a quicker apprehension or a more retentive memory. She had, he said, a mind which seemed to be free from female weakness, and her power of application was like a man's. She could talk intelligently on any intellectual topic and liked to spend three hours a day reading history. She spent hours, too, with a pen or a needle between her extraordinarily long, white fingers until her handwriting and her needlework were both of an exquisite beauty.

Her concentrated study, however, undermined her health. Already the nervous shock of her mother's execution and the events that had surrounded it, followed by the execution of Catherine Howard, a stepmother of whom she had been particularly fond, and the excitation of her awakening sexual instincts by the outrageous Lord Seymour, who had married another stepmother, Catherine Parr, after her father's death, had contributed, it seems, to do Elizabeth's 'nervous system and her sexual system an injury from which they never recovered'. Her menstrual periods were very few or none; she suffered from painful eyestrain, agonizing headaches and frequent breathlessness. The paleness of her skin, 'though tending to olive' when she was young, became so white through bleaching that it appeared almost to glow; and its whiteness was emphasized by the large pupils of her very bright eyes under faint, highly arched eyebrows and by straight reddish gold hair, which, like her clothes, plain and unadorned, scorned the current fashion.

Despite her hair and clothes, though, and her rigorous devotion to duty, she was far from either staid or unworldly. Indeed, it may well be that her modest demeanour and 'maidenly apparel' were calculated rather than instinctive, for the scandalous rumours that were spread about concerning her relationship with her stepmother's husband, Lord Seymour, were a threat to her future. Also, she was well aware that 'in the reign of her prim and Protestant little brother demureness was the becoming wear', while in Mary's reign 'the simplicity of her tastes helped her to make friends with what might be called the mammon of righteousness, that is, with the incipient Puritan party'. Certainly when she became Queen herself and Lord Robert Dudley, tall, dark-skinned, handsome and selfish, came to renew his friendship with her and to indulge her susceptibilities, he was immediately admitted to her service as Master of the Horse, an office — worth £1,500 a year and a table at Court — ideally suited to his talents, both as an expert in the riding, judging and maintaining of horses and as a showman. Dudley, created Earl of Leicester in 1564, retained the Queen's favour for thirty years, surviving the scandal of being sent away from Windsor when his wife was found with her neck broken at the bottom of a staircase in a lonely house in Oxfordshire, and surviving even his marriage to Lettice Devereux, which drove the Queen to fury. He was the epitome of those dashing, virile, gifted young men with whom the Queen delighted to adorn her Court.

She loved these men to tell her — they were expected, in fact, by a tiresome and elaborately stylized convention to tell her — how beautiful she was, that they would die of the passion that they had for her, that her skin (which she kept 'white as Albion rocks' with a lotion made of white of egg, powdered eggshell, poppy-seeds, borax and alum) was paler than snow. Indeed, as she grew older, her susceptibility to flattery, her delight in compliments however outlandishly extravagant, her inordinate vanity, were the talk of Europe. 'With her all is falsehood and vanity,' complained the Spanish ambassador maliciously, and Raleigh believed that if Essex had not said angrily that she had 'a crooked carcase' he need not have died. When the vile Robert Topcliffe said that he had been allowed to put his hand on Elizabeth's bosom and that he had seen her naked thighs, he was making an outrageous claim to favours that the Queen was rumoured to have bestowed elsewhere. Certainly she was always excessively proud of her body and liked men to see it. The French ambassador once noted in his journal how, one day during a private audience towards the end of her life, she kept pulling open the front of her white damask dress and lawn chemise so that he could see her belly 'even to the navel'.

She was sixty-four then. The gaps between her black teeth made it hard to understand what she said, her uncovered bosom was 'somewhat wrinkled', and she wore a 'great reddish-coloured wig'.

And yet she was not absurd; nor ever had she been absurd. She was not beautiful. Her nose was too long and her mouth too thin. She could not, apparently, feel a normal sexual passion, or perhaps it was that she was physically incapable of consummating it. But there was something in the liveliness of her conversation, her responsiveness, her ability to make men feel that she needed them, her spirit and energy and quick reactions, that was captivating.

Her courtiers and advisers often found her irritating and difficult, of course. For she was 'a great *prima donna*' in the realm of politics, and she had many personal foibles. She hated, for instance, to be ill or to be thought ill. In 1587 when a tooth was giving her pain and needed to be pulled out, her physicians dared not tell her so because she herself 'doth not or will not think so'. Eventually the Council decided that the tooth must come out, having listened to the opinion of a toothdrawer who said that the only other possibility was to dress it with fennygreek, but that might make the neighbouring teeth fall out as well as the painful one; and a body of councillors went to persuade the Queen that she must agree to the extraction. She refused to do so, however, until the Bishop of London allowed the surgeon to pull one of his own teeth out to demonstrate the ease with which the operation could be performed.

Illness was a personal affront, and she would never be affronted. Even in church she checked preachers who seemed to be disrespectful towards her. 'Do not talk about that,' she once called out to a dean who in a Lenten sermon attacked images and implicitly called attention to the crucifix. '*Leave that*,' she called out in an even louder voice when, not having heard her, he continued his sermon. '*Leave that!* It has nothing to do with your subject and the matter is now threadbare.'

But although she was dictatorial, high-handed and could be irritable, ungrateful and cruel, she had the endearing qualities of a gentler, less assertive and self-confident woman. She loved flowers and children and jewels; she changed her mind far more frequently than diplomacy required; she had a deep sympathy for those who were old or ill. She would refuse to take men into her service at Windsor if they were ugly and once refused employment to an otherwise handsome man who had a front tooth missing; but 'she was never known to desert them

Queen Elizabeth and her swordbearer. The Queen is shown taking part in a procession of the Knights of the Garter in 1578 with the castle, as seen from the north, in the background.

for age or other inferiority after they were once enrolled in her service'. They were paid 'good pensions', although her dislike of spending more money than she could possibly avoid was notorious.

It was, indeed, her parsimony which, intensified by the dictates of a shrewd financial policy, induced her to move her Court so often at the expense of her richer subjects. This was not the only reason, of course. She had, for instance, an extremely sensitive nose and the smell of a house occupied too long by too many people was peculiarly offensive to her. There were baths and jakes in most large houses — there were fine bathrooms at Windsor with ceilings and wainscots of looking-glass — but the water-closet installed at Richmond Palace in 1597 to the design of the Queen's godson, John Harington, was the first in any of the royal palaces.

There was, too, the smell of the horses. Henry III had felt compelled to regulate the number of horses that could be stabled at Windsor as they were considered a danger to Prince Edward's health; and in 1519 the regulation was repeated 'in consideration of a scarcyte and straitness of Lodgings as well as in avoyding and eschewing of the corrupt air'. For reasons of sanitation, therefore, the Royal Household had to be a mobile one, and Henry VIII, who was in the opinion of the French ambassador, Marillac, 'the most timid person in the world' when there was a threat of plague, forced it to move often enough, to trail from house to house with hundreds of carts carrying clothes and linen, tableware and documents, jewels and even furnishings, for many of the houses were too bare for a court. Not until the reign of Elizabeth, however, did it move so often, for no previous monarch had combined so sensitive a nose with so restless a determination to force the country's rich families to entertain the household in the interests of royal economy, or had combined so strong a desire for movement and activity with so great a gift for winning the hearts of the people she would meet on her way. Elizabeth's visits to Windsor were consequently never prolonged.

Her affection for the place was, however, undoubted. She was particularly happy there in the summer – in the winter she found it terribly cold – and she built a fine stone terrace beneath the windows of her apartments on the northern side of the Upper Ward. Here in the evenings she liked to walk, moving very fast, as though she were hurrying away from a ghost or trying to keep warm in ice-cold air, but never losing her dignity or appearing to bustle as her sister Mary had done. She built, too, a gallery next to the tower which her grand-father had built for his Queen, where she liked to walk when the weather was too bleak for exercise outside in the garden, 'full of meanders and labyrinths' that she made below the new North Terrace. She also liked to hunt in the Park, wearing clothes and jewels more suitable for the audience chamber than the hunting field, and riding her horse so fast that she tired out her frightened companions. She was capable of killing the 'great and fat stagge with her owen Hand'. And even when she was sixty-six she insisted on riding with the men. She was still 'excellent disposed to hunting' and rode for long periods 'every second day'.

The contrasts between her fragile figure and her strong will, her graciousness and her robust beer-drinking, spitting, swearing, coarse-ness, between her courage and her lapses into fear, her kindness and her cruelty, were contrasts to which her courtiers soon grew accus-tomed. They knew that she could not bear loud noises, that she slept badly and had a poor appetite, that she was sometimes as hysterical as her mother, but they knew, too, that she had her father's genius for authority, and that as an employer she was rigidly exacting – Leicester, Heneage and Hatton as members of the Council, and not only the Cecils and Walsingham as Secretaries, were all hard-working men. They knew that she did not shrink from giving instructions for men to be tortured, and that although she could forgive a man who had created a disturbance in the Sovereign's presence by firing a shot in her direction and could reprieve him at the gallows' foot in the castle courtyard, she could not forgive the Puritan John Stubbs for suggesting that she was too old to marry, insisting, rather, that his right hand should be cut off, saying she wished he could be hanged.

She was a woman of her time. In her room at Windsor she read and talked and laughed and played her virginals as any woman might have done. She sat on a cushion 'most curiously wrought by Her Majesty's own hands'. She slept in an immense and gorgeous bed 'covered with curious hangings of embroidery work'.

She would come to the window in her négligé to look down at Leicester's fool shouting on the Terrace and she would smile at Leicester himself when he came to see her in the morning and kissed him as he handed her her shift. But beneath that beautiful room, beyond the curve of the grey stone wall, was a place she knew in Windsor where the gallows were put in the time of the plague to hang anyone from the infected area who disobeyed the Council's order and came near the Queen's most precious person.

A bird's-eye view of the castle in 1607. This survey, done by John Norden, the topographer, shows the improvements and additions carried out for Elizabeth I between 1571 and 1576. The new stone terrace and gallery can be seen in the lower left-hand corner, also the new brick-enclosed 'Tennyce Court' on the easterly slope of William the Conqueror's mound. In the middle of the Upper Ward is a representation of the fountain set up in 1557–8.

III

STUARTS

1

JAMES I

Three days after the Queen died, a messenger spattered with mud and 'be-blooded with great falls and bruises', stumbled into the ante-chamber of King James VI of Scotland to tell him that the day for which he had been so impatiently waiting had come at last. Queen Elizabeth was dead and he was King of England. Almost immediately he set out to claim his rich inheritance.

The reports about him that had come through to the English Court during the Queen's last years had not been reassuring. He was grace-less, conceited, lazy and a coward. He was slovenly in his dress and he rarely washed. His narrow jaws and large tongue made it difficult for him to eat or drink without noisy and distasteful splashing. He spoke 'in the full dialect of his country' and in a very loud voice, expressing his opinions with a tiresome, irritating dogmatism. He hated to be beaten at games or, in fact, surpassed at anything. He was nervous, excitable and restless and walked up and down on his weak legs with a strangely erratic gait. His whole appearance was undistinguished — he was rather plump and looked ungainly even when he was standing still; his eyes were large and protuberant, 'ever rolling after any stranger that came in his presence'; he had a ruddy complexion with a skin left slightly pitted by smallpox, and thin sandy coloured hair; his small, trowel-shaped beard was 'scattering on his chin and very thin'. He was terrified of witches and naked steel, and he hated the sea and pigs. He had an almost obsessive interest in freaks and monstros-ities of nature and in sexual perversions, and he loved to listen to

James I. A miniature by Hoskins.

obscene stories and to recount them. He was married to Anne, the youngest daughter of King Frederick II of Denmark, an enterprising, ambitious, rather masculine, cheerful and affectionate blonde woman, given to childish tantrums and expensive and frivolous conceits; but he preferred the company of handsome young men whose cheeks he would pinch and kiss and whose clothing he would fondle as if it were the coat of a lap dog.

There were those who could find excuses for his unattractive failings in his narrow and unhappy childhood. His mother was Mary Stuart, the vivacious, passionately emotional Queen of Scots, and his father was Lord Darnley, drunken, faithless, unintelligent and insolent, although 'the lustiest and best proportioned long man' that Mary had ever seen. And when Mary was pregnant with James, this Darnley had helped to murder David Rizzio, Mary's Italian secretary, in her presence. This pre-natal shock alone, it was felt, accounted for much of her son's fears and physical peculiarities. In addition he had been handed over as a child to the care of George Buchanan, the Scottish scholar, once one of the most celebrated European humanists but now a dour and crabbed old man who poured into him the prejudices of a severely Calvinistic mind. At the age of four, James's syllabus included Greek, dialectic, and astronomy. By the time he was eight he could speak Latin and French, translate the Bible into either language with equal facility, and discuss high theological questions. But there was no affection in his life, no development of that understanding which makes learning both useful and admirable. Buchanan, about whom James continued to have nightmares at the age of fifty-three, did not like women and thought them all stupid and vain, and his pupil 'through all his life entertained most lofty views of the superiority of the male'.

He entertained also the most lofty views of his own superiority in particular, both as a person and as a king. 'The supreme consolation for everything he lacked lay in his kingship. The intense self-centredness which was to become his most dominating characteristic had its root in the importance which everybody else attached to his person and the kingship which it embodied.' He held that his subjects should 'fear and obey him as God's lieutenant on earth', and his English courtiers soon discovered that this belief in a divine mission made flattery, however grotesque, not merely acceptable but obligatory. In England his Court retained all the superficial vices of Elizabeth's, while losing most of those virtues that had made hers so virile and aggressively undegenerate. James's Court had vulgarity without panache.

The behaviour of Elizabeth's courtiers was governed not only by her own wishes, tastes and prejudices but also by standards which were beginning to be accepted throughout Europe as essential to the conduct of a gentleman. Authorities such as Castiglione's *Book of the Courtier*, first published in England during her reign, were having a widespread influence on the manners of courts by insisting that politeness and manliness were not contradictory. The true gentleman was a healthy, chivalrous, quick-witted sportsman with an instinct for self-advancement. Queen Elizabeth's ideal courtier was just that. King James's young friends, on the contrary, were encouraged to be all that Castiglione disliked. The most successful of them, according to one observer, 'exceeded any part of womankind' with their mincing walk and wanton gestures. Horseplay and practical jokes were *de rigueur*. The Earl of Pembroke disliked frogs, so the King put one down his neck; the King disliked pigs, so Pembroke put one in his bedroom.

Both the King and Queen delighted in masques and at one staged in 1606 for King Christian IV of Denmark, during whose visit the ladies of court were seen to abandon all 'sobriety and roll about in intoxication', there was more lack of 'good order, discretion and sobriety' than Sir John Harington had ever seen. The Queen herself often took part in such displays, for she loved dressing up and appeared in several of Ben Jonson's brilliant and ingenious masques, together with some of her heavily scented and lavishly bejewelled ladies, in extremely provocative dresses. The King encouraged them to do so for he liked watching women 'being immodest'.

His taste was for satire, low comedy and burlesque; and it seems that he liked best these aspects of the comedies of William Shakespeare, whose company continued to receive the royal patronage, as it had done in the time of Elizabeth when the Queen's wish that Falstaff might fall in love, had been, so it was said, the inspiration of *The Merry Wives of Windsor*.

The extravagance of these court entertainments was inordinate. One masque alone cost over £3,000 and Ben Jonson's *Metamorphosed Gipsies*, which James saw for the third time at Windsor in 1621, cost little less. During a Christmas holiday, in which another of Jonson's masques was performed, the Queen wore jewels worth £100,000. The King himself, despite his lack of interest in his own clothes and his insistence that his wife ought to make do with those outmoded ones that he had discovered in his predecessor's wardrobes, also spent immense sums on jewels with which he loved to decorate his clothes and his outlandish hats. He bought £92,000 worth in the first four years of his reign.

Meals would be served on the occasions of masques and holidays with 'dishes as high as a tall man could well reach, filled with the choicest and dearest viands sea or land could afford, and all this, once seen and having feasted the eyes of the invited, was thrown away and fresh set on to the same height, having only this advantage of the other that it was hot'.

Such extravagant waste at Court would have appalled Elizabeth. Her clothes (she had over two thousand dresses) and her jewels were magnificent; the splendour of her receptions and entertainments was dazzling. Such grandeur she believed essential to the maintenance of her position. But the castle, as all her palaces, was run with the most severe economy. She had an annual budget of no more than £40,000 allocated to the household and was very angry with the clerk comptroller when it was found not to be enough. The salaries of officials were kept as low as they had been during her father's time, and her maids of honour slept in an unheated room without a ceiling, open to a leaky roof and with a partition low enough for servants to look over.

These maids of honour were expected to do more than put up with disagreeable accommodation in the hope of making a good marriage. They had to entertain the Queen whenever she required them to do so, and they were expected to behave with the strictest propriety. The Queen was not above slapping them when they annoyed her, and she would have them put in the Tower if they became pregnant as Sir Nicholas Throckmorton's daughter did by Sir Walter Raleigh. She interfered with all their love affairs and became furious if they contemplated marriage without her consent, not so much because she was jealous — as sometimes, though, she may have been — as because 'like their manners and morals, their marriage was a royal responsibility, and it was a breach of duty as well as a gross personal affront to their Sovereign to marry without her leave'. They were required to obey the Queen in everything, to compose their inevitable and frequent quarrels for her sake, and to contribute as much to her fortunes as she did to theirs.

For James, such relationships were impossible. He could rarely command anything but the pretence of admiration, and so, abandoning himself to the pleasures of generosity and with little conception of the value of money, he lavished gifts on those whose affection he craved. He once presented one of those numerous Scottish friends — whose presence in England 'creeping into English lordships and English ladies' beds' enraged the English — with an order for £20,000; and on another occasion when walking along a corridor with one of his forty-eight Gentlemen of the Bedchamber and passing some servants carrying three thousand pounds in gold, he stopped them and made them take it to the lodgings of his companion who said he wished he had as much to spend.

Such munificence could not, of course, gain respect; nor could it be allowed to continue. James Hay, a favoured Scottish crony whose debts were settled by the King, was obliged to retire from the Wardrobe in favour of Sir Lionel Cranfield, who immediately made a saving of £14,000 a year. James, however, was not impressed. And when another of his officers had wanted to confess on his death-bed that he had been cheating him, the King forgave him immediately. 'I wonder much', he said, 'that all my officers do not go mad with the like thoughts, for certainly they have as great cause as this man hath.'

That James was fundamentally good-natured few men denied. Nor could it be said of him that he had an essentially vulgar mind. He swore with a lurid zest for obscenity and blasphemy; he never tired of lewd stories; but he had an acute intelligence and although his humour and puns were often too heavily facetious for even his contemporaries' taste, he was sometimes genuinely funny. 'He was very witty,' Weldon, who did not care for many of his other characteristics, said of him, 'and had as many jests as any man living, at which he would not smile himself, but deliver them in a grave and serious manner.' He did not like music – he was far too clumsy to dance – and his poetry was mechanical; but he had a sincere love of literature and wrote a vigorous prose himself. His *Counterblaste to Tobacco*, for instance, in which he suggests that smoking originated with the Indians, who indulged in the habit as an antidote to syphilis, is a fine piece of sustained tendentious polemics. He was undoubtedly lazy and governed England personally and self-indulgently in his spare time and mostly by correspondence; but his excuse that when he did work he could do a whole day's business in an hour or two was not entirely groundless. He had a real talent for business and made up his shrewd mind quickly. He also displayed an unexpected courage in moments of crisis. The fact remained that the King's virtues seemed swallowed up by the vulgarity of his behaviour and the gracelessness of his manner.

What did the people want? he asked crossly when they crowded round him in the street soon after his accession to catch a glimpse of their new King, frightening him with their numbers and staring, curious faces. They came of love to see his face, he was assured. But he had already grown tired of this adulation which he had at first found exciting, believing it to spring from love of himself rather than from pleasure in the occasion of welcoming a new King, and he cried out in Scottish, 'God's wounds! I will pull down my breeches and they shall also see my arse.'

It was, as his courtiers had quickly learned, a characteristic remark. Deal with 'this pantaloon', he once commanded Salisbury when an ambassador interrupted him with a business matter when he was out hunting, an activity which revealed far more unpleasant aspects of his character than the intimidation of crowds did.

He had an overwhelming passion for hunting. The discovery of so great a store of deer and game at Windsor was one of the most exciting pleasures of his first tour of his royal palaces. And within a few weeks of his arrival in England he was out after them. He hunted down the quarry with a fury which appeared insanely vindictive, riding after the hounds at a wild gallop, often with the ribbon of the Garter dangling above his left boot, disdainful of his customary timid caution, dismounting eagerly as soon as the stag was brought down to run at it and cut its throat. Then he would rip its belly open, put his hands and sometimes his feet inside and daub his companions with blood.

He liked to be accompanied, while indulging such tastes, by a few handsome young men. 'Handsomeness,' Sir Richard Bulstrode said, 'went a long way in our court.' For the King 'loved young men, his favourites, better than women, loving them beyond the love of men for women'. Sir John Oglander had never seen 'any fond husband make so much or so great dalliance over his beautiful spouse' as he had seen 'King James over his favourites, especially Buckingham'. Abroad he was sometimes referred to as Queen James, King Elizabeth's successor.

That anything more physically satisfying than kissing and petting took place between the King and these young men, most of his contemporaries doubted. Just as he rarely got drunk, preferring to sip the strong, sweet Greek wine and Scottish ale he loved throughout the day, so, perhaps, he had always preferred to sip at the men he loved.

When they married he continued to pet and fondle them in public as he had done before. The first morning after the Earl of Montgomery's marriage to Lady Susan Vere the King was in their room at an early hour and even, it was believed, in their bed. When Robert Carr, who had come from Scotland as the King's page and was created Earl of Somerset, went to face his trial for the murder of Sir Thomas Overbury King James 'hung about his neck, slabbering his cheeks, saying, "For God's sake, when shall I see thee again. On my soul I shall neither eat nor sleep until you come again . . . For God's sake, let me, shall I, shall I?" — then lolled about his neck. "Then for God's sake give thy lady this kiss for me"; in the same manner at the stair's head, at the middle of the stairs, and the stairs' foot.'

George Villiers, 1st Duke of Buckingham, after Cornelius Janssen.

After the King realized that, in Bishop Goodman's phrase, 'a choice of dishes best pleaseth the palate', and discarded the peevish Somerset in favour of George Villiers who was the 'handsomest bodied man in England' and had a 'very lovely complexion', he became more infatuated than he had ever been. Villiers, an energetic, talented and ambitious, as well as an extremely good-looking man, with 'that rather overripe masculine attraction that trembles on the verge of femininity', an 'exquisitely curved mouth, and the dark blue eyes of the highly sexed', was made a Gentleman of the Bedchamber in 1615, a Knight of the Garter and a viscount in 1616, an earl in 1617, and a marquess in 1618. By the time he was raised to the dukedom of Buckingham in 1623, he was one of the richest men in England and the country's virtual master. To the King he was 'Steenie' — he was said to look like St Stephen — his 'sweete boye', his 'dear child and gossope'. 'I wear Steenie's picture,' he confessed, 'in a blew ribbon under my wastcoate, next my hairte.' After Buckingham married, the Duchess, a pretty, kind, adoring woman, became 'Dere Dad's' pet, his 'Baby Kate', and even her children — although he had never shown any particular fondness for his own — became his pets, too, 'so that little ones would dance up and down the privy lodgings like fairies'.

Neither the King's own children nor the Queen came to Windsor often. There was little in the Queen to make the King uxorious, Bishop Goodman thought, and although she tolerated his peculiarities, 'they did not much keep company together'. She lived mainly at Greenwich and at Somerset House, then called Denmark House as a compliment to her native country, and she gave birth to seven children, four of whom died young. The eldest son, Henry, influenced by his mother, had little respect for his father who, in turn, was so jealous of his gifted, athletic and popular son that, when he died at the age of seventeen, cruel rumours circulated that his father had had him poisoned. And his son Charles, when he was old enough to make the choice, kept as far away as he could from a court whose behaviour disgusted him. He disliked Buckingham, until the Duke, recognizing, no doubt, the danger of 'quarrelling permanently with the heir to the throne of an ageing King', began to exercise his compelling charm over the son as well as over the father; and King James's appearance and manners cannot fail to have distressed so fastidious a boy as Charles.

As the King grew older and more infirm this appearance and these manners grew increasingly distasteful. 'His skin was as soft as taffeta sarsnet,' Weldon said, 'because he never washed his hands, but only rubbed his fingers' ends slightly with the wet end of a napkin.' He was always scratching himself, and as he was subject to over-heating and sweated profusely he had his clothes cut very loose. He also had them made stiletto-proof with 'breeches in great plaits and full stuffed; he was naturally of a timorous disposition which was the reason of his quilted doublets'. When he got too hot he would throw his outer clothes off, and so he caught cold and was for ever sneezing and blowing his nose. He lost all his teeth, and being unable to chew, bolted his food and so suffered from indigestion and heartburn. He was excessively fond of fruit and when he was brought the first strawberries, grapes or cherries of the season out of the Windsor gardens he would never wait till the man from the spicery had finished his speech of 'complimental words' and risen from his knees, but plunged his hands impatiently into the basket, so he suffered from intermittent diarrhoea as well. He also had arthritis and gout which he attempted to cure by standing up in the belly of bucks and stags slaughtered in the hunting field.

Hunting was one of the few pleasures that remained to him and he continued up till the last year of his life to insist on the observance of many forest laws and restrictions that had long since fallen into disuse. He had discovered at the beginning of his reign that the inhabitants of Windsor had, during the late Queen's time, been in the habit of walking through the Park with their dogs, shooting the little game, particularly hares, and collecting sticks and firewood. This he took as an affront and an importunity and he did all he could to prevent it. The old laws were revived and the brothers Richard and Jeffrey Richbell, who were imprisoned in 1621 for riding in Windsor Forest at night with 'staves and greyhounds', were neither the first nor the last to suffer for breaking them.

The King, however, had never much cared about the esteem of the public and as he grew older he cared less. He grew, indeed, indifferent to most things. He became ever more repellent physically, hiccupping and sneezing and belching, with sores on his lips from the 'bitter humours boiling from his mouth', with stones in his bladder and disease in his liver; and his devotion to Buckingham, now his 'sweete childe and wife', became ever deeper, more frenzied and more emotional, alternating between moods of angry reproach and tearful reassurance.

In March 1625 the King was attacked by a tertian ague and although it was agreed to be 'without any manner of danger if he wold suffer himself to be ordered and governed', the only people who had any control over him at all were Buckingham and Buckingham's fussy, managing mother. These two, apparently against his physicians' advice, decided to give him patent powders obtained from a doctor in Essex and to apply plasters to his wrists and stomach; and within a short time he was dead. The Buckinghams were naturally accused of having killed him, but when the doctors opened his body they found no poison. All his vitals were 'sound, as also his head, which was very full of brains; but his blood' — and this provided a sad and fitting epitaph — 'was wonderfully tainted with melancholy'.

2

CHARLES I

Charles, Prince of Wales, was twenty-four when his father died and everyone who had talked with him and looked into those sad, dark, reproachful, rather protuberant eyes knew that his Court would be a very different place from that of his father. And so, indeed, it was. Charles had no intimate companions apart from his 'sweet Steenie' for whom he conceived an affection which filled his whole horizon, as it had filled his father's. The sister whom he had loved was married and in Germany; the brother whom he had idolized was dead; the fifteen-year-old French wife he married within two months of his accession found at first his Protestant people tedious and himself at once solemn, priggish and unfriendly. Reserved, melancholy, restless, with little sympathy and less humour, meticulous, 'intellectual without being intelligent', disingenuous, so shy that he blushed at the sound of a coarse word, so hesitant and stammering when he spoke in his falsetto voice with its pronounced Scots accent that he infected most of those he met with his own ill-disguised embarrassment, he was not a man likely to inspire close friendship.

Immediately on his accession he let it be known that whoever had occasion to come to Court 'must never approach him by backstairs or private doors'. The Court became as ostensibly sober and moral as the King himself was, both in appearance and in fact. It also became rigorously formal. No other King in Europe was served on bended knee, and when the French ambassador asked for a chair to be brought for his wife, as would have been done for the English ambassador at the Court of Louis XIII, he was told that on official occasions no lady at the Court, except the Queen herself, was allowed to sit in the royal presence.

But although severely formal and exactingly decorous, it was not a parsimonious Court nor was it always a dull one. And after 1628 — when the murder of the Duke of Buckingham removed what had formerly been an insurmountable obstacle to a happy marriage between the King and the jealous, stubborn but eventually self-confident and charming little Queen Henrietta Maria — it became in the words of the Venetian envoy 'la piu sontuosa e la piu allegra del mondo'.

It was an abode of beauty as well as of 'ceremony, elegance and learning. The noble ladies in silks of pale saffron, and coral pink, sky-blue, willow-green and oyster, their ringletted hair framing plump, oval faces' were rowed in barges on the Thames to have their portraits painted by Van Dyck, while the smaller luxuries which surrounded them were 'etched in loving detail' by Wenceslaus Hollar, the royal children's Bohemian drawing master.

The King was not merely a patron of painters; he also had a real understanding and appreciation of their work. He was fond of music, too, and of the theatre. He liked hunting and riding as well as masques; he enjoyed swimming and tennis as well as dancing. He did not dismiss Archie Armstrong until the brash jester called Archbishop Laud a monk and a traitor, and when Armstrong was dismissed he was replaced by Muckle John. Both he and the Queen liked to have dwarfs about them. The Queen had several, including Jeffrey Hudson, the son of a bull-baiter, who was often at Windsor, and was said to have stood no higher than eighteen inches when he jumped out of a pie on to the dining-room table one day, in his miniature suit of armour, to bow politely to the Queen. He grew a little in the years which followed this youthful performance, but he remained small enough to fit into the pocket of the King's gigantic porter whose pretence of eating him as a tasty morsel between the two halves of a loaf of bread was greatly enjoyed at court masques.

In general, though, 'the fools and bawds, mimics and catamites of the former Court grew out of fashion; and the nobility and courtiers who did not quite abandon their debaucheries, yet so reverenced the King as to retire into corners to practise them'.

The reverence increased as the King grew older. For it seemed to those who knew him well that his chastity and sobriety, his deep religious sense, his perfect manners and gentleness, his insensibility to flattery, were not, after all, the affectations of a prig but the manifestations of a noble spirit. Even those whom his disastrous policies had made his enemies were as conscious of this nobility as they were exasperated by his 'ultimate power of complete refusal' to believe that his motives might be less pure, his friends less worthy of his loyalty, and his means less justified than he supposed them to be. But although he was reverenced as a good man, he was not greatly loved. Remote, sad, and mystical, he completely lacked the common touch. He expected his people to do their duty as his subjects, but what little he knew about their lives as human beings came by report and from books; he expected his servants at Windsor to be as stately and punctilious as he was and, so long as they were, he treated them justly and considerately; but the devotion those who remained in his service displayed towards him in his later years came not so much from affection as from pity. When the Civil War began and Windsor opened its gates to the forces of Parliament, many other servants came down from the castle to fight against him.

*

For eighteen years after the first battle of the Civil War was fought at Edgehill, Windsor Castle was a garrison and a prison. Colonel John Venn, a 'broken silk-man in Cheapside' as a Royalist historian described him, took possession of the castle in the name of the Parliament in October 1642. There was no opposition to his occupation and a week later, when Prince Rupert's artillery, firing from the grounds of Eton College, had failed to do any appreciable damage to the walls after bombardment lasting seven hours, the Royalists withdrew from the siege amidst scenes of 'great jubilation'.

Venn was instructed to 'take care that there be no disorders and disturbances made in the chapel at Windsor; and that the evidences, registers, monuments there, and all things that belonged to the Order of the Garter may be preserved without defacings'. And despite the charges made by many Royalist writers, he did his best to ensure that this injunction was obeyed. It seems unlikely that he 'caused St George's Hall to be filled with straw and hay', or that the Chapel, where services were held throughout the Commonwealth, was used as a stable. The altar plate was taken to help pay the cost of maintaining the parliamentary troops, as were many rich vestments, hangings, velvet chairs and brass ornaments. The metalwork of the unfinished tomb intended for Henry VIII, and Edward IV's coat of mail were both removed and melted down. The valuable Garter which had been sent to Gustavus Adolphus, King of Sweden, and returned to Windsor at his death, was taken from its hiding place and sold. But both the Chapel and the castle were plundered and damaged far less than has been maintained and far more circumspectly than many other churches and houses were damaged and plundered by the Parliamentarians in their hatred of ornamentation, of stained glass and 'superstitious pictures' and in their need for money.

The lack of money was felt no more strongly anywhere than at Windsor where the garrison's pay was ninety weeks in arrears by March 1646. The soldiers, constantly verging on mutiny, took to shooting the deer in the Park for food and tearing up the fences for fuel, and it was not until the summer of 1648, after General Fairfax had insisted on the 'great necessity of some present assignment of moneys for the better fortifying and victualling' of the castle, that they could at last be paid. By then the fate of the King had been decided.

At Windsor Castle on 11 November 1647 a meeting of the General Officers of the Army 'resolved that the King should be prosecuted for his life as a criminal person'. The decision was reached after 'earnest prayers, made at the very council by Cromwell or Ireton, or some other *inspired* person', and was followed some weeks later by a 'solemn fast' held at the castle where the officers 'prayed very fervently and pathetically; this continued from nine in the morning till seven at night'.

A few days before Christmas 1648 the King was brought from Hurst Castle to Windsor while preparations for his trial were being made in London. He rode into the castle on 25 December, a plot prepared for his escape on a fast horse in Windsor Forest having miscarried when the animal was lamed by a kick from another horse and the King found himself surrounded by a hundred cavalry soldiers each carrying a pistol 'ready spanned' in his hand.

Twenty pounds a day were allowed 'for the daily expenses of the King and his attendants'. And Colonel Christopher Whitchcott, who had succeeded Venn as Governor of the castle, was instructed by the House of Commons to 'discharge and turn out such of the attendants who wait upon the King, as are malignants'.

He was well treated, though, being allowed a choice of rooms in the royal apartments in the Upper Ward and as many visitors as he wished to receive. 'His Majesty hath three new suits,' *The Perfect Weekly Account* reported, 'two of them are of cloth with rich gold and silver lace on them, the other is of black satin, the cloak lined with plush. Since the King came to Windsor he shows little alteration of courage or gesture, and, as he was formerly seldom seen to be very merry, or much transported with any news, either with joy or sorrow; so now, although he expects a severe charge and tryal, yet doth he not shew any great discontent.'

On the fourth day of his captivity 'came the order that he was no longer to be treated with the ceremonial of kingship. The cup was not to be offered to him with a genuflection, nor his dishes brought covered to the table, nor the trumpets sounded at his meals. Therefore, for what he could save of his dignity, he determined to dine alone . . . His exercise was pacing up and down the long terrace, and for his solace he would pass hours in what Milton so curiously condemned in him, the reading of Shakespeare's plays.'

Dignified and adamant to the end, his head was cut off on the morning of 30 January 1649. 'The blow I saw given,' wrote a spectator, 'and can truly say with a sad heart, at the instant whereof, I remember well, there was such a grone by the Thousands then present as I never heard before and desire I may never hear again.'

The body was embalmed, wrapped in cere-cloth 'into the folds of which a quantity of unctuous or greasy matter mixed with resin' was melted so as to 'exclude as effectually as possible the external air', and an order was issued by Parliament that it 'should be buried at Windsor in a decent manner, provided that the whole expense should not exceed five hundred pounds'. The Duke of Richmond, the Marquess of Hertford and the Earls of Southampton and Lindsay were granted permission to attend the funeral, and the Bishop of London was permitted to officiate.

The Bishop was in tears when the coffin, covered by a black velvet cloth and carried by the four noblemen, was brought down towards the chapel from the darkened room where it had been kept while the vault, in which the bodies of Henry VIII and Jane Seymour lay, was being prepared to receive it. It was bitterly cold and the Thames below was frozen over from bank to bank. The sky, at first serene and clear, darkened; and then snow began to fall into the courtyards of the castle. 'By the time the corpse had reached the west end of the chapel, the black pall was white.'

3

DIEV ET MON DROIT

CHARLES II

On the afternoon of 15 March 1660, just before the Exchange closed, a workman 'with a ladder upon his shoulder and a pot of paint in his hand, set the ladder in the place where the last King's statue had stood'.

The statue had been taken down by order of the Government and in its place an inscription had been written: *'Exit Tyrannus, Regum Ultimus'* — The tyrant is gone, the last of the Kings. The workman painted out the inscription, and 'as soon as he had done it threw up his cap and cried, *God bless King Charles the Second*, in which the whole Exchange joined with the greatest shout'.

A few weeks later King Charles II returned home after his long exile and the people greeted him with such enthusiasm that his head was 'so dreadfully stunned' by their acclamations, so he told his beloved sister Minette who was still with their mother in Paris, that he did not know whether he was writing sense or nonsense. He did not disappoint his excited subjects, however, either by his behaviour or by his appearance.

He had an ugly mouth and his expression was seen sometimes to relax into one of mocking cynicism, but he bowed, he smiled, he took off his hat, he turned from left to right; he was tall and dark and slim and graceful; he was thirty and a bachelor. 'His face is rather grave than severe which is very much softened whenever he speaks,' one of his servants said of him in this year. 'His complexion is somewhat dark, but much enlightened by his eyes, which are quick and sparkling. Until he was near twenty years of age, the figure of his face was very lovely; but he is since grown leaner, and now the majesty of his countenance supplies the lines of beauty. His Haire, which he hath in great plenty, is of a shining black, not frizled, but so naturally curling into great rings, that it is a very comely ornament.'

Pleased as most of his people were to have their King back, however, there were soon to be few of them not shocked by the behaviour of his Court. At Whitehall, that magnificent and sprawling palace which was almost entirely destroyed by fire soon after his death, the King could be seen walking very fast up and down the galleries, doing his best to avoid the dreary, the impecunious and the ambitious, or, having been stopped, carelessly granting some expensive favour to an improbable-looking suitor. He could be seen in the Chapel Royal, kneeling on velvet cushions and going to sleep during the sermon; and in his Physic Garden, picking herbs for his laboratory where his chemists manufactured the famous King's Drops that made 'cunning tongues babble secrets'; and he could be seen in the Banqueting Hall, showing himself to his people as he dined in state. And everywhere he seemed to be surrounded by dogs and epicene courtiers and pretty pages and by expensive women, lush and wanton. Even at Windsor, where life was lived rather less publicly, people soon learned of the King's recklessly carefree behaviour — his dining 'almost every night' with the gorgeous Barbara Palmer, whose husband had been created Earl of Castlemaine (the honour to be tied up with the heirs of Lady Castlemaine's body), his getting so drunk after hunting in the Forest that he and his courtiers 'all fell a-crying for joy' in Sir George Carteret's house at Cranbourne, 'being all maudlin and kissing one another . . . and in such a maudlin pickle as never people were'.

Charles II in his robes as Sovereign of the Order of the Garter. The robes of the Order were, perhaps, at this time richer than they had ever been before or were ever to be again. The high crowned hat with its immense spray of feathers has now been replaced by a flat cap modelled on a much earlier style.

He took no trouble to hide from the world the pleasure he took in women and the presents and honours he bestowed upon them. Samuel Pepys was told how the King did 'doat upon his women, even beyond all shame'; and, in later years, John Evelyn, who said that he would never forget 'the inexpressible luxury and profaneness, gaming and dissoluteness of the Court', saw him 'sitting and toying with his concubines ... a French boy singing love songs, in that glorious gallery, whilst about twenty of the great courtiers and other dissolute persons were at Basset round a large table, a bank of at least 2,000 in gold before them'.

When he married, the King promised one of these concubines, Lady Castlemaine, that she should be a Lady of the new Queen's Bedchamber. The Queen angrily struck her name off the list of her Ladies, and the Lord Chancellor, the Earl of Clarendon, warned the King that his subjects would think him heartless, as indeed they did.

The trouble was, of course, that the Queen had fallen deeply in love with her husband within a few days of first seeing him, 'a solecism none of his mistresses was so careless as to commit' for they had learned that the King was a man 'easily irked by demanding affection'. The King's own passions were never aroused by this small, dark, nervous daughter of John of Portugal. He had chosen her not so much because her face in a miniature seemed 'not unhandsome' as because he needed a rich wife; and while he assured Lord Clarendon, having seen her in person, that there was 'not anything in her face that in the least degree could shame one' and that her conversation conducted in 'a most agreeable voice' was 'very good', he spoke of her in a less complimentary way to his courtiers. To Colonel Legge he complained that 'they had brought him a *bat* instead of a woman'. But although she was indeed 'a very little woman', as Sir John Reresby said, and with her sallow skin and prominent teeth and her 'very nervous distemper' could not hope to 'stand in competition with the charms of the Countess of Castlemaine', she had what Pepys called a good, honest and innocent look and was far more handsome than her formidable maids of honour — 'six frights' according to Count De Grammont — with their 'monstrous fardingales', their stern refusal to offend their virginity by sleeping in sheets once touched by a man and their entourage of 'very pious, very dirty Portuguese monks'. She might indeed have given 'little additional brilliancy to the Court, either in her person, or in her retinue', yet she was far from being the haughty, bigoted, parsimonious, unimaginative frump some writers have described.

Realizing that the King would not give up Lady Castlemaine for her sake, that he not only continued to make love to this mistress but was trying to seduce Frances Stewart at the same time, that he had other women besides, and that — or so she was advised — she would never change him, but might by changing herself win his love, she gave in. She stopped sitting alone and aloof, declining to join in the pleasures of the Court and going early to bed when she could bear no longer the insulting whispers and disdainful glances of her husband's friends. By 1668 she was apparently taking part in all the 'fashionable freaks' of the Court, going about the town masked or disguised as an orange girl, entering into houses to dance there 'with a great deal of wild frolic'.

This complete and astonishing change in the Queen's behaviour was noticeable, too, in her clothes. She abandoned her sombre and gigantic skirts held out by hoops of a vast circumference; she wore no more the high, stiff ruffs that concealed her throat; and she yielded to her husband's entreaties that she should conform to the current fashion of his Court. Indeed, whatever the fashion, the Queen's clothes not only reflected but exaggerated it. At a time when it was fashionable

The Knights of the Garter feasting in St George's Hall. Charles II sits alone at the high table
in the background, and the Knights sit along the wall on the left each served by his own attendant.
Garter King of Arms stands facing the King at the head of the twelve Officers of Arms.
The larger St George's Hall which visitors to the State Apartments now see was made by Wyatville
who pulled down the wall dividing it from Charles II's domestic chapel.

for a dress to be cut so low that the swell of the breasts was seen even to the nipple's aureola, the Queen 'exposed her breast and shoulders without even . . . the slightest gauze; and the tucker instead of standing up on her bosom, is with licentious boldness turned down and lies upon her stays'.

To those who knew him well there was nothing surprising about the Queen's surrender to the King's wishes and her rare objections to the insulting activities of his mistresses, for his bland charm was ultimately irresistible. He was self-indulgent, sometimes sarcastic, and often impatient; he had a tendency, without being permanently indolent, to dismiss serious matters with a flippant jest; and he also had a tendency, as Bishop Burnett said, to make 'fair promises, in which he was liberal to excess, because he intended nothing by them but to get rid of importunity, and to silence all further pressing upon him'; he was affected and he could be deceitful and unreliable, insensitive and even vindictive; he was capable of alarming outbursts of anger and moods of surly ill-temper, particularly as he grew old. But his innate kindness and generosity, his friendliness and tact, his love of children and animals, his tolerance, his ironical humour and conversation, his evident and disarming delight in all the pleasures of living, cast his failings into shadow. He may have been a 'lazy Prince' but he was a delightful man. He 'never lost his affability and courtesy. He touched people for the evil without evincing either nausea or a temptation to mirth. But on solemn occasions he could never play the King. He read his speeches to Parliament like a schoolboy . . . If he saw an acquaintance at play, in the park, or even in a State procession, he would nod to him with the easy familiarity of an equal; and if the gentleman happened to have a handsome wife with him, he would cast on the husband a glance of significant meaning.' And yet for all his carefree ways, he never forgot that he was King.

The household at Windsor was governed by rules which were occasionally relaxed but never abandoned. Many of his courtiers would have liked these rules to be more closely modelled on those of the French Court of Louis XIV which they had so much admired during their exile. But the King had little patience with the fantastic extravagance of formal etiquette that enforced upon French courtiers when performing their duties correctly — which it must be said they did not often do — the stylized movements of a parodied ballet. And when a visitor denied him the respect traditionally due to a King he would make a joke of the breach of etiquette rather than take offence, as he did with William Penn who 'thinking proper to bring his sectarian prejudices into the presence of royalty' kept his hat on when introduced and, seeing the King remove his own, asked him 'Friend Charles, why dost thou not keep on thy hat?' ''Tis the custom of this place,' the King replied, 'for only one person to remain covered at a time.'

Charles's daily life was consequently far less rigidly formal than many of his francophile friends would have liked it to be, and his Bedchamber, where the most secret affairs of State were transacted,

Preparatory drawings by Wenceslaus Hollar for his illustrations to Ashmole's 'Institutions, Laws and Ceremonies of the Most Noble Order of the Garter'. Ashmole and Hollar walked round the castle together in the 1660s; and Hollar's subsequent drawings show clearly how little its architecture can have appealed to Charles II who had grown to love the new Baroque style. The upper drawing is the view from the south-east, the lower one from the south-west.

A drawing by Hollar of the castle as seen from beyond the road from Datchet. The Queen's Tower is that on the far right.

frequently contained men and women whom a strict observance of court protocol would have denied entrance. To his closet only he and his trusted servant William Chiffinch had a key, but this was not so much because court etiquette required it as because Chiffinch was entrusted with the task of conducting women of the town into it; and here, when his male friends were admitted, the conversation, as in the Bedchamber and the Withdrawing Room, was gay and uninhibited. When he went to the lavatory, which he did every night before he went to bed, he liked to be accompanied by two attendants, one to hold the candle, the other to hold the paper, not because the rules governing his conduct required their presence, and certainly not because he shared the views of the King of Spain who would 'not piss but another must hold the chamber pot', but because he enjoyed their company.

He did not comb his hair or shave himself, but when these duties were being performed he was talking, flipping over the pages of a book, or sitting with his knees against the window looking out at his gardens and parks and planning alterations. Nearly every morning, whether he had been making love in the night or not, he got up early; and nearly every day he went outside to take some sort of exercise and so preserve his excellent health. He took pleasure in all kinds of sports, and at Windsor, where he could scull and swim as well as ride and hunt and play tennis in the new court he had built there, he was particularly happy.

*

The better he knew Windsor, the more he liked it. During the first few years of his reign, the duties and diversions of London life occupied most of his time and he came to the castle but rarely, and never stayed long. For although the squatters who had moved into the castle after the Civil War had been turned out, much of the fabric was still 'ragged and ruinous', and many of the items of repair, listed by a Commission of Inquiry into allegations of negligence and misappropriation of funds made against King Charles I's surveyor in 1629, remained neglected. After the King's execution the House of Commons had even resolved that 'the Castle of Windsore, with all the Houses, Parks and Lands there, belonging to the State, be sold for ready money'. But although a Bill was brought in, it was thrown out after a debate in which the price of £2,700 (for a fine house and 472 acres) obtained a few years before for Sunninghill Park nearby, apparently influenced many Members against taking so drastic a step for so small a price. It had been decided to sell the 'Little Parke and meadowes there' only. Within a short time, however, these were re-purchased for the Protector, and so passed back with the rest of the Windsor estates into royal owner-ship at the Restoration.

The Constable of the castle at the time of the Restoration was Bul-strode Whitelocke, who set out for the benefit of his successor the customary duties and perquisites of this office. The Constable 'is Keeper and Governour of the Castle,' Bulstrode wrote,

and commands any Garison or under officers there. Hee may make use of any Lodgings or Roomes in the Castle whereof the King hath not present use; Hee is Judge of the Castle Court for tryell of Suites of any value arising within the honor . . . He is Keeper of the Forest which is 120 miles compas, and hath care of the Vert and Venison there when it is stored, and power to hunt and dispose of them as he shall thinke fitt, not prejudicing the King's Pleasure.

He had power to punish and imprison in the castle's Colehouse all those who killed game without a licence or cut down any trees. He might dispose of the 'several Lodges and walkes in the Forest to whom he pleaseth' and was responsible for the collection of rents. His salary

A *bird's-eye view and a prospect of the Castle from the south-east in about 1670.* An engraving by Wenceslaus Hollar, formerly drawing-master to Charles I's children. The principal towers — to give them their present names and beginning at King Henry VIII Gate, the main entrance to the Castle in the bottom left-hand corner, and working to the east — are Mary Tudor Tower (rising in the middle of the Military Knights' Lodgings), King Henry III Tower, King Edward III Tower (at the foot of the mound steps), the Queen's Tower (on the south-east corner), Clarence Tower, Chester Tower, Prince of Wales Tower (on the north-east corner), Winchester Tower (opposite King Henry III Tower), Curfew Tower (on the north-western corner), Garter Tower and Salisbury Tower (on the south-western corner). The southern face of the Upper Ward (altered by Hugh May after this engraving was done) was altered again by Wyatville who made a new gate there. The Queen's Tower was rebuilt in 1680. Subsequently it contained the private apartments of Queen Charlotte and, after being remodelled by Wyatville, of all subsequent queens including Elizabeth II. The Horseshoe Cloister built by Edward IV for the priest-vicars at the western end of St George's Chapel can still be seen by visitors to the Castle. The annexe at the eastern end of the Chapel was started by Henry VII on the site of an earlier building erected by Henry III in 1240. It was restored by Queen Victoria in memory of the Prince Consort and is now known as the Albert Memorial Chapel.

Prospect of the Castle from the S.E.

WINDSOR CASTLE

1 Chancellors Tower
2 Castle Gate
3 St Francis Crames Buildings
4 Gouernor of the Alms Knights Tower
5 St Georges Chapell
6 Lieutennants Tower
7 Gainers Tower
8 The Wardrobe
9 Black Rods Lodgings
10 Earle Marshalls Tower
11 Kings gate
12 Winchester Tower
13 The Keepe
14 The ascent to the keepe
15 Watch Tower
16 Great gate to the Kings lodgings
17 St Georges hall
18 North East Tower
19 Bridge from ye Tarras into the little parke
20 Tarras Gate
21 Parke oate
22 Garters Tower
23 Bell Tower
24 Deanes House
25 Canons House
26 Petty Canons Houses
27 Alms Knights Lodgings
28 The Towne.

Geometricall Pases of 5 Feet

W. Hollar delineauit et Sculpsit

was only £20 a year and 'Tenn Load of wood for fuell and 40s. yearly to defray the charge of cutting it', so that, as Whitelocke complained, the office, although of 'very great antiquity, honour, power and pleasure', was of 'very little profit'.

One of Whitelocke's successors as Constable was Prince Rupert, by then prematurely old with a 'dry hard-favoured visage, and a stern look, even when he wished to please', but his life was as crowded and active as it had ever been. He hunted with vigour; he reorganized the garrison and tightened up its discipline; he experimented with mezzotint engraving; he wrote long letters to friends in Germany; he received visits from his mistresses; and, as John Evelyn noticed on a visit in August 1670, he began 'to trim up the keep, or high round tower, and handsomely adorned his hall with furniture of arms'. Indeed, the whole castle, Evelyn was glad to learn, was at last 'going to be repaired'.

Al prospict in the same Ward towards the West.

Al prospict from the East end of the Lower Ward towards the West.

Left: Drawings by Hollar of the Upper and Lower Wards. The top picture shows the Upper Ward looking towards the east with the Star Building and State Entrance to the left. The middle picture is the same Ward as seen from the opposite direction with the Round Tower in the centre. The lower picture shows the Lower Ward with St George's Chapel on the right and King Henry VIII Gate on the left.

Opposite: The castle in about 1680 by John Wijck. The view is of the north front from the river. The new State Apartments designed for Charles II by Hugh May can be seen on the left.

A few years before, Elias Ashmole, the antiquarian, had walked round it while gathering materials for his projected history of the Order of the Garter and had taken with him the engraver, Wenceslaus Hollar, whose most important engraving was the large bird's-eye view of the castle. This engraving, illustrating the castle's severe lines and its absence of windows in the outside walls, shows clearly how little its architecture can have appealed to Charles II, whose taste had been formed during his exile in Holland and France. The palace at Versailles and the Louvre, where the new Baroque style, born further south, was being revealed to admiring architects and patrons from all over the world, seemed to him incomparably finer than the severe lines of Windsor Castle which had remained largely unchanged in their main contours for five centuries. Christopher Wren, who visited Paris in the summer of 1665 and found a thousand hands at work on the Louvre, where twice a month 'an academy of painters, sculptors, architects, and the chief artificers' met to give magnificent reality to Bernini's design, thought that here indeed was the best school of architecture in Europe.

Wren had lived at Windsor for over twenty years, for his father had been Dean between 1635 and 1659; but he was not appointed Comptroller of the Works until 1684 when Charles II had only another year

to live. All the work that was carried out in the castle during the King's lifetime was supervised by another architect of far less fame but of considerable talent, Hugh May.

May was the friend of both Pepys and Evelyn. He was, Pepys thought, a most ingenious man; and although Horace Walpole did not include him in his list of architects, his designs for Berkeley House, Piccadilly, and for Cassiobury, 'a very noble place' in Evelyn's opinion, together with his work at Windsor, which was responsible for 'introducing the grand Baroque conception into the domestic architecture of the country', entitle him to high regard.

At Windsor, he entirely rebuilt the royal suite in the Upper Ward, known today as the State Apartments; and while from the outside this new Star Building – as it was called from the huge Garter Star on its northern face – presented an appearance which was plain to the point of dullness its interior was of an astonishing beauty.

On the ground floor, facing inwards towards the quadrangle, the fourteenth-century Gothic entrance hall was retained, but above this

Camera Præsentiæ
A. Verrio pinxit.   Regii Palatii Vindsorensis
                                      P. Vandrebanc sculpsit.

the domestic chapel, St George's Hall and the new saloons reflected all the rich exuberance of the Baroque taste. Delicately painted ceilings by the Neapolitan Antonio Verrio, in which the allegorical figures — one of which was Charles himself in the unlikely company of Prudence, Temperance and Fortitude — seem to move and float, and richly carved

Ceilings in the State Apartments painted by Antonio Verrio. Left, an engraving of the ceiling of the King's Audience Chamber (now destroyed) shows Verrio's patron, Charles II, in the unlikely company of Prudence, Temperance and Fortitude; above, the ceiling of the Queen's Audience Chamber — the Queen, Catherine of Braganza, is represented seated under a canopy spread by Time and supported by Zephyrs.

cornices and frames by Grinling Gibbons, in which the leaves and fruit, the fish and game have a graceful asymmetry at once intricate and sensual, give to those rooms, which have survived both the erosion of time and the Gothic revival, a splendour which is unexcelled.

John Evelyn on a visit to Windsor in the summer of 1683 was delighted with the newly finished works. Verrio's invention was 'admirable', he thought, 'his ordnance full and flowing, antique and original'. With 'the stupendous and beyond all description the incomparable' work of Grinling Gibbons he was particularly delighted, for he had himself discovered the artist, while walking near his home one day, in a 'poor solitary thatched house' which he had stumbled upon by 'mere accident'. He had happened to look through the window and seen Gibbons at work and some time later he had introduced him to the King. Seeing his work at Windsor he felt sure that he was 'without

controversy, the greatest master both for invention and rareness of work, that the world ever had in any age'.

Evelyn was delighted also with the surroundings of the castle. The terrace on the north side had been taken round the south and east flanks and had been made 'clean, even, and curiously turfed'. The Long Walk, an avenue three miles long, was not laid out and planted until 1685, but already other 'avenues to the new park had been planted with elms and limes'. There was 'a pretty canal and receptacle for fowl: nor less observable and famous' was 'the throwing so huge a quantity of excellent water to the enormous height of the Castle, for the use of the whole house, by an extraordinary invention of Sir Samuel Morland'.

Morland, a most versatile man credited with all sorts of inventions from the drum capstan for weighing heavy anchors to the speaking trumpet as well as with this machine for raising water, placed his remarkable engine beneath the base which Grinling Gibbons had carved for Josias Ibach's statue of Charles II in the Upper Ward. Morland amazed his contemporaries by forcing water 'in a continual stream at the rate of above sixty barrels an hour up to the top of the Castle'. There had been a fountain in the Upper Ward for generations and in Norden's drawing of the castle done in 1607 the Tudor fountain under its curious canopy occupies an imposing position; but Morland's seemed 'the boldest and most extraordinary experiment ever performed by water in any part of the world'.

The King enjoyed watching the machine at work and would stand by it with his watch in his hand, measuring the rate of flow. He had always been interested in mechanics and science and spent longer hours than ever in his laboratory as he grew older.

It was a quiet life at Windsor. 'There was little resort to him,' Sir John Reresby said after being shown round the castle when the improvements were in their final stages, 'and he passed his day in fishing or walking in the parks which indeed he naturally loved more than to be in a crowd or in business.'

And in these summer weeks, although he got up early as was his usual practice in London, he did little business. Occasionally there were days when he was obliged to discuss affairs of state; sometimes there was a visit from a foreign prince; and once the curious Ambassador from the King of Bantam came with 'several of his Retinue carrying Launces, and two of them umbrellas, besides two of his master's servants, who also carried two umbrellas over his letter of credence'. But most days were spent in quiet pleasure: fishing at Datchet, swimming in the river, hawking in the Forest, long walks in the Park, planting trees, playing tennis and bowls, watching cock-fights, looking at his pictures or the illustrations in his books, watching his exotic birds in their beautiful cages and, in particular, admiring 'Cockatoo', whose cage was kept in his eating-room, amusing his friends by his conversation, well informed and witty, and his store of anecdotes, embellished each time they were repeated. In the evening he would watch a play in St George's Hall or go to the Queen's apartments to play a game of basset or downstairs to the apartments assigned to the Duchess of Portsmouth to play crimp.

The Duchess of Portsmouth, formerly Louise de Kéroualle, an exceptionally pretty baby-faced Breton girl who had been his sister's maid of honour, was now his most favoured mistress, and perhaps, even, his closest friend. Lady Castlemaine, created Duchess of Cleveland in 1670 and the acknowledged mother of six of his numerous illegitimate children, rarely came to Windsor after the alterations were completed; while the other mistresses of his later years, the Duchess Mazarin, Catherine Peg, and Moll Davis, the actress, were also more often to be seen with the King in London. One of the Duchess of Portsmouth's rivals was, however, frequently at Windsor, where she lived in a fine house called Burford House after her son, who was created Earl of Burford in 1676.

The story of the elevation of this little boy to the peerage, whether true or not, is characteristic both of his father, the King, and of his mother, Nell Gwynn. Pepys first saw the lively little Cockney comedienne standing outside her door in Drury Lane. He admired her 'smock-sleeves and bodice' — something of a fetishist, he once confessed that it had done him good to look upon Lady Castlemaine's 'smocks and linnen petticoats' hanging up to dry — and he decided that Nell was a 'mighty pretty creature'. The King thought so too, and found her not only exciting and lovable as a mistress but enchanting as a companion. The daughter of a woman who had drowned herself when drunk, she had been brought up in a brothel and had been an orange-girl in a theatre before becoming an actress. She was a clever and impudent mimic and a mistress of tart and vulgar repartee. Once when her carriage was stoned by the mob who mistook it for the unpopular Duchess of Portsmouth's, she put out her head and shouted 'Don't hurt me, good people! I'm the Protestant whore,' and once when this rival went into mourning for a French prince to whom she was in no way related, Nell Gwynn dressed herself in even deeper mourning for, so she said, the dear departed Cham of Tartary. In Charles's presence she is said to have called to his son, 'Come here, you little bastard,' and when Charles reproached her for using such a rude word, she replied that she had no other name to give him. Immediately he was made Earl of Burford and afterwards Duke of St Albans.

Such stories delighted a people who detested the King's less honest and far less faithful mistresses. For, claiming no special privileges, Nell Gwynn excited no popular jealousy. She was appointed one of the Queen's Ladies in 1675, some years after the King's munificence had enabled her to leave the stage; but few except the Duchess of Portsmouth, who could tell she had once 'been an orange-girl by her swearing', begrudged her either this honour or her new-found wealth. 'Her joyous laugh, her wild extravagance of speech, her warm-hearted disposition, and imperturbable good-nature' established her not only in the affections of her Charles the Third (as she fondly called him, referring to her two previous lovers, Charles, Lord Buckhurst and Charles Hart, the actor) but also in the affections of her fellow people. She was, in fact, in her own time, 'the picaresque heroine she has ever since remained'.

Despite the presence of the Duchess of Portsmouth in the castle and of Nell Gwynn at Burford House, the Queen appeared to like Windsor as much as her husband did. She had long become resigned to his selfishness and constant unfaithfulness. Once going to his bedroom and noticing a tiny slipper beside his bed, she laughed and withdrew quickly, lest 'the pretty little fool', whoever it was, hiding behind the curtain, should catch cold.

Nell Gwynn by Sir Peter Lely.

She loved to go out into the Park on hot afternoons and share a picnic with her ladies and servants in the shade of the trees. 'All the Queen's servants treated her by everyone bringing their dish,' Lady Chaworth wrote, giving an account in a letter of one such alfresco meal, 'and she eat under a tree. Lady Bath's dish was a chine of beef, Mrs Windham's a venison pasty, but Mr Hall bought two dozen of ruffs and reeves and delicate baskets of fruit, Mr Chiffinch, for his daughter's behalf, twelve dozen of choice wine. The Queen wonderfully pleased and merry, and none but herself and servants.'

Informal as both the King and Queen liked to be, however, when taking their meals on ordinary occasions, the banquets given for the Knights of the Garter in the tapestry-hung St George's Hall at the time of the Feast of St George were as magnificent as they had ever been.

The celebrations lasted three days and at each meal the fare provided was a splendid display of English food and cooking at their superb and lavish best. The meals 'most costly and delicate, completely royal and set forth with all befitting state and grandeur', were eaten in a suitably ceremonious manner. For King Charles was determined to restore to the Order those ancient trappings of splendour which had never fully recovered their former ostentation since statutes, passed in the reign of Edward VI, had condemned their 'many despicable ceremonies of a Papist origin'.

As the Civil War approached, however, the Feasts gradually became less and less grand and imposing, and by the time of the Restoration the number of Knights had dwindled to half the statutory strength and there seemed even a danger that the Order itself might lapse into decay. Through the efforts of Charles II it did not do so. Within a year of his return to England he had restored the Order to its 'proper condition'; he had filled up all its vacancies and he had even 'thought it not unworthy' his care to 'descend unto the particulars of its clothing' by decreeing that undergarments which 'followed too much the modern fashion' should not be worn beneath the upper robes of the Order and thus detract from their 'decency, gravity and stateliness'. In future all undergarments, whether 'Trunkhose or Round Breeches' should be made of 'Cloth of Silver'. The effect of all this was, unfortunately, far from decent, grave and stately, for the Knights became so proud of their new clothes that, so Evelyn told Pepys, they 'did wear them all day till night, and then rode into the Park with them on'.

While Pepys and Evelyn were both distressed by the conduct of the Knights who disregarded the King's wishes for their dignified appearance and behaviour, they were both gratified that the restoration of the Order had led to the restoration also of St George's Chapel, 'a noble place indeed' in Pepys's opinion, with 'a good Quire of voices'. 'Great bowing by all the people, the poor Knights in particular, to the Altar,' he noticed when taken to a service there one day by the organist. There were those who were shocked by these repeated obeisances; but Pepys made no complaint. It was a memorable day and he was happy that the Stuarts had come back. And Windsor, after all, was truly the 'most romantique Castle in the world'.

The interior of St George's Chapel as it appeared in the reign of Charles II. The chancel of the Chapel as seen from the east showing the stalls. The Sovereign's stall is on the left of the choir doors, the Prince's stall on the right. The organ was replaced in the eighteenth century by one built by Samuel Green and presented to the Chapel by George III.

4

JAMES II

Although most Englishmen shared Pepys's view of the Restoration, few of them could look forward happily to the accession of Charles II's brother, James, Duke of York, who, since it seemed unlikely that Queen Catherine would ever have a son, would regrettably be his successor.

Once when taking one of his long walks with two of his friends, Charles came across the Duke of York returning from hunting in his coach. The Duke expressed surprise at seeing his brother endanger his life by walking about with 'so small an attendance'. 'No kind of danger, James,' said the King, 'for I am sure no man in England will take away my life to make you King.'

It might well have been true, for the Duke of York, as Burnet said of him, had the 'strange notion' that no regard was 'to be had to the pleasing of the people'.

When Charles died in 1685 the Duke was fifty-one and he had the reputation of being as great a threat to female virtue as his brother had been. According to De Grammont, the Duke of York's principal if not his only occupation was adultery.

He had few other vices, apart from an impenetrable obstinacy which made him believe that all those opposed to him were guilty of treason or worse and deserved the most ferocious punishment; but his virtues were not attractive ones. He was provident, but it was a providence close to parsimony; he was rarely drunk but was censorious of those who were; he was a firm friend but 'a heavy enemy'; he was brave but entirely lacking in understanding of what makes some good men cowards; he was sincere but self-righteous; he was industrious but unimaginative; he was desperately concerned about the strength of his sexual needs. He was believed at the time of his accession to be suffering from a venereal disease which had impaired his mental faculties, and certainly the loss of what little sense of proportion he had previously enjoyed, his erratic impulses and excessive *hauteur* can be thus explained. Apart from a passion for hunting which rivalled that of his grandfather — he was one of the earliest of aristocratic fox-hunters, foxes previously being considered fair quarry for yeomen farmers and the lesser gentry but not for noblemen who had confined their attention to stags and hares — he had few other interests. Music appealed to him a little, but literature and painting scarcely at all. Like most egotists he had no humour. The principal objects of his life — the conversion of England to Roman Catholicism and the establishment of a monarchy on the model of Louis XIV's — were never realized, and the means he took to achieve them resulted in his final exile and the Glorious Revolution of 1688.

In his younger days he had served with distinction in the French and Spanish armies, both of which he had for some time commanded, and had proved himself, as Lord High Admiral in England, a good naval commander as well as an excellent administrator. He had demonstrated his skill in military tactics at Windsor, when, with the Duke of Monmouth, 'at the foot of the long Terrace below the castle' he attacked with a little army a representation of the City of Maestricht, 'newly taken by the French. Bastions, bulwarks, ramparts, palisadoes, graffs, hornworks, counterscarps, etc., were constructed', John Evelyn, one of the spectators, wrote in his diary:

On Saturday night they made their approaches, opened trenches, raised batteries, took the counterscarp and ravelin, after a stout defence; great guns fired on both sides, grenadoes shot, mines sprung, parties sent out, attempts of raising the siege, prisoners taken, parleys; and, in short, all the circumstances of a formal siege, to appearance, and, what is most strange, all without disorder, or ill accident, to the great satisfaction of a thousand spectators. Being night, it made a formidable show.

But admirable as James may have been as a tactician, his interest in the Army after his accession was taken as being a threat to the Constitution, and his determination to have a large standing army as a means of establishing an arbitrary power and himself as supreme ruler of a Roman Catholic state.

How far he was prepared to go in realizing his ambition was demonstrated in July 1687 when the Papal Envoy was received in State at Windsor. 'The Duke of Somerset (one of the lords of the bedchamber) being in waiting refused to attend in that ceremony, for which he was forbid comming to Court and lost all his places. Five of the six gentlemen of the Privy Chamber were put out of their imployments for the same caus.' Already the King, who had publicly celebrated Mass at Windsor and bought vestments and candlesticks and a new organ out of Secret Service money, had discharged the 'Dean of the Chappell and the Chaplaines from attending any more at that office'. Now he and his second wife, Mary of Modena, were to the horror of most of their subjects prepared to 'parade the Papal Envoy' if not before the 'vast population of the capital' at least before the 'great multitudes that flocked' to Windsor to see the long procession of thirty-six coaches each drawn by six horses led by the Knight Marshal's men and 'a long train of running footmen'.

It was one of James's last acts of provocation towards a people far from ready to accept the kind of religious toleration he advocated; and when in the following year seven bishops were tried for refusing to read in their pulpits a Declaration of Indulgence, which exempted Catholics and Dissenters from penal statutes, and a son was born to the Queen, an invitation was sent to William of Orange, James's nephew and the husband of his daughter Mary by Anne Hyde, the King's first wife.

William landed at Torbay on 5 November 1688 and made his way to Windsor, which became the 'Dutch headquarters'. Here as the year and James's reign ended, William of Orange demonstrated a gift for statesmanship which his father-in-law had never possessed.

5

WILLIAM III AND MARY II

Apart from a strong taste for hunting and an autocratic manner, there was little in common between James II and his nephew. The new King was thirty-eight and his character had long ago 'been shaped in the iron mould of disillusionment'. He had grown up among enemies and was distrustful, cold, artful, always severe and on occasions ruthless. 'He hid his slow brain, his growing distrust of men, behind an impassive exterior. He heard his Ministers out in chilling silence, chewed over their advice until they had almost forgotten it themselves, then acted, relying only on his powerful memory and his exact judgement of men in politics.'

His father had died eight days before he was born, and his mother, the eldest daughter of Charles I, had quarrelled both with his grandmother and the government about his custody. At the age of nine he was taken to the University of Leyden, where he showed himself to be a conscientious pupil, a good linguist, a strict Calvinist and precociously conscious of his stern destiny. Married to King James's daughter Mary at St James's at eleven o'clock on the night of his twenty-seventh birthday, he had consistently treated her with a harshness which she appeared never to resent or even to regret. She was pious and charitable, modest, gracious, sweet-natured and retiring. She loved to work and, as Horace Walpole was sardonically to observe, she 'contented herself with praying to God that her husband might be a great hero, since he did not choose to be a fond husband'. Her Court at The Hague had been 'remarkable only for dullness and decorum' and when she returned to England to be proclaimed joint-sovereign with her husband she ran about, talking a great deal and 'looking into every closet and conveniency, and turned up the quilts of the beds, just as people do at an inn, with no sort of concern in her appearance'.

Much as her new courtiers despised her, however, they considered her husband's behaviour far more unseemly than that of their tall, gentle Queen with her interests in housework, gardening, music and collecting porcelain. William kept his mistress, the Countess of Orkney, out of public sight. But his two close and extravagantly rewarded Dutch friends, Hans Willem Bentinck (created Earl of Portland and given, among many other sources of revenue, the Rangership of Windsor Great Park) and Arnoud van Keppel (created Earl of Albemarle, a Lord of the Bedchamber, Keeper of the Robes, and a Knight of the Garter), were believed to be something more than friends. According to the Duchess of Orleans, the King was 'in love with Albemarle as with a woman . . . and used to kiss his hands before all the Court'; while Portland's jealousy was obvious to everyone and was believed to be impossible to explain outside the context of a homosexual affection. The King, however, provided his many enemies with no satisfactory proof of an illicit relationship. And more sympathetic observers might have seen in his emotional attachments to these two men the sad hunger for friendship of a man without friends, the desire for a father of a man who had never known his own father, the desire for a son of a man who did not have one.

Aloof and unsociable, with a 'coldness in his way' that damped 'a modest man extremely', so reserved that often at dinner he would eat the entire meal in silence, by turns phlegmatic and irritable, seldom laughing 'but when he had outwitted others and then it was in the most ungraceful manner', he struck most of the English nobility with his awkward movements, his pitted face, his slow speech and constant cough as a thoroughly distasteful interloper. Unprepared to recognize his qualities as a brave soldier, a statesman and a diplomatist, or to sympathize with his high aims and ideals, they disliked him for the apparent callousness of his means — pointing to the massacre of Glencoe as a characteristic example — they despised him for his atrocious manners and lack of any social graces.

The castle by Leonard Knyff. The view is from the north in about 1708.

One of Princess Anne's ladies gave an instance of his vulgar behaviour at his own table: 'There happened to be a plate of peas, the first that had been seen that year. The King, without offering the princess the least share of them, ate them every one himself. Whether he offered any to the queen I cannot say; but he might do so safely enough, for he knew she durst not touch them.'

The Court became as unutterably dull as only five years before it had been gaily licentious. The King avoided it as much as he could. He suffered badly from asthma and found the air of London oppressive; nor did he feel either well or at ease at Windsor and was 'never so happy as when he could quit the magnificence of the Castle for his far humbler seat at Loo'. Occasionally he came to Windsor for the hunting, but after his wife died in 1693 he visited it less and less.

Queen Mary's death, in fact, had a profound effect upon him. During her sickness he had been 'in an agony that amazed us all,' Bishop Burnet wrote,

fainting often, and breaking out into most violent lamentations. When she died his spirits sunk so low that there was great reason to apprehend that he was following her . . . He turned himself much to the meditations of religion and secret prayer. He entered upon solemn and serious resolution of becoming in all things an exact and exemplary Christian.

He married off his mistress to an army officer and he kept his wife's wedding ring and a lock of her hair next to his heart. He began to drink heavily, usually alone, and his voice, already weakened by his asthma, became fainter than ever. His body shrank to a pitiful thinness, while his legs swelled to an immense size. When he pointed this out to his lugubrious physician, Dr Radcliffe heartlessly replied, 'I would not have your Majesty's two legs for your three kingdoms.' His manners became gentler and he who had been known to lash out at servants with his cane now treated them with marked consideration. One day when driving from Windsor in his coach a woman ran up close to the windows to see him. 'Is *that* the King?' she said to a friend in a voice which surprise had made louder than she had intended, 'Why my husband is a handsomer man than he.' William 'stooped towards her and said, very seriously, "Good woman, don't speak so loud; consider I'm a widower."' To his sister-in-law, Anne, with whom both he and his wife had been on the worst possible terms, he gave the dead Queen's jewels.

As his character seemed to change towards the end of his life, so did his people's attitude towards him. Their indifference and even their dislike developed into a wary respect.

6

ANNE

His sister-in-law's dislike of William long outlived him. She could not forgive him for being so rude both to her dearest confidante and to her husband. When she became Queen she continued on occasions to refer to him as 'Mr Caliban' and the 'Dutch Monster'. Anne was, of course, no Miranda herself. As a child her mother, who, according to De Grammont, was 'one of the greatest eaters in England', encouraged her daughter's good appetite and she had grown extremely podgy. When she succeeded William III in 1702 at the age of thirty-seven, although

Queen Anne, after Sir Godfrey Kneller.

not as stupendously fat as she later became, she was nevertheless a very stout woman whose early good looks had long since been lost.

Her husband, Prince George of Denmark, was also fat, and on asking Anne's uncle how he might stop himself from becoming more so, Charles II had replied, 'Walk with me, hunt with my brother and do justice to my niece.' And no one could deny that he followed the last part of this advice. During her life Anne became pregnant nearly twenty times. She miscarried frequently, however, and most of the babies that survived their birth died of hydrocephalus in their infancy, and the one that lived longest, the Duke of Gloucester, died at Windsor, also of hydrocephalus, shortly after his eleventh birthday had been hopefully celebrated with an exciting party and a magnificent display of fireworks.

These painful experiences seriously affected the health of a woman who had never been strong. She suffered recurrently from gout, and her round and serious face, always ruddy, eventually became so discoloured and blotchy that she was obliged to paint her skin to disguise it, and she often felt too ill to get up in the morning. Because of this it was often suggested that she was a heavy and secret gin drinker, but the rumours, in the opinion of the Duchess of Marlborough, a far from sympathetic observer at the time of its expression, were 'utterly groundless'. She had, in fact, most of the virtues of her father with few of his peculiar vices. She was deeply attached to her husband, the good-humoured, rather stupid, quiet, asthmatic George with his kindly ways, his love of the bottle and his atrocious accent, and she was deeply affected by his death. Her passionate attachments, first to Sarah Jennings (whom as a mark of intimacy she called Mrs Freeman and was in turn called Mrs Morley) and in later years to Abigail Hill, were whispered to be homosexual, as indeed they no doubt were, although she was probably not even conscious of the sexual root of her love for them.

Sarah, Duchess of Marlborough, after Sir Godfrey Kneller.

Sarah Jennings, who married the future Duke of Marlborough in 1678, had clearly fascinated her when they were both young girls. She was pretty, lively, strong-willed and amusing. The friendship of so vivacious and unusual a girl was flattering and exciting.

As soon as Anne became Queen she heaped honours on both Sarah and her husband. He was made Captain General of the Forces and a Knight of the Garter; she became Groom of the Stole, Mistress of the Robes, Keeper of the Privy Purse, and in place of the Dutch Earl of Portland, Ranger of Windsor Park, with emoluments totalling £5,600 a year. The Rangership of the Park carried with it the use of an attractive house, Byfield House (later to be known as Cumberland Lodge), so that the Queen was to have her dear friend close to her whenever she made one of her frequent visits to Windsor, which she loved.

Preferring a quiet country life to any other, she had spent as much time at Windsor as she could before her accession. She had lived for some years in Burford House after Nell Gwynn's death; and when Nell Gwynn's son, the Duke of St Albans, had come of age and taken over the house that had been given to his mother, Anne bought another house nearer to the South Terrace on Castle Hill. This 'little retreate out of the Palace', as the energetic traveller Celia Fiennes called it, was a charming house, all the rooms in which were panelled in plain unvarnished oak, which looked 'very neate'. The chairs were covered in white, crimson and yellow damask and there were beautiful marble chimney-pieces and pier glasses between the windows.

At both Burford House and this house on Castle Hill, Sarah Jennings had been a frequent visitor; and both Sarah and Anne, for their different reasons, continued to find their close companionship enjoyable for the first few years of the reign. By 1707, however, it had become evi-

A Prospect of the House att Windsor, Belonging to his Grace Charles
Addington Capt. of the Honble. Band of Gentlemen Pensioners, March of his Majte.

Beauclerck Duke of St. Albans, Earle of Burford, and Baron of all & Surveyour of the Hawkes to his Majne & one of the Gentlemen Bed Chamber.

A prospect of Burford House, Windsor, in the reign of Queen Anne after Leonard Knyff. Burford House is the large house on the left of the picture to the south-west of Charles II's tennis-court. Once the home of Nell Gwynn, it now belonged to her son by Charles II who was created Earl of Burford in 1676 and the Duke of St Albans in 1684. Queen Anne's house is the one with four dormer windows to the south of William the Conqueror's mound. Charles II's long walk is on the right of the picture. It was not until the reign of George IV that the Long Walk was taken up into the Upper Ward and the medieval Rubbish Gate, which can be seen behind Queen Anne's House, was demolished.

dent that the Duchess was finding the Queen increasingly tiresome and that the Queen was finding the Duchess insupportable. It was clear that their uneasy relationship would soon be damaged beyond repair. And then suddenly it was. The Duchess discovered that she had a rival, who 'came often to the Queen when the Prince was asleep'. One day Sarah had been in the Queen's room in the castle when a woman 'unlocked the door in a loud familiar manner', and tripped 'across the room with a gay air' until, catching sight of the Duchess, 'she immediately stopped short and acting a part like a player, dropped a low curtsey . . . and in a faint low voice cried "Did your Majesty ring?"' The woman was Abigail Hill, a poor relation of the Duchess who had been introduced to Anne by Sarah herself. Sarah discovered that this plain and red-nosed girl, who nevertheless possessed her 'own share of the Jennings' charm', had secretly married Samuel Masham, one of Prince George's attendants, and that Anne had been present at the ceremony without telling her anything about it. The quarrel became an open one, and often it seemed to those who knew of it that the Queen's obsessive passion for hunting was a means of escape from the bickering of her erstwhile friend.

Being now too fat to ride, she drove after the hounds in Windsor Forest at a furious pace, 'like Jehu', Jonathan Swift told Esther Johnson, the 'Stella' of his *Journal*. The Queen drove herself in a narrow one-seated, one-horsed calash with extraordinarily high wheels which carried her rattling through cornfields and across the most formidable obstacles. The taking of the quarry was celebrated by a loud blowing on a great number of horns and a knife was presented to the highest ranking man present who cut off the animal's head. Young spectators were smeared all over with blood, and in 1696 the six-year-old Duke of Gloucester was given a lavish 'baptism of blood' from hands dipped into the carcase of a deer that had been brought into the yard and killed for this specific purpose.

After the Duke's death Anne became more addicted to hunting than ever and drove as many as fifty miles on the hottest summer days. She built new kennels for the hounds at Windsor and restocked the Forest with deer. Apart from hunting and racing – she was responsible for transferring the main local race meeting from Datchet Mead, where Charles II had 'appointed races to be made', to Ascot in August 1711 – she had, however, no compelling interests. She had strong, indeed often obstinate views, but she never seemed to understand what was happening in the world or even in her own country. She paid little attention to the art, the drama or the literature which were making her reign a time of fresh renaissance. She is said to have been fond of music and she played the guitar as a girl, but in her later life she did not even listen to her own band. Her conversation was the conversation of a good-natured, unambitious, and unimaginative woman who liked her food, enjoyed playing cards and gambling, and was excessively concerned with the niceties of etiquette. She spoke, in a very pleasant voice (and with a disarming habit of 'blushing frequently'), chiefly 'upon fashions', the Duchess of Marlborough said, 'and rules of precedence, or observations upon the weather, or some such poor topics, without any variety of entertainment'. She had an extraordinarily retentive memory, 'but chose to retain in it very little besides ceremonies and customs of courts, and such like insignificant trifles'.

Her knowledge of court procedure and protocol was, in fact, immense; and her Court was consequently at once peculiarly dull and extremely ceremonious.

Her behaviour at one of the tedious receptions at Windsor has been described by Swift:

There was a drawing-room today at Court but so few company that the Queen sent for us into her bedchamber, where we made our bows, and stood about twenty of us round the room while she looked at us round with a fan in her mouth and once a minute said about three words to some that were nearest to her; and then she was told dinner was ready, and went out.

The North Terrace by Paul Sandby. On the left where the soldiers are marching is the tower which Henry VII built for his Queen. It was here while sitting in the oriel window that Queen Anne received the news of Blenheim in 1704. It now forms part of the Royal Library. Next to it is the gallery that Queen Elizabeth I made for her walks when it was too cold or wet to go outside. The tower beyond the line of trees, which conceal a buttressed curtain wall of about 1180, is Winchester Tower which was originally built by Henry III but was largely reconstructed between 1357 and 1358 by William Wykeham. It was again reconstructed by Wyatville who lived in it from 1824, when he began supervising the alterations he carried out for George IV, until his death in 1840.

She noticed at once if anyone present was improperly dressed and would express her disapproval of any man who appeared before her in the wrong sort of wig. Once Lord Bolingbroke came to her in a tie-wig instead of a full-bottomed one, and although she had sent for him in the greatest haste she was thoroughly disconcerted. 'I suppose', she said crossly, 'that the next time his lordship appears at Court he will come in his nightcap.'

With regard to her own dress she was particularly careful and despite the dullness of the result and her negligence when she was feeling ill, she spent a great deal of time each day at her toilet, an operation performed with all due ceremony, the clothes being handed by the bedchamber woman to a Lady of the Bedchamber who helped the Queen put them on.

Rigorous as she was in the observance of etiquette, however, and susceptible as she was to even the most outlandish flattery, Queen Anne was, as the Duke of Marlborough said of her, 'a very good sort of woman'. She was extremely conscientious, deeply religious, self-restrained and more ready to spend money on presents or pensions for others than on herself or on her palaces.

Most of the money she spent at Windsor was in improving the lay-out of the grounds and gardens, in which she took much interest, rather than in improving the castle itself. William III who had spent a great deal on Hampton Court 'contemplated improvements to the

A view across the Park to the south in the middle of the eighteenth century. In the foreground are the greenhouses of the Garden House, the Garden House itself and Burford House. The Long Walk stretches towards the skyline on the left.

Castle in a similar style, and on an equal scale of grandeur' and the 'talents of Sir C. Wren were called upon for a design to convert the Castle, as far as might be practicable, into a regular edifice and to connect with it an extensive and magnificent suite of gardens'. Nothing came of the scheme, however, and many parts of the castle towards the end of the Queen's reign began gradually to fall into disrepair, while many encroachments were made not only in the castle ditch where several 'Tenants and others pretended to have Interest', but also within the walls of the castle itself where there was even a small shop, the building of which inside the Gate in the Lower Ward had been permitted by Wren, then Comptroller of the Works, as it did not render any 'inconvenience to passage'.

*

The Queen, growing fatter and more gouty in her advanced middle age, lived on at the castle, a sadly pathetic figure. She could not manage to walk up the stairs during her last years and had to be carried up and down in her chair and eventually had to be lowered through a trapdoor into the room below and hauled up again by means of ropes and pulleys as Henry VIII had been. For a time she hoped that the waters which she had brought up to the castle every day from a well near Chalvey on the far side of Eton would cure her dropsical complaint, but they proved useless. She spent long hours looking out across the fields and woods, sitting in the window where in 1704 the messenger with the news of Marlborough's victory at Blenheim had found her in her large and heavy chair. Her once beautiful hands were red and swollen and swathed in bandages and it was 'only with the greatest difficulty that she could sign her name'. Her face was more blotchy than ever. On a cold rainy day in February 1714 she left Windsor for the last time, a dying woman. Throughout the spring she insisted on touching for the King's Evil, a scrofulous disease which it was believed could be cured by contact with the royal hands.

Throughout the early summer the Queen's death was intermittently reported and on 1 August she died. As her servants wept for this 'entirely English' queen, messengers were already on their way to Hanover to inform her German distant relative that he was, by virtue of his Protestantism and his descent from a daughter of James I, their new King. George I came to England to claim his inheritance, accompanied by a large retinue of German attendants, two Turkish valets and an uncertain number of German mistresses. And for sixty years Windsor was virtually abandoned as a royal home.

IV

HANOVERIANS

1

GEORGE III – THE ROYAL FARMER

Shortly after seven o'clock on the morning of 25 October 1760 George II, having drunk his customary cup of chocolate, went into his water-closet. A few moments later 'the German *valet de chambre* heard a noise, listened, heard something like a groan, ran in, and found the hero of Oudenarde and Dettingen on the floor, with a gash on his right temple, caused by falling against the corner of a bureau. He tried to speak, could not, and expired.'

His son Frederick, Prince of Wales, 'a nauseous little beast' to his mother and 'the greatest ass and the greatest liar, the greatest *canaille* and the greatest beast in the whole world' to his father, had died, un-lamented, in the arms of a dancing-master nine years before; and so it was to George II's twenty-two-year-old grandson that the Crown now passed.

The new King, it was generally admitted, was an honest, healthy and good-natured young man. Despite his bulging eyes, the rather flabby lips and undershot chin characteristic of his family, he was not bad looking. He spoke well in public; he was dignified; he was religious; and his morals, compared with those of his father and grandfather, were beyond reproach. He was, in fact, a good and amiable man. And it is at Windsor, where he loved to be, that he is to be seen at his best. Here, surrounded by a respectful family and a restful countryside, he had no longer to strive to be a king, an occupation which called for greater talents than he possessed, but he could instead behave as a country squire, a way of life more suited both to his temperament and to those undoubted capabilities which could find expression nowhere else. Like most men who suffer from a recurrent sense of inferiority and a consequent need for self-assertion, he often appeared to be less intelligent than he was and more brusque than he intended to be. At Windsor, however, retired from a life which he did not fully under-stand and removed from people he did not trust, he could feel at ease. His brusque rudeness was softened into the acceptable abruptness of an acknowledged and beloved eccentric; his celebrated conversational method became no longer an object of ridicule but an endearing and highly personal idiosyncrasy. Away from those who thought him stupid, he did not seem stupid. He was at home.

He did not discover the pleasures of this home until he had been King for several years. As his grandfather and George I had both pre-ferred Hampton Court and Kensington Palace to Windsor, most of the castle had remained neglected since the death of Queen Anne, and several parts of it were occupied by families with real or pretended claims upon royal favour.

The courtyards, the gateway, the ditch and the terraces had become playgrounds. 'The deserted courts of the Upper Quadrangle often re-echoed on the moonlit winter evenings' with the shouts of running children. 'The rooks and a few antique dowagers,' the son of a local bookseller remembered, 'were the only personages who were disturbed by our revelry. In the magnificent playground of the Terrace, away we went along the narrow wall, and even the awful height of the north side could not abate the rash courage of *follow my leader*.'

While children played, visitors, beggars, idle soldiers, higglers sell-ing fish and vegetables, women crying out oysters and oranges, all passed unhindered through the gates into the courts, and 'disorderly persons and women in red clogs or pattens' wandered up and down along the terraces shouting to each other and making assignations.

For almost twenty years the King left the castle and those who lived within its walls undisturbed, using his mother's house at Kew as a retreat from St James's Palace where he did most of his work, and

A View of Windsor Great Park by Benjamin West.
West was a favourite painter of George III who preferred his work to that of Reynolds.
He came to England from America in 1763
and was appointed historical painter to the King in 1772.

from Buckingham House which he bought for the Queen from Sir Charles Sheffield for £21,000. The Queen also had the use of Ormond Lodge in Richmond Old Park which had been set aside for her by Parliament, together with the generous promise of £100,000 a year, in the event of her husband's death. These four houses satisfied his never extravagant tastes so long as his family remained small, but as year followed year and the Queen gave birth to children with seasonal regularity, a larger country house became essential. He had never cared for Hampton Court which, like Kensington Palace, was associated with the family quarrels that had disturbed his childhood, and so his mind turned to Windsor Castle. Instead of turning out its occupants, however, and making it suitable for a King and Queen who by then had eleven children, he decided in 1776 to build a new house on the site of the one on Castle Hill which Queen Anne had occupied. He had taken over this house on its being relinquished by the Lord Steward, Lord Talbot, as the Queen had 'expressed a strong wish' to have it; but it was too small to extend and Sir William Chambers, Governor General to the Board of Works, was asked to design a much larger one,

Queen's Lodge in 1783 from a drawing by George Robertson. George III and his family are walking on the South Terrace. In the middle of the picture is Queen's Lodge built for the King's large family in 1778 on the site of Queen Anne's almost entirely demolished house. Behind it is Burford House which Queen Charlotte bought from the Duke of St Albans, Nell Gwynn's grandson, in 1777 for £4,000. The high cusped castle wall which can just be distinguished in the background above the King's hat was replaced by the present low wall so as to improve the view from Queen's Lodge. Queen's Lodge was demolished in 1823 by George IV after having been in existence for only forty-five years.

making use of what few features in the original one he could. The new building, constructed at a cost of £44,000 and more like a barracks than a country house, was referred to by its architect and by some local people as the Upper Lodge.

By the summer of 1778 King George was able to move into Upper Lodge, or Queen's Lodge as it was more generally called, with the rest of his still growing family; and for the first time in his life he seemed to be happy. He loved his good-looking children passionately (particularly the girls) when they were young, frequently weeping when they were ill or when he was parted from them, and his elder sons, who were soon found suitable apartments in the castle itself, were not yet causing him the distress they were to do later. He was not a good father to them as they grew older, for his strict enforcement of a well-intentioned, although stultifying and provocative regime allowed no imaginative modifications; but for the moment he ruled benevolently over an apparently contented family. And he seemed, at this time, to be fond of Charlotte, his wife.

He had married her in 1761 on an evening in September, a few hours after he had seen her for the first time. She had been chosen for him because she was a Protestant princess likely to bear children, and Prince George, who had recently fallen passionately in love with the beautiful Lady Sarah Lennox, took her as his wife without marked enthusiasm. She was small and thin and plain. Her skin was pale, her nose rather flat, her mouth excessively large. Her beautiful, fine brown hair, her 'pretty' eyes and her regular teeth were all that those who have described her appearance have found to praise in it. But George soon overcame his initial reluctance. She was young — only eighteen — and her expression was lively and her movements graceful. She seemed sensible and friendly, and although as the daughter of the Duke of Mecklenburg-Strelitz she had, as she herself confessed, led a life of 'extreme retirement' in Germany and was consequently not very entertaining, her husband did not appear to resent the fact. She could not talk English when she was married and, in fact, never did learn to speak it idiomatically, but her French was tolerable and the King could talk to her in German, which remained throughout their lives the language they always used together when they were alone.

Sharing a taste for a life of quiet regularity, the King and Queen introduced at Windsor a form of court life more uncompromisingly domestic and virtuous than ever before had been known there. Those chosen for court appointments were accordingly compelled to spend weeks on end in stupefying boredom. Life at St James's, as Lord Hervey had complained, was bad enough. But at Windsor where no Drawing-Rooms were held as they were at St James's; where few dances ever took place, as they quite often did at Buckingham House; where, in fact, scarcely any entertaining of any sort was done, there was nothing to relieve the appalling monotony of the days.

*

For the attendants it was a life of misery. Fanny Burney, who was one of them, had never conceived how miserable she would be.

The choice of this remarkable woman for such unsuitable employment seemed to her contemporaries extraordinary. She was the second daughter of Dr Charles Burney, the musical historian, at whose house in London she had met many of the leading actors, musicians, painters and writers of the day, including Garrick, Burke, Sir Joshua Reynolds and Dr Johnson. She herself had written two novels, *Evelina* which had an immense success — to the great surprise of her father who did not even know that she was the author of it until six months after it had been published — and the less successful *Cecilia*. Dr Burney had been disappointed when he had not been made Master of the Queen's Band; and it seemed that here was an opportunity of making amends to him through his daughter, by giving her a court appointment which commanded a salary of £200 a year, the services of her own footman, her own maid, and the use of a coach.

Fanny Burney by her cousin E. F. Burney.

And so Fanny Burney at the age of thirty-five became Assistant Keeper of the Wardrobe to Queen Charlotte. She proved to be far from an ideal assistant; and the long, introspective entries in the journal she kept at Windsor reveal a great deal more than she can have intended to expose. Her extreme shyness and frequent blushing, her nervous uncertainty and occasional absentmindedness were, for instance, disabilities of which she seems to have been unconsciously proud; and Mrs Schwellenberg, the pretentious and intolerably self-satisfied German Keeper of the Wardrobe, may well have been justifiably irritated by what appeared to be wilful efforts to exaggerate them. Whether or not she was 'utterly unfit for any place requiring punctuality, neatness and manual dexterity' as one antagonist commentator has maintained, she was certainly often to be seen racing half-dressed down the windy corridors of Queen's Lodge to Her Majesty's apartments and she never did manage to tie the bow of her necklace without getting the Queen's hair caught up in the knot. Her days were not only emotionally exhausting but physically exhausting too — and the exhaustion was increased by her not being allowed to wear spectacles, for this would have been a breach of court etiquette.

She got up each morning at six o'clock and waited for the bell to ring, giving her the first of her daily summonses to attend the Queen. The summons usually came at half-past seven and Fanny immediately rushed to the Queen's apartments. When she arrived there, Her Majesty's hair had already been dressed by her wardrobe-woman, who handed Fanny the clothes that were to be worn that day. No maid was allowed in the Queen's room while it was occupied, so Fanny always had to do all the dressing herself.

By eight o'clock the Queen was dressed and ready to go to prayers in the now cleaned and restored St George's Chapel with the King and Princesses; and Fanny, unless she was asked to look after the Queen's favourite dog, Badine, was free to return to her room. The next hour, while she read a book alone at her breakfast table, was the only pleasant one in the day.

After breakfast a long time had to be spent preparing her own clothes. On an 'ordinary' day at Windsor her dress 'required no finery' but merely had to be 'neat, not inelegant, and moderately fashionable'; but there were so many days that were not ordinary. There were Court-Days; there were the numerous birthdays of the royal family, all of which necessitated a new dress; and there were days when a journey had to be made to London or to Kew. Sometimes Fanny had not finished getting her clothes ready until a quarter to twelve when she was called again to attend the Queen. On Wednesdays and Saturdays she was called earlier, for on those days Her Majesty's hair had to be curled and craped, an operation which took the hairdresser, who always needed about two hours for the normal daily treatment, an additional hour to perform. While the hairdresser was at work, the Queen read the newspapers, occasionally reciting a paragraph aloud to lessen the boredom of her attendants. Fanny liked listening to her voice, which she described as very prettily foreign with a 'varying emphasis' which gave an interest to everything she said; and she thought that the Queen's insistence that she should go away during the process of powdering so as not to spoil her clothes was yet another example of a 'consideration' which one would not have expected 'belonged to her high station'.

The labours of the toilette were over at about three o'clock and Fanny was set free to get ready for dinner, which was served at five o'clock. It was a dispiriting meal, sometimes eaten alone with the forbidding Mrs Schwellenberg, more often with the attendants of any guests whom the King and Queen might have staying with them, or with the guests themselves; but it was always eaten in tedium. After dinner, coffee (which Fanny did not like) was served upstairs in Mrs Schwellenberg's room; and when the royal family had finished their habitual evening stroll on the Terrace — usually at eight o'clock — the poor woman, almost stupefied by boredom, came down again to the dining-room to have tea with the equerry and any gentlemen that the King or Queen might have invited for the evening, as it was 'only a very select few' that could eat with Their Majesties, and those few were always ladies, 'no men, of what rank soever, being permitted to sit in the Queen's presence'. An hour later the equerry led the guests away to the concert-room and left Fanny with Mrs Schwellenberg for two more long hours during which, every evening, she was obliged to play piquet.

At eleven o'clock she had supper and then waited, as after breakfast, for the bell to ring. As soon as she heard it she ran along the corridor again to the Queen's room to take Her Majesty's clothes off.

Only occasionally was the dreary routine altered or enlivened by a visitor; very rarely did she see any of those entertaining people who had made her earlier life so much more stimulating. Even when one of them did come to Windsor she was hesitant about allowing him to come to see her for fear of what her mistress or Mrs Schwellenberg would think. Once James Boswell came to stay with the Bishop of Carlisle in the Canons' Lodgings and it was suggested that he should be brought down to Queen's Lodge to see Miss Burney. But although she 'really wished to see him again', not only for the amusement which his own oddity and good humour gave her but also out of respect for the 'object of his constant admiration', her revered Dr Johnson, she dared not permit a visit and felt constrained to suggest what might appear to be a chance meeting outside St George's Chapel after evening service.

This, however, was quite as embarrassing. 'I am extremely glad to see you, indeed,' Boswell told her in his loud and cheerful voice. 'But very sorry to see you here. My dear ma'am, why do you stay? It won't do, ma'am! You must resign! We can put up with it no longer! I told my good host the Bishop so last night. We are all grown quite outrageous.'

Laughing nervously, Fanny hurried away from him terrified that these 'treasonable declarations' would be heard. Boswell, not in the least put out, however, followed her, continuing his advice with that deep and urgent seriousness that heightened the effect of his humour. By now, though, Fanny was thoroughly alarmed. Mrs Schwellenberg was looking out of her window, the royal family were coming towards them from the Terrace, and a crowd was gathering round the railings. She made a quick apology and hurried inside, immediately to be asked who the unknown and uninvited gentleman was and to be warned that she must never allow him to come beyond the limit of the railings.

*

In the hours that remained to her between dressing and undressing, having her hair done, and eating and sleeping, the Queen, herself, had a no less uninteresting time than Fanny Burney. She did a little embroidery; she occasionally read a book; she took a great deal of snuff; she shared her husband's liking for music and sometimes sang to her own accompaniment on the spinet; she usually went for a walk or a ride in the afternoon and in the evening played a game of cards, although her husband did not altogether approve of women enjoying themselves in this way; she professed a taste for conversation but had few opportunities to indulge it, as she found difficulty in expressing herself in English. With her husband she could speak German, but conversation with George was never easy. She does not, though, appear to have been an unhappy woman in these early years, and according to her Chamberlain, Colonel Desbrowe, the 'bloom of her ugliness' began to wear off. She never appeared to resent the fact that the King, who never discussed politics with her, forbade her to make many acquaintances in England where, so he said, 'there never could be kept up a Society without party, which was always dangerous for a woman to take part in'.

6

_____

The west end of St George's Chapel
By Paul Sandby. The entrance gate to the Horseshoe Cloister is on the left with the Curfew Tower behind.

7

_____

The summer house
By Paul Sandby. This wooden gazebo used to stand in the Home Park to the east of the north terrace.

8

*Roque's survey
of
Berkshire, 1752.*

Fanny Burney, who could not — it remains a national idiosyncrasy — judge her Queen as a woman without regard to her queenship and was always acutely conscious of her 'condescension', thought her 'a most charming woman'. She remembered vividly her kindness, forgetting — or, at least, rarely recording — her contradictory meanness and selfishness; she remembered her good nature, dismissing her frequent peevishness. Yet the picture of a fundamentally contented woman which Fanny Burney has drawn has not been satisfactorily contradicted. The Queen was lonely, of course, and her pleasure on seeing the King whenever he came upon her unexpectedly was moving and unfeigned.

The King was not so lonely, and far more self-contained. He had, in fact, an extraordinary variety of interests apart from all the normal duties and recreations of a country squire. He was interested in botany as well as music, in architecture as well as genealogy. He was devoted to fireworks and to the history and traditions of Eton College. He had

George III in Windsor uniform by Peter Edward Stroehling.

a little-known but deep concern for social reform and both Robert Raikes, the Sunday School enthusiast, and John Howard, the prison reformer, had long conversations with him at Windsor. He had a passion for pottering about with bits of machinery. He could use a lathe with skill and even managed, so it was said, to turn out several respectable buttons. He loved to take clocks and optical instruments to pieces, and it was his deep interest in telescopes that led to his appointing Sir William Herschel as Royal Astronomer and to providing him with a house and observatory at Slough. It was, of course, the detail and predictability of machinery that appealed to him, for he was a man who detested uncertainty, unpunctuality, untidiness and change. Any suggested alteration in the details of a military uniform or the prescribed customs and trivialities of etiquette disturbed him profoundly. When the shape of the hats worn by the Guards at Windsor was changed, he was deeply shocked. 'What!' he protested to the Duke of Richmond. 'What, Richmond! Who ever saw Guards in round caps?' 'Oh, yes, Sire,' said the Duke. 'My own hat is round.' 'Aye! And so is my night-cap.'

He loved uniforms. He spent hours studying military prints until he could recite the details – as he could recite the names of all the ships in his Navy – by heart. He often wore the uniform of the Royal Horse Guards because he liked the colours so much and he created a special Windsor troop and made himself a captain. In 1778, borrowing perhaps an idea of Frederick the Great's, he designed a purely personal uniform to be worn at Windsor, blue like that of the Horse Guards with scarlet and gold accessories. Even when he went out riding or walking through the royal estate he often wore a uniform, a less striking variation of the Windsor uniform made in country colours of country cloth. When he went hunting with the Princesses they all wore 'blue habits faced and turned up with red, white beaver hats and black feathers'. Sometimes he found a black jockey's cap more suitable, for eighteenth-century rides were often fast and long – eighty miles being a not uncommon distance – and, by modern standards, ferociously cruel to the horses.

The King loved the country. He had a sound knowledge of agriculture, writing letters under a pseudonym to the *Annals of Agriculture*, and the farms in the Great Park were well and profitably run. He was never so much at his ease as he was with country people. He would stroll into their cottages unannounced and talk to them about simple things in a friendly, wholly natural way. If they were poor he did his best to help them.

In many respects he was niggardly, and the tips he gave to servants frequently amounted to a single penny produced after a long search between the folds of a leather purse, while the hospitality usually offered at the castle was severely economical if not actually parsimonious. But his heart was moved by poverty. A mill in the Park ground corn at a special rate for the needy; and it was his habit to leave money behind him when he left a cottage whose tenants seemed in want of some comfort they could not afford. A committee appointed to examine the state of his private finances during his first long illness discovered that nearly a quarter of his personal income was given away in charity. The smaller, spontaneous gifts were made with the greatest good humour and without a hint of patronage.

He knew all his servants, and often spoke to them about their lives and families. He did not allow his guests to give them vails (to tip them) as was the custom in most other big houses — and this led to a demonstration by his London servants at a theatre where the King 'bore all their taunts and uproar with the greatest composure' — but he insisted that they received all the other perquisites which were due to them. And it was for this reason, more than for reasons of economy, that as soon as the last evening card game was over in Queen's Lodge and as soon as the benediction was pronounced in St George's Chapel, he saw to it that the candles were immediately blown out, for partly used candles were still an important part of the perquisites of royal servants. In addition to candles (on which by 1812 the household at Windsor was spending £10,000 a year) the servants' perquisites included all unconsumed food and wine once it had been laid upon a table. So, although they often had to wait for long periods before they received their wages, they were never unduly discontented. Certainly the King himself did his best to make them feel at home. All new servants were likely sooner or later, usually in the first week of their employment, to be startled by His Majesty appearing suddenly in front of them to make some cheerful and friendly if confusing inconsequential remark.

Inside the stables one morning he found the grooms arguing so urgently that they did not notice his arrival. 'I don't care what you say, Robert,' one of them said, 'but everyone else agrees, that the man at the Three Tuns makes the best purl in Windsor.'

'Purl? Purl? Purl?' whispered the King in his quick excited way to Robert who was standing next to him. 'Purl? What's purl, Robert?'

Robert said it was a tankard of warm beer with a glass of gin in it.

'I dare say a very good drink, grooms,' said the King so loudly that they all turned round and recognized him, 'but, grooms, too strong for the morning. Never drink in the morning, grooms.'

He never expected that they would take his advice, and many years later, arriving at the stables much earlier than usual, he found them deserted except for a small lad who did not know him.

'Boy! Boy!' the King asked. 'Boy! Where are the grooms?'

'I don't know, sir, but they'll soon be back because they expect the King.'

'Aha! Then run, boy, run, and say the King expects them. Run to the Three Tuns, boy. They are sure to be there, boy, for the landlord makes the best purl in Windsor.'

He often went down to the town himself. He liked strolling along the streets, tapping the stones with his long stick, looking in the shop windows, occasionally walking in to give the tradespeople instructions on how to vote in a local election. Sometimes he was to be seen sitting on a high stool at the counter of Charles Knight's bookshop, looking over the latest publications. One afternoon his eye caught Paine's *Rights of Man* and he picked it up and began to study it intently. Absorbed, he 'continued reading for half an hour', the bookseller's son remembered, 'and he left the shop without saying anything; but he never afterwards expressed his displeasure'. In fact, when he returned to the shop later, he was as good-humoured as ever. On another occasion, though, the title of Bishop Watson's *Apology for the Bible* upset him. 'What! What! What! Apologize for the Bible! What! What! What!'

He was profoundly and sincerely religious, with the Low Churchman's belief in the virtues of a straightforward simplicity of worship. He refused to wear his crown when attending Holy Communion after his coronation, and he later decided that new Knights of the Garter should not be required to attend that part of the service after their installation because the Sacrament was not to be 'profaned by our Gothic institutions'. Every morning at Windsor, before his visit to the stables at seven o'clock, he devoted an hour to reading the Bible and to solitary prayer; and every day he went to St George's Chapel, where he accompanied the time of the music with the printed form of the service rolled up into a baton. Anyone near him who showed the slightest symptom of having lost his place in the prayer book he was sure to put right, and a visitor once received a few smart taps on the back of the head for having sat in the wrong place.

Despite the rigidity of his political views he was not the religious bigot he appeared to those who did not know him. He refused to countenance any measures designed to remove the disabilities imposed upon Roman Catholics, but this was more due, it seems, to a confirmed belief that to do so would be to deny his coronation oath than to any violent prejudice against their religion. To Nonconformists he was openly sympathetic. The Methodists, he believed, were 'a quiet, good kind of people and would disturb nobody'. Towards the end of his life he told one of his doctors that the Lutheran religion was superior to that of the Church of England.

It was, of course, the simple virtue of the Nonconformists that made its appeal to him. One of his first acts as King had been to issue a proclamation 'for the Encouragement of Piety and Virtue, and for preventing and punishing of Vice, Profaneness and Immorality'. Addressed to 'all persons of whatsoever degree or quality', it was particularly intended for 'those who were employed near (the) royal person'. And it was the Court that suffered most. Playing at dice, cards and other games was theoretically prohibited everywhere on Sundays; but it was only at Court that the prohibition was strictly observed. Here, gambling died away on week days as well as on Sundays, and the Sunday Drawing-Rooms became entertainments of the past.

The abolition of Sunday receptions could be justified, so it seemed to the King, on other grounds, too. They were expensive. And an economic Court he was determined to have. He himself set the example.

The King's Presence Chamber in the reign of George III.

People could point as they liked at the great number of his costly children, but no one could say that his own life was an indulgent one. He refused to have a carpet in his bedroom, and there was no heating in the passages of any of his apartments. St George's Chapel was always fearfully cold. 'Princesses, governesses, equerries, grumbled and caught cold; but cold or hot, it was their duty to go; and wet or dry, light or dark, the stout old George was always in his place to say amen to the chaplain.'

One of the equerries, Colonel Goldsworthy, warned Miss Burney at the outset of her career that she would certainly die of cold. He himself, like every other equerry when in waiting, had always to be ready to accompany the King whenever he felt like going out for a ride. It was the King's 'delight to mount his horse before the equerry-in-waiting could possibly be aware of it; often in severe or unpleasant weather which rarely deterred him'. Sometimes the King was halfway down Windsor Hill before the equerry had had time 'to pull up his stockings under his boots'.

'Oh, Ma'am,' Colonel Goldsworthy lamented, 'what lives we do lead!' Of course, he comforted her, 'You won't have the hunting, to be sure, nor amusing yourself with wading a foot and a half through the dirt, by way of a little pleasant walk, as we poor equerries do! It's a wonder to me we outlive the first month.' And the final hardship was that 'after all the labours of the chase, all the riding, the trotting, the galloping, the leaping, the — with your favour, I beg pardon, I was going to say a strange word — the, the' — he was not allowed to say sweat — 'wet perspiration, and — and all that — after being wet through over head and soused through under foot, and popped into ditches, and jerked over gates', they were expected to get warm again by drinking — barley water.

'Running along in these cold passages,' he went on despairingly, 'bless us! I believe in my heart there's wind enough in these passages to carry a man o'war! And there, you'll have your share, ma'am, I promise you that! You'll get knocked up in three days, take my word for that.'

But at least Colonel Goldsworthy could not complain of the food in the castle. There was always enough to eat, for the equerries did not have to share the King's table, which was exceedingly plain and very sparse, since the King, as he had once told a friend, dreaded becoming as fat as so many members of his family had been. He took great pains never to allow himself to suffer the indignities of such obesity. He not only rode and hunted with furious energy; he not only walked twelve of the twenty-three miles between Windsor and London; he not only drank little but water, lemonade, barley water or very weak wine, but he ate nothing which he thought might lead to corpulence. Frequently his dinner was limited to cold mutton, green salad and stewed pears. Only occasionally were there plovers' eggs or cherry tart. On Sundays, like any English farmer, he had a plate of roast beef with plenty of vegetables. This, though, was a rare treat. His one regular indulgence was fresh fruit which, as it grew plentifully in the Windsor orchards, he did not consider an extravagance.

Banquets were, of course, events of extreme rarity except on royal birthdays, although, when they were given, the guests admitted that they had been well treated. And the King himself would go round the kitchens, ensuring 'that all was going on right, and that proper cheer was provided, not merely for the higher orders, but even for the soldiers in attendance'.

Friendly and hospitable as he appeared to his guests, however, he never forsook the custom of dining alone with his family at a table raised to a slightly higher level than the other tables in the room, for life at Court, simply as the royal family usually lived and much as the King insisted on the virtues of plainness and economy, was bound by the strict regulations of an invariable etiquette.

*

Every guest or attendant at Windsor was obliged to retire to the nearest wall and stand quite still as soon as any member of the royal family appeared in sight. And even amongst themselves the family maintained this severe formality. When the King entered one of their rooms, preceded by a page who made that 'particular kind of scratch' which had to be used on royal doors instead of knocking, the Princesses were expected to stand up and they were not allowed to say anything unless asked a question. Nor were they allowed to leave a room — walking backwards as everyone else did — until they were dismissed with the formal command, 'Now I will let you go'. They could sit down with permission, but the ladies-in-waiting, whose rules went so far as to forbid them to walk past the open doorway of a room which contained a royal personage, had always to remain on their feet, sometimes for hours on end. Even Her Majesty's Reader had to stand up at a lectern while she read to the Queen who, in her efforts to demonstrate that the standing circle around her was less formally constrained than it appeared, always had a small table at her elbow on which she could place her needlework or tea cup.

The etiquette during the royal family's evening stroll on the Terrace was observed with equal strictness. Usually the royals walked sedately up and down, the spectators backing away from their path, while two bands played alternately. The King wore his Windsor uniform with a star on his chest and a hat with a gold button and loop, mounted by a

George III and the royal family walking on the Terrace. The King and Queen bring up the rear. In front of them are the Prince of Wales and Prince Frederick, Princess Charlotte and Prince William, Princess Augusta and Prince Edward, Princess Elizabeth and Prince Ernest, Prince Adolphus and Prince Augustus, Princess Mary and Princess Sophia, and (in their nurses' arms) Prince Octavius and Prince Alfred. Princess Amelia had not yet been born.

black cockade, which marked him out 'conspicuously from the rest of the company'. A police officer was in attendance with a little switch to keep 'individuals from pressing too much on the King' when he stopped to talk to anyone. But this was done 'with the greatest urbanity'. Even on less formal occasions if a visitor happened to come across any member of the royal family while walking in the grounds, he was expected to back away respectfully.

Inside the castle or Queen's Lodge a visiting Minister was rarely asked to sit down. And Pitt was once kept standing for two hours when suffering painfully from an attack of gout. Later the King asked Pitt if he had had any ill effects from his having to stand so long; but he seems not to have considered the possibility of asking him to sit down.

Conversation on these occasions was appallingly difficult. Although the King was nearly always pleasant and good-humoured, he had no idea of how to make educated people feel at ease with him and often asked them to repeat several times things he found amusing, laughing just as much the last time as the first. His tastes were as limited as his opinions were erratic, and he expressed himself forcibly, talking very fast in a series of questions which expected no answer and interrupting most of them with a series of rapidly repeated ejaculations.

'Was there ever', he once asked Fanny Burney, expressing a celebrated and understandable opinion, 'such stuff as great part of Shakespeare? Only one must not say so! But what think you? What? Is there not sad stuff? What? – What? . . . Oh, I know it is not to be said! But it's true. Only it's Shakespeare and nobody dare abuse him.'

Despite this, however, and although he thought Voltaire a 'monster', he was not the philistine that most of his ancestors were. He had a genuine interest in literature and accumulated an excellent library as well as a fine collection of works of art, relying on the advice of others for his own taste was not well formed. He admired Sir Joshua Reynolds who became the first President of the Royal Academy founded in 1769; but he preferred the less subtle Benjamin West, whom he put to work on an immense representation of the Resurrection for the east window of St George's Chapel. He had a passion for Handel, but was content to listen to the same facile work of lesser composers time after time. He played the flute himself, but not very well. He went regularly to the theatre, but he enjoyed a simple farce better than anything else. He delighted in the broad comedies performed at the little theatre in Windsor and roared his appreciation of the actors of whose familiar faces and antics he never grew tired. He preferred Mrs Siddons to Garrick, and asked her frequently to come to Windsor to read a play for his family – and characteristically he did not pay her anything for doing so.

These limited interests, his lack of general knowledge and slow understanding all added to the difficulties of talking to him – difficulties which have been well described by Fanny Burney, whose own extreme shyness emphasized them.

Mrs Delany by John Opie (detail). Of this portrait Horace Walpole wrote in February 1782, 'Opie has done a head of Mrs Delany for the King — oui, vraiment, it is pronounced like Rembrandt, but as I told her, it does not look older than she is, but older than she does.' The pendant, with the initials G R, was a gift from the King.

Fanny had met him for the first time at the house near Queen's Lodge in which the King had installed his old friend, Mrs Delany, widow of an Irish clergyman, as a life tenant. The old lady had already given Fanny a short lecture on how to talk to the Queen, whose service she had not yet entered. The Queen, Mrs Delany said, often complained that she could not get any conversation and when she did she not only had to 'start the subjects, but, commonly, entirely to support them' for people could often think of nothing to reply to her except 'yes' or 'no'. Fanny experienced a similar difficulty with the King.

She was in the drawing room with Mrs Delany's great-niece Georgiana, a little girl who was Georgiana's cousin, and the little girl's father, when the noisy Christmas game they were all playing was interrupted by the entrance of Mrs Delany followed by a large man in deep mourning with a glittering star on his chest.

'The King! — Aunt, the King!' Georgiana called out nervously while Fanny retreated to the wall, intending to slip out of the door as soon as she had sidled near enough to it. But before she could fulfil this design she heard the King's loud whisper: 'Is that Miss Burney?' Mrs Delany said that it was and the King, with 'a countenance of the most perfect good humour', approached her.

'How long have you been come back, Miss Burney?' the King asked her.

'Two days, sir,' Miss Burney answered in a very soft voice.

'Unluckily he did not hear me,' she wrote later in her diary, 'and he repeated his question; and whether the second time he heard me or not, I don't know, but he made a little civil inclination of his head and went back to Mrs Delany.'

Fanny was eventually to become accustomed to the King's unnerving manner of conducting a conversation, his habit of walking about a room to ask a question of one person in a tone of voice at once good-natured and hectoring, and then to turn away and repeat the answer to someone else; but for the time being it confused her pitiably.

After telling Mrs Delany that Princess Elizabeth, his tragically fat fifteen-year-old daughter, was recovering from a recent illness, having been blooded twelve times in a fortnight, and after reminding her that the fault of his own constitution was a tendency to excessive fat which he kept under control by the most vigorous exercise and the strictest attention to a simple diet, he went up to a table to look at a book of prints which had caught his eye. He turned over a leaf or two, and then said, 'Pray, does Miss Burney draw, too?'

The *'too'* was pronounced very civilly.

'I believe not, sir,' answered Mrs Delany; 'at least she does not tell.'

'Oh!' cried he, laughing, 'that's nothing! She is not apt to tell, she never does tell, you know! — Her father told me that himself. He told me the whole history of her *Evelina*. And I shall never forget his face when he spoke of his feelings at first taking up the book! — he looked quite frightened, just as if he was doing it that moment! I can never forget his face while I live!'

Then going up close to Fanny, he said in his abrupt and alarming way, 'But what? What? How was it?'

'Sir,' Fanny said nervously, not knowing what he meant.

'How came you? How happened it? What? – What?'

'I – I only wrote, sir, for my own amusement – only in some odd idle hours.'

'But your publishing – your printing – how was that?'

'That was only, sir, – only because – '

She hesitated, as she confessed, 'most abominably, not knowing how to tell him a long story, and growing terribly confused at these questions'. She was also trying not to laugh at the urgently repeated *'What? What?'* that followed so many of his questions.

Another *'What?'*, more earnest than ever, suddenly burst from his lips and Fanny stammered out, 'I thought – sir – it would look very well in print.' It was, she thought, the silliest speech she had ever made, but she felt compelled to say something for fear of laughing. It was, however, the King who laughed. And he laughed, she remembered, very heartily and walked away from her, crying out, 'Very fair, indeed! That's being very fair and honest.' Then, as was his custom, he turned abruptly round and went back to her to continue the investigation of her motives, occasionally going over to Mrs Delany to tell her what the girl had said.

Suddenly a 'violent thunder' was made at the door. Fanny felt certain it was the Queen and longed again to escape. Georgiana backed out of the drawing-room into the hall to light Her Majesty in.

'Oh!' said the Queen as she came into the room, making her husband a low curtsey as etiquette demanded, 'Your Majesty is here!'

'Yes, I ran here without speaking to anybody.'

The Queen crossed the room towards Mrs Delany holding out both her hands; then she turned – or Fanny's weak eyes registered the impression that she turned – and made another curtsey. Not being sure that the Queen had made it to her, if, indeed, she had made it at all, and whether or not, therefore, she ought to return it, Fanny became more nervous than ever. She knew that etiquette forbade a formal introduction except at a court Drawing-Room. The King saw her distress and said something to his wife about her so that Fanny would know she must curtsey. She did so, the Queen curtseyed again and 'with a very smiling countenance' went up to her. 'But she could not speak, for the King went on talking, eagerly, and very gaily,' repeating to his wife every word Fanny had said during his conversation with her.

When tea was brought in and the Queen went to sit down, the King began all over again, with marvellous energy, on a different tack:

'Are you musical?'

'Not a performer, sir.'

He rushed to the Queen with this intelligence: 'She does not play.'

He stayed with his wife a few minutes to tell her some encouraging news he had had about Princess Elizabeth from the doctor, and then returned to Fanny.

A View of the north front of the castle from across the Thames by Paul Sandby. Sandby's brother, Thomas, was Deputy Ranger of Windsor Great Park. They lived together at Windsor of which Paul painted numerous pictures in the 1770s.

'Are you sure you never play? Never touch the keys at all?'

'Never to acknowledge it, sir.'

Soon Fanny grew extremely fond of the King, for, in spite of all his foibles and the disastrous effects of his misguided sense of duty, he was undeniably a lovable man. Her heart could not fail to warm to him when she saw how much he adored his children. It was ridiculous, of course, to allow the three-year-old Prince of Wales to make a short speech of thanks to a charitable organization and to allow him to hold a Drawing-Room after he had been created a Knight of the Garter at the age of seven. It was absurd to permit Princess Amelia to march along the Terrace at Windsor in front of the rest of the family, 'in a robe coat covered with fine muslin, a dressed close clip, white gloves and a fan', turning from side to side to watch the spectators retreat before her, as a celebration of her third birthday. But the King's so obvious delight in his 'little darling', the way he held her hand and picked her up to kiss her, his concern for her and all her sisters when they were ill, his excitement and pride when his second son the Duke of York and his next one the Duke of Clarence came back as young officers to Windsor, the one from Germany where he had been studying military science, the other from his service in the Navy, all the pleasure that he took in being a father, and most of the mistakes he made as a father, were too moving for ridicule.

Fond of him as she became, Fanny Burney could not, therefore, fail to be deeply shocked and upset when in the spring of 1788 it became clear that the King was in danger of losing his reason.

2

GEORGE III – THE ROYAL PATIENT

The King's behaviour in the past had often given cause enough for alarm. Outbursts of disconcerting hilarity had been followed by moods of silent depression. He had always been liable to violent headaches and attacks of overwhelming nervous excitement, accompanied by palpitations and sweating, when worried about something, however trivial it might be. The problem of what to do about Lady Beaulieu's application for the Earldom of Montague, reduced him, for instance, as he confessed himself, into 'the greatest state of uneasiness' he ever felt, an uneasiness no less intense than that he endured when General Burgoyne surrendered at Saratoga bringing nearer the dreaded day when the independence of the American rebels would have to be recognized, and, with that precedent set, the Empire would begin to crumble. His feverish illnesses in 1765 and 1766 had been accompanied by excessive nervous agitation and a delirious incoherence. But all this had been little known outside his family and Court. In 1788, however, his behaviour and appearance became too outlandish for secrecy.

Middle-age had emphasized the peculiarities of his face. His eyes no longer merely protruded, they goggled; his complexion was not so much healthy as florid. Thickened lips and a flabbier chin made his rapid speech even more difficult to follow than it usually was. When he walked, waving his arms, nodding his head and rolling his shoulders, he looked like a drunken penguin. In the spring of 1788 his Principal Equerry, General Benjamin Carpenter, committed suicide and after this shock the King became more erratic than ever. Sir George Baker, his doctor, alarmed by his 'up and down condition' which has recently been diagnosed as that rare metabolic disorder known as porphyria, consulted other physicians who 'prescribed a regimen without riding, to which His Majesty refused to submit, and the mildly purgative waters of Cheltenham, to which he consented'. The holiday seemed to do him good. But one day, not long after his return, he stopped Miss Burney, who was on her way from the Queen's room to her own, and talked about his health for nearly half an hour 'still with that extreme quickness of speech and manner that belongs to fever'. He was 'all agitation, all emotion,' Miss Burney said, 'yet all benevolence and goodness, even to a degree that makes it touching to hear him speak. He assures everybody of his health.'

He admitted, though, that he could not sleep any more; and once, in the Queen's dressing-room, Miss Burney heard him tell his wife 'at least a hundred times' not to speak to him when he got to his own room next door for he was greatly in need of rest. He lost weight through lack of sleep and began to look very frail. Even music now failed to comfort him, for it hurt his head to listen to it and one day he suddenly burst into tears after riding in the Park and cried out, 'I wish to God I may die, for I am going to be mad.'

In the middle of October his illness began to reach its climax. Yet he insisted on holding a levée to prove there was no cause for alarm.

A view through Queen Elizabeth's Gate by Paul Sandby. This drawing indicates the decayed state into which the castle (a playground for Windsor children) had been allowed to fall during the reigns of the first two Georges. The view through the arch is of the sharp turning in Thames Street where the road coming up south from the river turns west round the castle walls.

Four views by Paul Sandby.
Above left, Henry VIII's Gateway. This is the main gate to the castle. First mentioned in 1194, it was rebuilt by Henry VIII and bears the pomegranate badge of Queen Catherine of Aragon over the arch. Castle Hill is in the foreground and Salisbury Tower in the centre.

Below left, The South Entrance. This was how the south front of the Upper Ward appeared in 1777 before the old Rubbish Gate, approached by the Moat Bridge, was demolished and the Long Walk was taken into the Upper Ward.

Above right, The Round Tower and Devil's Tower.

Below right, The Norman Gate. This gate leads from the Middle to the Upper Ward. The Deputy Governor's house is at the far end of the Moat Garden.

But his appearance in London with his disordered dress, his legs wrapped up in flannel, his vacant gestures, his lips moving so quickly as he talked away in a hoarse, scarcely coherent voice, had, of course, quite the opposite effect. In chapel the next Sunday, in the middle of the sermon, he stood up suddenly, so it was reported, threw his arms round the Queen and the Princesses and said loudly, 'You know what it is to be nervous. But was you ever as bad as this?'

At the beginning of November he seemed a little better. On the 5th he went for a ride in his chaise with the Princess Royal and, although he gave numerous orders to the postillions and got in and out of the carriage several times with an agitation which was painful to watch, he was smiling cheerfully when he set off.

That afternoon, however, the Prince of Wales arrived at Windsor from Brighton and at dinner the King in a delirium of rage seized his infuriating son by the collar and threw him out of his chair against the wall. The Queen, who for weeks had been close to a nervous breakdown herself, fell into violent hysterics. The Prince burst into tears and was only prevented from fainting by his distracted sisters who rubbed his forehead with Hungary water.

That night a most uncommon stillness 'reigned over the whole house. Nobody stirred; not a voice was heard; not a step, not a motion'. Shortly after one o'clock a page came to Miss Burney's room to tell her that the Queen wanted her.

My poor Royal Mistress! [Fanny Burney wrote in her diary next day.] Never can I forget her countenance — pale, ghastly pale she looked; she was seated to be undressed . . . I gave her some camphor julep, which had been ordered by Sir George Baker. 'How cold I am!' she cried, and put her hand on mine; marble it felt! and went to my heart's core!

Fanny offered to spend the night in the little room next door but the Queen would not let her. The King himself was in the second dressing-room and would be sure to wander about in the dark. The previous night he had got up in sudden fear that his wife had left the house, and had spent half an hour looking at her through the curtains of her bed, a candle in his hand, muttering to himself. He was still talking the next morning (one day some weeks later he was to talk without stopping for sixteen hours) and the Queen asked Miss Burney to listen and tell her what His Majesty was saying.

'I am nervous,' Fanny heard him say. 'I am not ill, but I am nervous. If you would know what is the matter with me I am nervous. But I love you both very well; if you would tell me the truth: I love Dr Heberden best, for he has not told me a lie: Sir George has told me a lie — a white lie, he says, but I hate a white lie! If you tell me a lie, let it be a black lie!'

He was an appallingly difficult patient; and the methods used to combat his outbursts of violence and constant ramblings were both painful and humiliating. He was continually given overpowering purges and emetics until the Queen in looking at his eyes could compare them to 'nothing but blackcurrant jelly. The veins in his face were swelled, the sound of his voice was dreadful. He often spoke till he was exhausted and, the moment he could recover his breath, began again while the foam ran out of his mouth.'

After Sir George Baker, worn out by his duties, handed over the case to Dr Warren and Sir Lucas Pepys, the King's shaven head was blistered 'to draw the noxious substances from the brain to the skin surface'. And this treatment was so painful that it led to paroxysms 'so violent that his attendants had to sit on him to hold him down'. Often a strait-jacket had to be applied to prevent him tearing off the bandages.

9

The castle from the Great Park
in the
late eighteenth century
A water-colour by Thomas Girton.

10

The Guard Room in the Round Tower
in the
early nineteenth century
A water-colour by James Stephanoff.

While the King struggled with his pages and they retaliated by 'behaving with a degree of familiarity and insolence that often irritated and hurt him', the doctors argued about the best way of dealing with their patient. On only one matter could they agree; and that was that perfect quiet must be maintained throughout the house.

The silence and gloom within the walls of the Lodge was something terrible [one of the royal attendants told his wife]. Every precaution was taken to preserve this state of quiet. No bells were rung, and all arrangements were made among the attendants that the necessary changes should take place at stated hours without any bustle or confusion. The park gates were locked and no stranger was permitted to enter. Three gentlemen porters were added at the Royal entrance-gate, and four sergeant porters at the gate in the Home Park, and an additional number of kitchen boys was ordered down from London to fetch everything from these gates.

While the Queen spent her days sitting at a table with her suddenly greying head resting on her outstretched arms, refusing to eat anything and drinking nothing but barley water, the King in his calmer moments energetically performed a succession of imagined duties with determined industry. He wrote dispatches, he bestowed orders, he kept a journal, filling it with details of everything that took place around him and every conversation that he overheard. Occasionally, for brief intervals, he would talk rationally. Once he asked if Lord North had been to inquire about him, and when told that he had been, he said, 'He might have recollected me sooner. However, he, poor fellow, has lost his sight, and I my mind. Yet we meant well to the Americans, just to punish them with a few bloody noses, and then make bows for the mutual happiness of the two countries. But . . . we lost America. Tell him not to call again. I shall never see him.'

And then his mind wandered and he began talking about something else.

By the end of the month there was so little improvement in his condition that it was decided, at last, to call in an acknowledged expert in mental diseases. There was only one man in the whole country who was considered to deserve this title – Francis Willis, an old clergyman who had taken a medical degree at Oxford and acted both as priest and doctor to his parishioners. Dr Willis had shown himself so skilful in his long career in treating symptoms of madness and so many patients had come to him for help, that he had founded an asylum in Lincolnshire where his treatment, based on kindness and sympathy rather than upon forcible subjection, had had remarkable results.

He came with his two sons to attend the King and they were greeted with predictable suspicion.

Wasn't he ashamed of himself, the King asked the father in a lucid moment, to exercise the profession of medicine when he was an ordained clergyman?

'Sir,' said Dr Willis, 'Our Saviour Himself went about healing the sick.'

'Yes,' agreed the King, adding with a rude wit which promised his ultimate recovery, 'but *He* had not £700 for it.'

Eventually, however, the King was persuaded to accept the help of the Willises on condition that they allowed him to shave himself, to cut his own nails and to have the use of a knife at meal times. Previously the King had been shaved by one of his pages and the operation of clearing the cheeks alone had taken nearly two hours, owing to the patient's compulsive need to talk all the time.

The King himself was not much quicker, and although he managed to do it without cutting his skin too badly, he was glad, having asserted his authority, not to have to handle the razor again.

Before the Willises took charge of his case a suggestion had been made that the King should be taken to Kew. Here there were 'grounds and gardens in which His Majesty could take air and exercise privately, and without any annoyance, while at Windsor the whole of the private garden could be seen from the Terrace; and to exclude the public suddenly from what they had hitherto had the privilege of using would give rise to comments and surmises that were best avoided'.

The King, unfortunately, in recent years had taken a dislike to Kew and when the move was first suggested to him he had been 'very vehement in his objections'. The Willises felt sure, though, that the change must be made whether he liked it or not; and it was settled that the Queen and the Princesses should leave Windsor quietly without his knowledge so that when he discovered he had been left behind he might more easily be persuaded to follow them.

On Saturday morning 29 November at about ten o'clock they left. The Queen, 'drowned in tears', climbed softly into the leading carriage with Lady Courtown and two of the Princesses, who were also in tears, while Lady Charlotte Finch, the royal governess, and another Princess got into the next one. Fanny Burney thought that a more melancholy scene could not be imagined. 'There was not a dry eye in the house. The footmen, the house-maids, the porters, the sentinels — all cried bitterly as they looked on.'

These servants were instructed to follow later, as Dr Willis insisted that the King should have as few new faces around him as possible; but one of the footmen, Fortnum, 'begged to resign from ill health'. He was given leave to do so and soon afterwards went to help in his family's grocery shop in Piccadilly.

When the King was told that the Queen had left Windsor he was extremely angry. At first he refused to get out of bed and insisted that the Queen must return and beg his pardon. His physicians and equerries and even the Prime Minister pleaded with him to be reasonable, but it was not for several hours that he was at last persuaded to pull back the bed curtains and get dressed.

He came out to his coach in his Windsor uniform and while 'sentries, footmen and porters wept as though they would never see him again, he drove off with an escort of cavalry'.

*

The Oatlands Stakes, Ascot, in 1791. Queen Anne had transferred the main local race meeting from Datchet Mead to Ascot in 1711. In this picture by Sartorius the Prince of Wales's horse Baronet is seen winning the race.

Gradually that winter at Kew, under the skilful and sympathetic care of the Willises, the King's health began to improve. At first the weather was fearfully cold and he was kept inside, breathing the powerful fumes of musk in whose therapeutic qualities Dr Willis believed so strongly that the whole place was pervaded with them. But as the warmer weather came at the beginning of 1789, he was allowed out more often to walk in the garden, where he occasionally caught sight of the Princesses watching him anxiously from the windows. He peered back at them and complained to Dr Willis that his eyesight was not good enough to see his dear Amelia as clearly as he would have liked.

The exercise did him good. He began to look better and to walk with more control over his limbs. He talked as quickly as ever but more sensibly than before. He had, however, one intermittent delusion which, becoming persistent later, caused profound grief to the Queen, and that was that he was no longer married to her.

One day Dr Willis persuaded him to see the Queen, and when he saw her he kissed her and burst into tears. He wanted to tell her 'of all his sufferings, but she said she was aware of them, and had known of all that had passed both by day and by night'. The interview was short; and although they saw each other every day from then on, their behaviour towards each other, even after the King's recovery, never again suggested that 'most cordial confidence and happiness' that Fanny Burney had noticed three years before. At the crisis of his illness he had repeatedly insisted not only that he was going to retire to Hanover – he had threatened this before, preparing the most elaborate details of the new liveries to be worn there — but that all marriages were to be dissolved both there and in Britain by Act of Parliament. It was an obsession that Charlotte, now so stout that she looked, so it was said, as if she were bearing all her fifteen children at once, found it impossible to forget.

As spring approached, however, the King showed so much improvement that the Regency Bill, although passed by the Commons, seemed unlikely to pass into law. One day Fanny Burney came across the King in the gardens at Kew and noticed this appreciable improvement.

She was strolling on the lawn when she saw a group of figures and recognized one of them to be the King. As Dr Willis had given instructions that the King's walks were on no account to be disturbed, Fanny turned and fled. Terrified, she heard the men run after her. Then she heard shouts and the King's voice, loud and hoarse, calling her name, and then a shriller voice: 'Stop! Dr Willis begs you to stop.'

At length she did stop, and turned round to see the King between two panting doctors hurry on towards her.

'Why did you run away?' he called out.

Not knowing how to answer him, she overcame her fear and walked up to him. He put out his arms and she felt a sudden horror that he was going to crush her like a bear. But he put his hands on her shoulders and to her relief and astonishment he kissed her fondly on the cheek.

He was overcome by the pleasure of seeing her alarmed but friendly and familiar face and he talked to her with an excitement that was almost feverish. He spoke of anything that came into his mind, and although he still had little control over his speech he was, Fanny thought, nearly in his perfect state of mind as to his opinions. He spoke of Fanny's father, and the thought of Dr Burney brought him to his favourite theme — Handel. He recounted numerous anecdotes of the great composer and 'ran over most of his oratorios, attempting to sing several airs and choruses, but so dreadfully hoarse that the sound was terrible'.

He walked away from the doctors with Fanny by his side, asking about other people whom she knew. This reminded him of his Ministers and he told her how dissatisfied with them he was and how he would alter things as soon as he was able to 'get loose again'. He took a paper from his pocket and showed her his list of names for a new Government. 'When once I get away,' he said passionately, 'I shall rule with a rod of iron.'

Hearing the vehemence in his voice, the doctors became alarmed again and insisted, this time successfully, that the conversation must stop. Fanny hurried back to the house, 'inexpressibly thankful to see the King so nearly himself'.

In March he returned to Windsor, where he was welcomed with unfeigned enthusiasm by cheering crowds. The following month he drove in state from Buckingham House to St Paul's for a service of thanksgiving for 'God's Mercy in giving the King his health and reason once more'. And as the bells pealed and the guns boomed, the crowds

Queen Charlotte
by Peter Edward Stroehling.

cheered him more wildly than ever. He had never been so popular. Disliked and distrusted before his illness, all was forgiven him now by a people with a traditionally sincere and spontaneous sympathy for the afflicted and the ill-used. His two elder sons, chatting unconcernedly during the service in St Paul's, were greeted coldly when they came out of it; but the applause for the King was deafening.

Nothing could have done more to hasten his full recovery. He drove back to Windsor in the highest spirits and allowed the Princess Royal to organize a gala, at which all the ladies wore bandeaux with 'God Save the King' embroidered in front; and the dinner — there were no fewer than twenty different sorts of soup alone — was adjudged the best that had been given there for a hundred years.

In July the royal family went for a summer holiday to Weymouth where the King, cheerful and relaxed, could enjoy once again the company and obvious loyalty of simple people. When he played cards in a private apartment in the Rooms, he left the door open so that everybody could see him; when he went to the theatre he leant forward in his box to acknowledge the cheers; when he went bathing in his blue serge costume followed by a machine filled with fiddlers playing 'God Save the King', he waved happily to his female companions, upon whose bonnets as well as upon the cumbersome sashes they wore round their waists, were embroidered letters expressing the same universally popular sentiment.

On his return to Windsor the King seemed as happy as he had ever been. He resumed the habits of his former quiet life with contentment. He walked; he rode; he hunted; he farmed; he listened to concerts in the new music room overlooking the Terrace; he pottered about, fiddling with Herschel's telescope and the castle's recently completed organ; he played chess and backgammon with his equerries; he read his newspaper; he dozed. Usually in the summer after the races at Ascot and Egham he went to Weymouth. He never seems to have considered going anywhere else. The idea of foreign travel appalled him — indeed, few Kings can have travelled less in their own country than he did. Regularly, out of a sense of duty, he attended his levées in London, where his manners were as startlingly unconventional as ever. Once when a Scots colonel was presented and bowed so low that his ill-fitting kilt came up at the back to an embarrassing height, he called out in a loud and cheerful voice, 'Keep the ladies in front! Keep the ladies in front!' This, no doubt, was innocent enough. On other occasions, though, he could be distressingly ungracious. It was nevertheless a tactlessness which those who knew him best in these years found easy to forgive, for his fundamental good nature was as always unquestionable.

Dr Johnson, a man also without much tact, decided that George III was the 'finest gentleman' he had ever seen. As the holder of a royal pension, Johnson was predisposed to this opinion, of course, but others shared it who had no cause for gratitude. John Adams, for instance, the first envoy to the English Court from the United States of America, to whom the King confessed that he was the 'last to consent to the separation' of America from Britain but now was the 'first to meet the friendship of the United States as an independent power', thought that George III had all the 'affability of Charles II' with all the 'domestic virtues and regularity of Charles I'. And although the subsequent interviews were less pleasant because the Queen was so cold and aloof, Adams continued to hold the King in high regard. Benjamin Franklin thought him 'the best King any nation was ever blessed with'.

*

When Fanny Burney became ill and she was obliged to give up her appointment, she parted from the King and Queen with a deep and sincere regret. And as she said goodbye, the Queen, who, despite Fanny's protests, insisted that she would continue to pay her half her present salary as a pension, had to keep dabbing her eyes with a handkerchief and Fanny, too, was almost in tears.

> The King then came into the room [Fanny recorded]. He immediately advanced to the window, where I stood, to speak to me. I was not then able to comport myself steadily. I was forced to turn my head away from him. He stood still and silent for some minutes, waiting to see if I should turn about . . . and perceiving me quite overcome he walked away, and I saw him no more.
> His kindness, his goodness, his benignity, never shall I forget.

*

Even those who had cause to detest him as a King found it difficult to maintain their hatred of 'Farmer George' as he pottered about at Windsor in his political retirement. They warmed to him when they heard that he had said to Colonel Landmann, 'I should like to fight Bony single-handed, I'm sure I should. I should give him a good thrashing. I'm sure I should. I'm sure of it.' For they knew he meant it; and the thought of that emphatic voice and those emphatic gestures as the excited figure in his Horse Guards uniform regularly inspected the Volunteers drawn up under the Round Tower at Windsor during the autumn of 1803, when a French invasion seemed imminent, was curiously inspiring.

But he was growing old now and each new crisis in his public or family life seemed to threaten a return of insanity. Pitt, on whose calm good sense he had grown accustomed to rely, shocked him profoundly when he sought to bring about the long overdue emancipation of the Roman Catholics, and he was soon 'in the height of a phrenzy fever — as bad as the worst period' of his former attack. According to the Prince of Wales he spoke of abdication and again of retirement to Hanover and now even of going to live in America. He got better but it was only a temporary recovery, and as his fear of permanent insanity grew he became increasingly suspicious of all those around him who seemed to be watching him to discern symptoms of its onset. He began to hate his doctors; he refused to see the Prince of Wales, whom,

George III leaving Windsor in 1806, from a painting by R. B. Davis.

although he loved as his son, he 'hated as his heir'; he took pains to avoid the company of his wife, whose nervousness increased the cold hostility of a dying marriage. He took to dismissing servants for imagined slights or insults; and once more lay in bed at night unable to sleep, talking breathlessly to himself.

He had moved now from Queen's Lodge and was living in the castle itself, on the north side overlooking the Terrace, where all his predecessors had lived, while his wife and daughters occupied apartments in the southern wing, changing, so the Queen lamented to Lady Harcourt, 'from a very comfortable and warm habitation to the coldest house, rooms and passages that ever existed'. Their life there soon became set into a rigid pattern.

The King got up at half-past seven and walked over towards the Queen's apartments, where one of the Princesses, who took it in turns to attend him, met him and accompanied him to chapel. At breakfast he sat at the head of the table with the Queen, the five Princesses sitting, in order of seniority, down the side.

After breakfast he went riding if it was fine or played chess if it was wet. He dined at two o'clock and at five visited the Queen and the Princesses (who dined at four) for a glass of wine thinned with water. Then he went back to his study to transact business with his secretary, and afterwards he played cards in the Queen's drawing-room. Occasionally guests were invited but they never stayed long, for at the stroke of ten they were expected to retire. When they had gone supper was laid out; but that was 'merely a matter of form', because no one ate anything.

The King always went back to his apartments in the north front at an early hour and was soon in bed. His ground-floor bedroom was still uncarpeted but it was otherwise 'neatly furnished partly in a modern style' and was newly decorated. Indeed, the whole castle was now gradually changing its appearance.

James Wyatt had succeeded Sir William Chambers as Surveyor-General to the Board of Works in 1796. By then he had turned his attention to Gothic architecture which had become so fashionable since Horace Walpole's extravagant fancies at Strawberry Hill and Gray's elaborate house at Stoke Poges had caught the imagination of a class to whom the severe lines of Palladio were becoming arid and lifeless. Wyatt, although he was never fully in sympathy with the Gothic taste, was one of its most influential popularizers, and he found in George III and Windsor Castle both a client and a building sympathetic to his ideas.

Work began in 1800 to give the buildings round the Upper Ward — which were then as plainly unornamented as Hugh May had left them in the time of Charles II — the more elaborate appearance suggested by the romantic details of Gothicism. Rectangular windows were taken out to be replaced by arched openings with surrounds and transoms cut from Portland stone; and in the entrance tower to the State apartments a new staircase, wide, tall and gloomy, approached from a vault under the Queen's Guard Chamber, took the place of the two staircases whose ceilings had been painted by Verrio in 1678.

The new Grand Staircase was far from being an improvement, but it seemed to the King a more suitable setting for the Garter ceremonial in which he was now taking a renewed interest. And in April 1805, when the new Knights were installed, they were able to walk up a staircase which resembled those built during the days of their Order's founder.

This installation was, in other respects, a memorable occasion, for the King had been determined to revive as many as possible of the ancient customs associated with the Feast of St George. The dinner which began at six o'clock was even more splendid than that held in the castle to celebrate his recovery in 1789. The royal princes sat at the Sovereign's table, on which there was £12,000 worth of gold plate and a 'variety of splendid ornaments consisting principally of several figures of knights on horseback, composed wholly of silver, surmounted by the Star and Order of the Garter in solid gold'. After the meal, eighteen tables were set out in the castle yard covered with provisions and nine hogsheads of ale. Police officers from Bow Street helped to keep the crowds outside in order, but when the gates were opened the scene of confusion which ensued exceeded 'all description. Everyone being more anxious to plunder than to eat, they carried off that which came soonest to hand.'

The King, watching the tumult from one of the windows of the Queen's apartments, was seen to be extremely agitated. All the excitement, particularly the anxious supervision in the kitchen of the roasting and spicing of a baron of beef, weighing 162 pounds, had clearly been too much for him. In St George's Chapel, surrounded by an array of Knights whose dispiriting appearance, 'fat, limping and leaden', took much from the splendour of the scene, the King's face was 'unusually red and anxious' and the vast, outmoded, powdered and curled periwig he wore gave the impression of a man in the most absurd fancy dress.

He was no longer able to withstand the effects of these exciting alterations in the rhythm of an unvaried routine. So long as he observed this routine and so long as nothing surprised, worried or shocked him he was able to control the agitation which otherwise overwhelmed his mind. But as he refused to shut himself away in the care of a crowd of detested doctors, he suffered the consequences. In 1809 his favourite son, the Duke of York, Commander-in-Chief of the Army and a man who in that position had shown himself possessed of a far greater talent than his detractors would allow, was accused, without possibility of contradiction, of having commissioned and promoted officers on the recommendation of his consequently rich mistress. This shocking scandal, preceded by the retreat of the British Army under Sir John Moore to Corunna and followed in the same year by the disastrous expedition to Walcheren, had its predictable effect on the King's health. And then, in the following year, his fifth son, the Duke of Cumberland, was involved in a criminal case which received widespread publicity.

The Duke, a strange and ugly man of the most reactionary opinions, had, so he claimed, been woken up in bed one night at St James's Palace by a light blow on the head which he thought at first had been caused by a bat attracted into his bedroom by the light of the lamp that was kept burning there all night. He sat up and his eyes caught the flash of a sabre blade. He reached up, gripped the blade and almost severed his right thumb. He felt for the bell rope, could not find it, jumped out of bed and ran next door to his page's room, pursued by his assailant, who managed to cut him superficially on his buttocks and thigh and more seriously on his head. Hearing the Duke shout 'I am murdered! I am murdered!' other servants and some soldiers ran into the room and he immediately asked them where Sellis, his Corsican valet, was. Sellis was found in his room, half undressed and with his throat cut. The official verdict was suicide but there were many who thought that Sellis had not cut his own throat, and that the Duke, who was reported not only to have been found once in bed

The Hundred Steps by Paul Sandby. The steps led up towards the North Terrace by Winchester Tower from Thames Street.

with Mrs Sellis, but also to have been blackmailed by her husband after the Duke had made homosexual advances to him, was the murderer.

This was in the summer of 1810 and the King had scarcely recovered from the shock of it all when in November his beloved Amelia died at Windsor. Towards the end of her illness the King had become progressively more distracted and unbalanced, talking so loudly while out riding on a horse led by a hobby groom — for he was almost blind now — that his voice could be heard a long way off, and then relapsing into paroxysms of weeping. As often as he could he would go into Princess Amelia's room and 'hold her hand and bend over her to scan the face in which he was too blind to discern the onset of death'.

He accepted the news of her death with a low mumble of incoherent talk and although he recovered sufficiently to arrange 'everything relating to the ceremony of the funeral', except for short intervals he was never sane again.

He lived on for nine more years, a shrunken old man with a white beard, dwelling in a world of his own imagining. It was difficult to tell how much he knew of the real world outside, for when he was not violent he rarely showed emotion now and even cried silently. The doctors were at first concerned to prevent him learning anything which might upset him, though they soon understood that their concern was unjustified. They had dreaded, for instance, his discovering that Princess Amelia had left all her possessions to General Fitzroy, one of his equerries, of whom she had been so fond that there were rumours of a secret marriage, and to whom she, at any rate, so she told her brother, the Duke of York, 'considered herself married'. But when the King learned the contents of the will he seemed unperturbed, contented even. Later he believed Amelia to be still alive, happily married and living in Hanover.

Queen Charlotte was all but forgotten. For years it had been known that they no longer slept together, and that she went so far as to lock her door against him. She never dined with him now and refused to see him alone. When she did go to see him she was usually accompanied by one of her daughters. 'I went down with the Queen,' wrote Princess Mary after one of these distressing visits, 'and it was shocking to hear the poor, dear King run on so, and her unfortunate manner makes things worse.' Princess Mary thought that this 'unfortunate manner' of her mother's was attributable partly to 'extream timidity' and partly to an inborn deficiency in 'warmth, tenderness, affec.' The Queen seemed to find her husband frightening as well as distasteful and in her unhappiness she made others unhappy too. She quarrelled with the Princess Royal, who decided that she was a 'silly woman'. She quarrelled with the Princess of Wales, whose daughter Charlotte was brought up at Windsor in the care of her grandparents. She behaved badly to her attendants. She became increasingly ill-tempered, withdrawn and aloof.

She spent much of her time at Frogmore, a small estate in the Park which was bought for the Crown by Henry VIII and had subsequently been let to a succession of tenants. Queen Charlotte acquired the adjoining estate, Little Frogmore, in 1790 and Great Frogmore, in 1792. She demolished Little Frogmore and added its ground to Great Frogmore. Here, in her 'little paradise', she retreated from the formal and aggravating life of the castle and found pleasure in creating the lovely gardens which still exist. In earlier years she had entertained here and given fêtes; but now she came only for peace. Sometimes her daughters came with her, but whenever they could they excused themselves and stayed behind at the castle, sometimes spending their afternoons in a hexagonal cave in the slopes beneath the North Terrace. This cave, ventilated by a chimney which opened on to the turf above their heads and made less gloomy by walls of looking-glass, no traces of which remain, was their favourite hiding-place from a difficult mother, who died in 1818, a sad, unloved old woman, after a long and painful illness.

The King still lingered on, although he sometimes believed himself to be dead as well. The thought did not seem to distress him; often indeed, he seemed strangely happy. He walked about his rooms in his flannel dressing-gown and ermine night-cap, holding conversations with Ministers long since dead. He still liked to play his flute and his harpsichord and when he had given an uncertain rendering of one of his favourite tunes he would say that he had been very fond of that particular tune when he was in the world. His meals often appeared before he was expecting them and he would say, 'Can it be so late? How time flies!' He had a good appetite, particularly for cold meat, which he usually ate standing up.

He did not lose his appetite and until the last few weeks of his life he never lost the pleasure of dressing up. Every afternoon he changed for dinner, wearing his Orders, up to the day of his death. Occasionally he decided to wear mourning 'in memory of George III, for he was a good man'. He found comfort in praying to God and on at least one occasion, apparently, he administered Holy Communion to himself. He liked to believe that he possessed supernatural powers and he would sometimes stamp his foot when one of the doctors annoyed him and say that he would send him down to hell.

But he was rarely upset now. It irritated him when he was denied his favourite meal or when it was proposed to shave his beard. If they insisted on shaving him, he warned them once with magnificent authority, he would have the battle-axes called in. It was a rare outburst, though. Most of his days were passed quietly and without complaint in the dark room overlooking the Terrace, where he refused now to go because he could no longer see the countryside beyond it which he loved. On the evening of 29 January 1820, quietly and without complaint, he died.

3

GEORGE IV – THE *COTTAGE ORNÉ*

For several weeks the Prince Regent had been seriously ill himself at Brighton and he had begun to fear that he too might be dying. He was already fifty-seven. The handsome, chubby young man who had fallen so helplessly in love with 'Perdita' Robinson at the age of seventeen and who had secretly contravened the Royal Marriage Act by marrying the handsome, devout and intelligent Roman Catholic Mrs Fitzherbert when he was twenty-three, had become gouty and immensely fat. He was often breathless, frequently in pain, exaggerating the minor complaints of a fundamentally strong constitution by a

George IV. A miniature by John George Paul Fischer painted in 1820, the year the King ascended the throne.

hypochondriacal self-concern. He had, indeed, though, much to worry him, apart from his health.

Nine years after the illegal marriage to Mrs Fitzherbert he had felt obliged, partly by the need for an heir, more, no doubt, by debts, which amounted to £400,000 in 1792, to marry again. His father had refused to increase his allowance until he chose a suitable wife; and the Prince of Wales, who clearly could not tell his father that he already had a wife, agreed to choose his cousin Princess Caroline of Brunswick, a short, coarse, highly-sexed, fair-haired woman who wore dirty under-clothes and was, according to the diplomatist sent out to bring her back from Germany, consequently rather smelly. The Prince married her with sulky desperation, caused his lovely mistress Lady Jersey — he had temporarily forsaken Mrs Fitzherbert — to become one of her ladies-in-waiting and in 1795 took her to Windsor for the first part of their honeymoon.

By the time the summer came and they went on to Brighton they were already no longer sleeping together. Indeed, according to a journal purported to have been kept by the Princess, the Prince was so drunk 'the night he married that, when he came into her room, he was obliged to leave it again; and he remained away all night and did not return again till the morning; he then obliged her to remain in bed with him and that is the only time they were together as husband and wife'.

'Judge what it was to have a drunken husband on one's wedding-day,' the Princess told Lady Charlotte Campbell, 'and one who passed the greatest part of his bridal-night under the grate, where he fell and where I left him.' Certainly the Prince, for his part, decided that he would rather see toads and vipers crawling over his 'victuals than sit at the same table with her'. When Princess Charlotte was born, nine months less one day after the wedding, the Princess of Wales went to live in a different house.

She was an irritating, vulgar, vapid, unbalanced woman; but it was she who had the people's sympathy.

The Prince's fantastic extravagance, the fortunes he spent on his idiosyncratic house at Brighton and on Carlton House in London, the widespread reports of his vast losses at racing, his drinking bouts, his extravagant parties, his flippant friends, his unsavoury brothers whose publicized vices put emphasis upon his own, his taste for middle-aged grandmothers who would indulge his need to be fondled and fussed over like a child, the sight of his grease-painted face, of his bulging though corseted figure in its richly coloured clothes and of his yellow Berlin coursing, with purple blinds drawn down, to his mistress's house in Chelsea, were alike angrily condemned by a country at war with France and forced to pay for the cost of it all.

Nor were his wife and the public all that the Regent had to worry him. His daughter Charlotte, who had grown up into a high-spirited, capricious, rather rowdy, fat and clumsy girl, passionately attached

The memorial to Princess Charlotte in St George's Chapel. This white marble monument in the Urswick Chapel was commissioned by her father from Matthew Cotes Wyatt, Jeffrey Wyatville's cousin.

to her friend Miss Mercer Elphinstone yet provocatively flirtatious with most presentable young men, much preferred her mother's *outré* household to the stifling atmosphere at Windsor.

At her mother's life was much more exciting. It was here that she was allowed to meet Captain Hesse of the Light Dragoons, supposedly an illegitimate son of her uncle the Duke of York, whom she had met while out driving in her carriage at Windsor. The affair with Captain Hesse lasted for several weeks until, at a party at Carlton House, she met Prince William of Orange, whom her father wished her to marry and of whom she became quite fond. In the summer of 1814, however, when for that one 'year of revelry' the war with Napoleon was over, she decided that Prince William was less attractive than most of the dashing young princes with whom London was filled and far less desirable than Prince Frederick William Henry Augustus of Prussia with whom she fell passionately in love. She told her father that she would not marry the Prince of Orange after all. He was furious with her. She rushed out of the house and took a hackney-coach to her mother's. She was at length persuaded to return, and her father sent her down to Cranbourne Lodge at Windsor in the care of several ladies who might be relied on to ensure that she would not be left alone with the unsuitable Prussian Prince again.

The newspapers and the public took the side of the young Princess against that of a tyrannical parent whose conduct was likened by a Member of Parliament to that of a 'Prussian Corporal'. Worse, though, was yet to come. In 1816 Charlotte married Prince Leopold of Saxe-Coburg, a handsome, ingratiating, ambitious, self-satisfied and somewhat unctuous man with no possessions and little money. Her father persuaded his Ministers to grant him an income of £50,000 a year and he gave the couple the beautiful house of Claremont as a wedding present. Here the following year Charlotte died, having given birth to a dead baby, and the shocked Regent, who 'received the tidings of the death of his Beloved Daughter with the greatest grief', was once more reminded by the newspapers of his previous cruel treatment of an idolized heroine.

Meanwhile the idol's mother, the public's other heroine, was providing Europe with a scandalous amusement which delighted her husband's enemies. Dressed in the most *louche* attire, she wandered from town to town accompanied by a crowd of excitable Italian attendants. At Genoa she was drawn through the streets in a gilt and mother-of-pearl phaeton; at Baden she appeared at the Opera in 'an enormous head-dress, as worn by the Oberlander peasants, and decorated with flying ribbons and glittering spangles'; on the way to Constantinople she spent her time in a tent on board ship with her Italian chamberlain, a lively young man, 'six feet high, with a magnificent head of black hair, pale complexion, mustachios which reach from here to London', whom she made Grand Master of the Order of Caroline which she had created in Jerusalem; at Geneva she attended a dance, *en Vénus*, naked to the waist, 'displaying a bosom of more than ample proportions'.

In 1819 the Prince Regent was told by his legal advisers that there was sufficient evidence for a divorce on the ground of adultery. The following year George III died and the new King began his reign under the shadow of the fear that his wife would return to England. She did so and was received with boisterous enthusiasm. The King felt that he could not but pick up the gauntlet of her defiance, and so she was brought before the House of Lords to answer a charge that her 'scandalous, disgraceful and vicious conduct' had made her unworthy

The Kettle calling the Pot ugly names.

of the title and rights of Queen Consort. She answered the accusation of adultery with the spirited reply that she had only once committed adultery and that was with the husband of Mrs Fitzherbert. It was a response which found wide sympathy, and, after proceedings lasting almost three months, the Government realized that they would never get their Bill of Pains and Penalties through the House of Commons and so the charge was withdrawn. The celebrations were immediate and rapturous; for three nights flambeaux and lights were kept burning all night in London and those who refused to express their joy had their windows smashed by the mob. The King, more than ever an object of ridicule, retired to Windsor, lonely and depressed.

Here in the grounds of the Great Park, to the designs of John Nash, he had converted a small house, formerly occupied by the Deputy-Ranger, into a large Gothic *cottage orné*, officially known later as the Royal Lodge. Its roof was thatched and its windows mullioned; it was beautifully decorated and furnished; it was surrounded by newly planted trees and shrubs, and it was estimated to have cost £200,000. Everything inside was in faultless taste, and the dinner parties the King gave there after his delayed coronation were both lavish and amusing. For His Majesty was, by general if sometimes grudging consent, still an excellent host, attentive, entertaining and constitutionally generous. He had always been so, undeniably, but the worries of his middle age and the gloom of his recent career had driven him to long moods of despondency and irritation, while the proceedings against the Queen had exhausted him. The coronation, though, had been a tonic. It was, in the first place, a magnificent and moving spectacle; and the King, gorgeously attired and looking unusually virile, was greeted with an enthusiasm which he had long since grown accustomed to believe was the prerogative of his enemies.

Above left, 'The Kettle calling the Pot ugly names', a caricature by John Marshall, 12 August 1820. This print, suggesting the King and Queen Caroline were equally to blame for their quarrel, was published shortly before the Queen's conduct was investigated by the House of Lords.

Above, A miniature of Mrs Fitzherbert by Richard Cosway. When he was dying George IV earnestly asked the Duke of Wellington, whom he had appointed one of his executors, to ensure that he was buried in his nightclothes 'with whatever ornaments might be upon his person at the time of his death'. Later, noticing a black ribbon round the King's neck in the open coffin, Wellington was driven by curiosity to see what was suspended from it. He drew aside the collar to reveal a miniature of Mrs Fitzherbert.

The Royal Lodge. George IV's *cottage orné* was built for him by John Nash. Most of it was demolished by William IV. Around what remained of it George VI built the present house where Queen Elizabeth the Queen Mother now lives.

As the cheers of the people rose above the boom of the guns, Queen Caroline who had unsuccessfully demanded to be crowned with her husband presented herself at Westminster Abbey and asked at least to be admitted. She was jeered derisively. She drove back to Piccadilly and the spectators shouted at her that she ought not to stop there but go on back to Italy. A few weeks later she was dead.

*

The King, released after twenty-five years from the humiliations of a disastrous marriage, and encouraged by triumphant visits to Ireland and Scotland, felt a resurgence of a youthful *joie de vivre*. His wonderful gift for mimicry was unimpaired, and the charm of his conversation, when too much drink had not made him excessively garrulous, remained fascinating. He had always taken great pains to make even the least brilliant of his guests feel at ease with him, and although he clearly preferred the conversation and company of such witty, worldly, scintillating men as Charles James Fox and Richard Brinsley Sheridan, of Beau Brummell and the Duke of Orleans, his ability to disarm a man of Dr Burney's more staid character had never failed him. Dr Burney, indeed, was 'astonished to find him amidst such constant dissipation possessed of so much learning, wit, knowledge of books in general, discrimination of character, as well as original humour . . . He may with truth be said to have as much wit as Charles II with much more learning.'

He had a real interest in books and music, as in architecture and painting, furniture and in objects of art. And his taste rarely faltered. His collection of pictures, chosen with great care and discrimination, might alone now be said to justify all his other inordinate extravagances, while his patronage of great artists like Gainsborough and

Sir Thomas Lawrence, his encouragement of sculptors and architects and those writers like Sir Walter Scott and Jane Austen from whom political antagonism had not estranged him, went a long way to excuse the shortcomings of a man, who, as Dorothea de Lieven, the Russian ambassador's wife said, while not bad in himself was 'capable of bad actions'. 'He was', she added, 'full of vanity and could be flattered at will. Weary of all the joys of life, having only taste, not one true sentiment, he was hardly susceptible to attachment, and never I believe sincerely inspired anyone with it . . . No one trusted him.' Yet, Dorothea de Lieven had 'never known a person like him, who was also affectionate, sympathetic and gallant'. This fragmentation of his character, at once selfish and generous, vain yet sensitive, occasionally vindictive and heartless as well as sincerely good-natured and kind, was also commented upon by the Duke of Wellington. He was, the Duke said, the 'most extraordinary compound of talent, wit, buffoonery, obstinacy and good feeling – in short a medley of the most opposing qualities, with a great preponderance of good' that he had ever known in his life. Thackeray confessed that he could see nothing of George IV behind the clothes, beyond the bow and the grin. 'There must be something behind, but what?'

There *was* something, though, behind the clothes and the bow and the grin. His frustrated sisters adored him. His difficult mother forgave him and grew to love and respect him; and she died holding his hand. His tiresome brothers quarrelled with him from time to time, but the fault was theirs more than his own. His behaviour to his father was often cruel, but George III was not a father likely to inspire obedience or devotion in a high-spirited, sensual son; and the gulf between the two mutually antagonistic characters was not so deep that the son could not cry when he visited his father, old and frail, and saw him so pathetically and helplessly insane. He fell out with Sheridan and Brummell. But he offered Sheridan an apartment in Carlton House and sent him £500 in his last illness; and Brummell was a highly provocative man. The King was unfaithful to his wife as well as to Mrs Fitzherbert, but he never suggested that he would remain faithful to Caroline and he died with Mrs Fitzherbert's picture round his neck. To his other mistresses he gave more loyalty and affection than they had any reason to expect; and it was not, in any case, an age in which fidelity was a common virtue, nor did he come from a family whose forbears had ever shown much inclination to faithfulness.

He was flamboyantly self-indulgent, of course; but he raised £50,000 so that his brother, the Duke of York, could settle his debts, and asked him never to refer to the gift as he wished the rest of their lives to be spent 'in uninterrupted friendship and the warmest affection'; and he gave £15,000 to Charles Arbuthnot to settle debts incurred as Ambassador at Constantinople, saying, 'Take this and never let the subject be mentioned again and, above all, do not let it cause any shyness or embarrassment between us.' It could not have been done, Mrs Arbuthnot decided, 'with more kindness and delicacy'.

But then, the King was always 'kind and good-natured', when he acted upon his impulses and had 'no ill-natured person to check him'.

This kindness and humanity is reflected in the support he gave to the reform of the criminal code and in the numbers of death sentences he commuted. Often he would write to his Ministers insisting on his right to exercise his prerogative of mercy; and there is something both revealing and touching in the story of his sending for Peel in the middle of the night because the imminent execution of a criminal upset him so. Peel agreed to pardon him and the King excitedly kissed him; then, noticing the poor quality of the Home Secretary's dressing-gown, he said suddenly, 'Peel, where *did* you get that dressing-gown. I'll show you what a dressing-gown ought to be.' And he made Peel put on one of his own.

His Ministers found him trivial and vain; and he had, indeed, where matters of State were concerned, an undeniably frivolous mind. Like many kings before and after him he set great store by the observance of what to outsiders seemed the absurd rigmarole of protocol and the petty rules of dress. Nothing appeared to upset him so much, when Caroline returned from the Continent, as that she rode in a carriage through the streets of London sitting next to 'that beast Wood', an alderman who was a chemist. And nothing appeared to upset him as much at a ball as that an officer should be improperly dressed. Once, seeing Lord Charles Russell without the regulation aiguillette, he called out in a loud voice, 'Good evening, sir. I suppose you are the regimental doctor.'

His vanity was legendary, and one of its least distressing manifestations was his affected belief that he was to a considerable extent responsible for all the triumphs of the age which has been named after him, including the military and naval ones, victories that were attributable to his 'own original and indefatigable exertions'.

Less attractive, though, was the King's indifference to most of the aspirations of the country's more enlightened politicians. His only political objects were to avoid trouble, to indulge his own whims and prejudices, and to ensure the continuance of royal patronage. It was a selfish programme which might be said to justify his unpopularity.

The youthful association with the Whigs that had enraged his father was more the result of personal predilections than political convictions. As Prince Regent he became an obstinate Tory, and as King he developed into a constitutional monarch, and all the time his opinions were a reflection of his friendships, prejudices and lazy selfishness.

He objected to George Canning succeeding to the Foreign Office when Lord Castlereagh cut his throat, partly because he thought Canning too liberal, partly because he did not approve of his views on Catholic emancipation, but mainly, it seems, because he had opposed the proceedings against Caroline, with whom, he believed, he had had an affair. Nor, when the King was obliged to accept Canning into the Cabinet, did he scruple to invite to the Royal Lodge the Princes Ester-

hazy and Polignac and Count Christopher Lieven, representatives of
Austria, France and Russia, the most powerful reactionary governments in Europe.

Eventually the King promised Canning that the 'continental gossip-
ings' at the Royal Lodge would come to an end. But here again, he was
not so much influenced by a change of heart as by the knowledge that
Canning's policy had improved his own prestige in Europe, by the
recognition of Canning as a man with much of Fox's wit and charm,
and by gratitude for his having appointed as his Under Secretary
one of the sons of the woman with whom he shared the last years of
his life, and for having dispatched her tiresome lover on a diplomatic
mission to South America.

*

This woman was Lady Conyngham, with whom he fell in love so
helplessly that to many observers he seemed not merely embarrassing
but even disgusting in his mawkish sentimentality. Both he and his
new companion were over fifty and yet he behaved towards this far
from beautiful, far from amusing, rather fat, kindly but rapacious
mother of five grown-up children, as if he had been a boy again and
she a brilliant beauty. Mrs Arbuthnot, the highly intelligent but somewhat priggish High Tory friend of the Duke of Wellington, thought it
was all 'very ridiculous', and thoroughly indecent. She recorded with
distaste in her diary that at a ball in the summer of 1821 the King
made a complete fool of himself, remaining by Lady Conyngham's side
all evening and at last shutting himself up in a room with her and
placing a page outside the door with instructions to let no one in.

The King told Madame de Lieven that 'he had never known what
it was to be in love before, that he was himself quite surprised at the
degree to which he was in love, that he did nothing from morning till
night but think what he could do to please Lady Conyngham and make
her happy, that he would do anything upon earth for her . . . and that
she was an angel sent from Heaven for him. He cried, Lady Conyngham cried, and Madame de Lieven said later, being nervous and easily
agitated, she had cried also; and all this passed in a crowded Drawing-
Room.'

A few weeks later, to Mrs Arbuthnot's horror, the King drove down
from Carlton House to the Royal Lodge at Windsor with Lady Conyngham '*tête-à-tête* in his carriage' to spend a day alone with her there.
Mrs Arbuthnot could 'hardly believe this', when the Duke of Wellington told her, but he assured her it was true. 'Lady Conyngham has no
sense of shame about her connexion with the King,' Mrs Arbuthnot
went on, 'she continually boasts of her influence over him.'

The influence was certainly considerable. And in time she 'gained
the summit of her ambition' and had 'all the honours paid to her as a
royal mistress'.

Her whole family came to Court. Her husband was made a Marquess
and, on Lord Hertford's retirement, the King wanted to make him Lord

'A Short Ride in the Long Walk or the Ponies Posed', a caricature by William Heath, 28 March 1824. George IV takes Lady Conyngham for a ride in a four-wheeled pony-chaise.

Chamberlain as well. This, however, Lord Liverpool, the Prime Minister, would not consider, though obviously some appointment must be found for him. 'After all,' as the Duke of Wellington sensibly observed to Lady Conyngham herself, 'you are going abroad with the King; and depend upon it, the first remark at all the courts you go to will be, "Who the Devil's Lady Conyngham? What post does she hold? What business has she with the King?" All of which would be easily answered if Lord Conyngham was in the Household.' It was an argument which Lord Liverpool could not overlook, and so he agreed to Conyngham being appointed Lord Steward of the Household.

His children benefited from his wife's position, too. One of his sons, 'a very good boy', in the King's opinion, although there was 'nothing in him', became Master of the Robes and later Under Secretary for Foreign Affairs; another son, through the King's influence, was offered the command of the Clare Militia; and his eldest daughter married Lord Strathavon from the Royal Lodge.

It did not appear, however, that Lady Conyngham's new life at Windsor, and the favours which it enabled her to bestow upon her family, made her happy. This was her own fault though, people believed, since she had succeeded in excluding from Windsor most of the King's amusing friends. The Duke of Wellington told her, when she confessed to him that she found life so tedious she felt she could no longer stay with the King at Windsor, that the blame was entirely hers. She could have a hundred people there every day if she wanted to; and to suggest that she was 'afraid of her character', as she had begun to do, was surely a little late in the day.

Her frustrations drove her, the Duke noticed, to behaviour which was 'really quite shocking'. The King was still most attentive to her, but she 'shrugged her shoulders at him and seemed quite to loathe him, so much so that everybody observed it'. She grew more and more 'wonderfully haughty and high and mighty'. She made less and less effort to disguise her boredom and her irritation with the King, but she would never leave him, continuing to content herself with the nursing of her grievances and ill-humour and still accepting all his presents. The trouble with Lady Conyngham was, so Dorothea de Lieven concluded, that 'though she can do without sentiments, she can't do without diamonds'.

The further the King retired into seclusion at Windsor the less he was liked. People gossiped about the trouble he took not to be seen when he went for a ride in the Park, how the ponies' heads would be turned sharply round if anyone was sighted on the road, how he always used private roads when he could, how he was constantly planting new avenues 'from which the public were wholly excluded', how furious he became when workmen or maid-servants stared at him when he drove out of the lodge or castle to Sandpitgate Lodge, where he liked to visit the animals in his menagerie and then come back to sit in his pony chaise with his favourite cockatoo on his arm and a glass of cherrygin ('which was always kept in preparation for him') in his hand.

He was fatter than ever since he had abandoned the diet that his love for Lady Conyngham had imposed upon his vanity, and this distressed him. And after the autumn of 1822, when he became ill again and his legs began to swell and he showed symptoms of dropsy and was constantly sweating, he became more and more depressed and disinclined to show himself.

Madame de Lieven during a visit to the Royal Lodge in 1823 described the extraordinary life that was now led there. It was raining in torrents and field mice came in from the garden and ran about the rooms; the King was limping and often in tears; and one night he began to sing and 'in order to produce the sole musical sound of which his throat is capable he closed his eyes, shed tears'. Madame de Lieven got up at nine, went out into the garden, went into luncheon with the King between eleven o'clock and one, went out for a drive or on the river between two and four and then came back for dinner.

After dinner the piano [she told Prince Metternich]. After the piano, *écarté*, and at twelve to bed. Occasionally, the conversation is interesting; but usually, it is so stupid that one begins to doubt one's own intelligence. I look into my mind and, honestly, I find nothing in it; if you were to beat me you would not get a sensible idea out of me. I was reflecting yesterday that there were better ways of spending an evening, and I remembered Verona. At this moment I looked up: the King was gazing at Lady Conyngham with an expression in which commonsense battled against love; Lady Conyngham was gazing at a beautiful emerald on her arm; her daughter was toying with a ruby laying round her neck . . . I was very close to tears.

To overcome his depression and alleviate his boredom, the King began to drink heavily. According to the Duke of Wellington 'the quantity of Cherry brandy he drank was not to be believed' and without it he could not bring himself to eat anything. As the months passed it became more and more difficult for his Ministers to get him to concentrate on matters of State. He was 'extraordinarily ingenious in turning the conversation from any subject he did not like', so Wellington said, and it was often impossible to discover what his true feelings about it were.

There were, however, two matters upon which the strength of his feelings was never in doubt. One was Roman Catholic emancipation, a reform which, encouraged by his brother the Duke of Cumberland, he opposed with all the vehemence of his father, becoming so heated about it that Lord Mount Charles 'verily believed he would go mad', as, once he got on to the subject, there was 'no stopping him'. The other was the necessity of transforming Windsor Castle into a palace suitable for the kings of the greatest country in Europe.

4

GEORGE IV — THE GOTHIC CASTLE

For the first few years of his reign he had lived always at the Royal Lodge, staying at Carlton House when he had to be in London and occasionally visiting Brighton. But the Royal Lodge was, in Greville's words, although a 'delightful place to live in', too small 'for very large parties'. And so in the summer of 1823 the King decided to close the terraces of the castle — except on Sundays — and to stop the people of

Windsor walking and playing in the Home Park. In the autumn, having given orders for the demolition of Queen's Lodge, he moved into the castle for two months to see what living there was like, choosing to occupy the rooms that his mother and sisters had used rather than the gloomier north front which his father had occupied and which was for the future to be reserved as State Apartments for distinguished visitors. Neither front, however, seemed to the King sufficiently splendid and dignified, and Parliament was asked to vote money for the extensive rebuilding which was considered necessary.

The scheme was approved and James Wyatt's nephew, Jeffrey Wyatt, was chosen as architect in charge of the reconstruction. Wyatt, a man of 'low stature and inelegant personal form, redeemed by liveliness of expression and sincerity of manner', immediately moved into the castle, to be ready to direct the labours of over five hundred workmen who were soon to start work on the Upper Ward. In August 1824 the King drove up from the Royal Lodge to lay the foundation stone of a new archway which was to bear his name and was met by Mr Wyatt, described now as 'a busy, bustling, vain little man', who asked him if he might change his name to Wyatville, to avoid confusion with other members of his family some of whom were mere builders. 'Ville or mutton,' the King is said to have replied cheerfully, 'call yourself what you like.'

Wyatville was soon in difficulties. His original estimate, submitted in competition with Robert Smirke and John Nash – John Sloane was also asked to compete but declined – was for £122,500. This figure seems to have been arrived at in a curiously unorthodox way. Before he was invited to submit his estimate by the commissioners appointed to supervise the work, Wyatville was asked by the King personally to draw up some designs. Later, so he said, the Chancellor of the Exchequer, one of the commissioners, told him that the Government could afford £150,000; and so he adjusted his estimate accordingly.

From the beginning it was clear that this sum was completely inadequate. A further £150,000 was voted by Parliament and when it was obvious that even £300,000 was far from sufficient and had been greatly exceeded, Members began to show their alarm.

A design for the east front of the Upper Ward by Sir Robert Smirke. Smirke was one of various architects who were invited to submit plans and estimates for the rebuilding of the castle for George IV. This drawing of the proposed east front shows Smirke's scheme for a bridge leading on to the Long Walk.

Nash's design for a bridge over the Long Walk. John Nash was one of the architects invited to submit plans and estimates for the rebuilding of the castle. This bridge indicates the style he presumably had in mind.

Within a few years the cost of the works at Windsor rose to £800,000; and when they were asked to vote an additional £100,000 Parliament rebelled. Who could say, protested one Member, whether there would be any 'limit to such extravagance'. Daniel O'Connell — who seemed to the King at least one very good reason for keeping Roman Catholics out of the House of Commons to which they had at last been admitted — said that he thought £100,000 would come in very useful in Ireland and there was 'abundant reason for opposing such profligate expenditure' at Windsor.

The Chancellor of the Exchequer was obliged to withdraw his motion and the Duke of Wellington, spelling the Chancellor's name with disdainful inaccuracy, reported his failure to Windsor. 'The question is a bad one,' Wellington continued. 'We are in the wrong for bringing forward for the third or fourth time a vote for a fresh grant without an estimate of the whole expense.'

The rest of the Government was constrained to agree with him and a select committee was appointed to try to discover the likely amount of this expense. The original estimate was made, Wyatville reported to this committee:

... when the King was residing at the Castle. I could not go and strip the apartments to see the walls and timbers when the King was there, and therefore they were calculated, as any person might do, at probable expense. When the King retired, and I stripped the walls, the timbers were all found rotten, and necessarily the whole of the floors were removed ... and the roof was in an equally bad state, and obliged to be taken off also, and many of the walls were cracked through, and many holes had been cut in, the Castle having been divided into different residences; it was very much dilapidated by each inhabitant cutting closets and cutting through the walls without any regard to the destruction of it. Then when the roof was removed, as there was not sufficient room for the King's servants, advantage was taken to put the roof higher, and make another storey over, which of course would increase the estimate.

The Grand Corridor by Joseph Nash. This corridor was designed by Wyatville to link the private apartments and to provide a picture gallery as well as a covered way between the north front and the east. It was 550 feet in length.

The committee took Wyatville's point and as a large part of the £100,000 which was requested had, in fact, already been spent, they could not but recommend (while deploring the evident disregard of economy) that 'the complete repair of this ancient and Royal Residence', being an 'object of national concern', should be provided for. They also recommended 'for the sake of uniformity of character and design' that the works – of which, incidentally, they entertained 'a favourable opinion' – should be completed under the same direction.

Their favourable opinion of the works was not, however, shared by everyone who visited the castle during the years of its reconstruction, and Wyatville's alterations and embellishments have been severely criticized since. No one could complain about the completion of the Long Walk, the beautiful elm-lined avenue which Charles II had begun in 1685 and which by the demolition of Queen's Lodge could now be taken through the new George IV Gate up into the quadrangle. No one could complain, either, about the magnificent Grand Corridor which, providing a much needed covered way between the north front and the east, would have saved George III many a cold walk across the quadrangle when he went to see his wife and daughters. No one should blame Wyatville – as he has often been blamed – for filling in the medieval ditch round the castle, for this was done in the 1770s. But it was possible to complain about the somewhat arch manner in which Wyatville continued on a much more ambitious and grandiose scale, the Gothicization of the castle which his uncle had begun in 1800, going so far as to introduce excessively picturesque machicolations to overhang the summit of his new towers, although examples

Wyatville's proposals for the Great Drawing Room. Wyatville's watercolour shows his design for the decorations of the east wall. The room was to be furnished for the most part in scarlet and gold, the window bay being dominated by a circular stand and the floor covered by a carpet designed by J. J. Boileau. This room is now known as the Crimson Drawing Room.

of this architectural contrivance – originally designed for the medieval warrior so that he could accurately pour molten lead on his enemies from between the corbels – had hitherto been unknown at Windsor and were, in the nineteenth century, it was to be hoped, no longer of practical use.

Wyatville might also be criticized for his architectural *blague*. He inserted bogus portcullis-grooves in his gates; he cut long, straight indentations in his freestone blocks and filled them with mortar and flint chippings to give an impression of regularity at once improbable and unsightly; he increased the height of the Round Tower by providing a stone crown thirty feet higher than the former structure, and while this structure had already been much altered over the centuries, its original proportions were now destroyed for ever.

It can, however, be argued that while most of Wyatville's architectural deceits are inexcusable, an essentially Gothic structure demands Gothic treatment and even those to whom the Gothic taste does not appeal might agree that Wyatville's work has successfully imparted to the castle that appearance of solid grandeur which has made it one of the most distinctive monuments in the world.

A View of the Mandarine Yatcht and Belvedere belonging to His Royal Highness the Duke of CUMBERLAND. at WINDSOR

This Yatcht is above 40 Foot in the Keel, carries above 30 Tun, and the Grand Room is 20 Foot by 14. Price 1s plain 2s 6d Colour'd. Publish'd according to Act of Parliam.t Dec.r 26 1753 by T. Hayne.

Above left, The Duke of Cumberland's 'Mandarine Yatcht' and belvedere at Virginia Water in 1753. William Augustus, Duke of Cumberland, third son of George II, was appointed Warden of Cranbourne Chase in 1751 and Ranger of Windsor Great Park in 1758. Assisted by Thomas Sandby, the Deputy Ranger, he greatly improved the Park and began the formation of Virginia Water. The belvedere was probably designed by Isaac Ware. Mrs Delany visited it in 1757 and described it as being 'in a triangular form, at each corner a square or octagon turret. One of them is the winding stone staircase that leads to the great room which is a hexagon, the other two are closets, one painted and carved [blue and gold] with shelves filled with books, the other gold and green with shelves filled with China. The middle room is in stucco adorned with hanging festoons of fruit and flowers painted in their natural colours, the ground white; in the middle hangs a lustre of Chelsea china that cost six hundred pounds and is really beautiful.'

Below left, A design for a fishing pavilion at Virginia Water by Frederick Crace. Crace, who had worked for Nash at Brighton, was working on the decorations in the castle in the 1820s. In 1825 Wyatville was instructed to build 'a small Fishing Temple . . . for His Majesty's convenience' at Virginia Water. He left most of the work to Crace and this was the result. The design, which allowed for a lakeside gallery where the King could sit while fishing, was probably based on 'The House of Confucius' in Kew Gardens. There was one large room with a dressing-room on each side, and a separate kitchen.

Many of Wyatville's contemporaries thought that it was not, however, nearly grand enough despite the sumptuously gilded woodwork and plaster of the private apartments, the richly brocaded walls and the fine doors from Carlton House. Charles Greville decided that not enough had been 'effected for the enormous sums expended'. Thomas Creevey thought so, too. 'Went in the carriage yesterday to see all that is going on at Windsor,' he told his step-daughter, 'and Mr Wyat-*Ville* himself did us the honour of conducting us thro' all the new apartments and showing us all the projected improvements. All the New Living Rooms make a very good Gentleman's or Nobleman's house, Nothing more.' But he thought the Grand Corridor, '16 feet wide and 560 feet in length, above all price'.

And once the Corridor was decorated and furnished, there were few who disagreed with him. Indeed, the resplendent decorations of the castle as a whole, which reflected the King's taste more than Wyatville's, were almost universally admired, even though, as Croker said, they were perhaps more in the style of Louis XIV than accorded with the general character of Windsor. Wyatville, also, thought them too 'Frenchy' and was often persuaded with difficulty to incorporate some finely wrought door or fireplace from Carlton House in his designs. 'Wyatville hummed and hawed at first a good deal', when asked to incorporate some painted glass from Carlton House in the walls of a staircase, the King told Knighton, his indispensable Keeper of the Privy Purse. 'However, I brought him at last to say that he thought "he cud pleace soom of't to adwantage, though 'e 'ad not joust then fix'd where."'

*

As well as collaborating on the reconstruction and redecoration of the castle, George IV and Wyatville worked together on improving its surroundings. The East Terrace was laid out with a central pool surrounded by lawns, flower beds and groups of vases and statuary; the Moat Garden, south and west of the base of the Round Tower, was cleared and improved, and some miles across the Great Park, to the south-east, ornamental temples were built to decorate the shores of a lovely artificial lake.

This lake, known as Virginia Water, had been made by the King's great-uncle, the Duke of Cumberland ('Billy the Butcher' of Culloden), who for all his faults was a man of aesthetic sensibility. He had been made Ranger of Windsor Great Park after his return from Holland in 1758 and had given employment to as many discharged soldiers as he could find work for in building roads and planting trees and lawns. He lived at Cranbourne Lodge, the house which Nell Gwynn's grandson, the Duke of St Albans, had occupied as Lord-Warden of Windsor Forest; and his Deputy Ranger, Thomas Sandby, lived in the smaller house which the Regent had converted into the Royal Lodge. Sandby, the brother of the painter Paul Sandby, who shared the house with him, was responsible for the operations at Virginia Water, which were carried out with more artistry than practicability. In order to make the lake, he dammed the small rivulets with soft banks of sand and clay which during a heavy thunderstorm in 1768 were washed away by floods 'causing £9,000 worth of damage'.

After the dams were rebuilt, a Chinese temple was put up on an island in the middle of the lake, and it was this that gave George IV the idea of building other ornamental temples around its shores. Wyatville helped him design a fishing temple, also a folly which was to be built out of various classical remains that had for some time been kept in a courtyard of the British Museum and which was to be decorated with Greek statues captured in a French frigate during the Napoleonic wars.

On warm days in the summer the King liked to drive down in his phaeton to Virginia Water followed by guests in landaus. When he reached the landing stage, his band, seated in a boat moored in the lake, would strike up 'God Save the King' and he and his guests would step into a barge to spend an afternoon fishing or go aboard the junk, *The Mandarin*, which had been brought to Virginia Water by the Duke of Cumberland. Sometimes there were tents on the shore and the King's guests would have dinner in them while the band went on playing; and afterwards they would stroll on the lawns by the water's edge.

Once the little Princess Victoria went with her uncle across the lake in his barge. It was 1826 and she was seven and he asked her to kiss him, and more than half a century later she remembered it as being 'too disgusting because his face was covered in grease paint'. But he was kind and she had liked him then.

'When we arrived,' she remembered, 'the King took me by the hand saying "Give me your little paw." He was large and gouty but with a wonderful dignity and charm of manner. He wore the wig which was so much worn in those days. Then he said he would give me something to wear, and that was his picture set in diamonds, which was worn by the Princesses as an order to a blue ribbon on the left shoulder. I was very proud of this — and Lady Conyngham pinned it on my shoulder.' The next day she went for a drive with her mother and they met the King who was driving his sister, the Duchess of Gloucester, to Virginia Water in his phaeton. 'And he said, "Pop her in" and I was lifted in and placed between him and aunt Gloucester who held me round the waist. (Mamma was much frightened.) I was greatly pleased.'

She was taken fishing; she was taken to see the King's menagerie at Sandpit Gate and she looked at the wapitis and chamois and gazelles; and in the evening she was allowed to go to listen to the band, which was playing in the conservatory by the light of coloured lamps. But best of all she liked going in the phaeton with her uncle and her aunt Gloucester.

The King was sixty-three then and had only four more years to live; and these trips in his phaeton to Virginia Water were becoming more and more rare.

The classical ruins at Virginia Water. The stones from the Temple of Augustus at Leptis Magna were erected by Wyatville in 1826.

Most days at Windsor during the rest of his life were, in fact, spent indoors wearing flamboyant and not always very clean dressing-gowns and turbans in stuffy, overheated rooms, reading, drinking cherry brandy and punch, dosing himself with laudanum, eating strange meals with quantities of pastry and vegetables at irregular times, talking to his pages and *valets de chambre*, to his stud groom, Jack Redford, or to O'Reilly, Surgeon to the Household.

Mount Charles told Greville that he led 'a most extraordinary life'. The curtains of his room were opened between six and seven. He had breakfast in bed and then 'read every newspaper quite through'. Occasionally he read a novel and was always pleased when a new book by Walter Scott came out. The rest of the morning was spent dozing. He rarely got up before six or seven o'clock in the evening, and when he felt too ill to get up at all, Lady Conyngham would visit him in his room. But otherwise she never entered it and he went to hers for an hour or so — not to make love, for 'he sought affection rather than sensual delight'; and perhaps he never had made love to her, even in the beginning. She still sometimes talked of leaving him, although she remained incapable of doing so; and for hours on end when he seemed really unwell she would devote herself to prayer. Once, although like Mrs Fitzherbert she knew that 'he always wished everyone to think him dangerously ill when there was little the matter with him', she burst into tears on being told he was 'very ill'. She and Knighton were on better terms now and this, Greville thought, was because the calculating Knighton opposed every kind of expense except that which was 'lavished on her'. The amount she had accumulated by savings and presents must have been 'enormous'. The malicious Lady Anne Hamilton said she had been 'very credibly informed' that the total sum was more than £500,000. Certainly Lady Conyngham's servants and those of her husband were all found situations in the royal household so that they did not have to pay their wages themselves, and even in London when the Conynghams gave a dinner at Hamilton Place the food was cooked at St James's and brought over by hackney coach in machines specially made for this purpose.

The Conynghams, nevertheless, were one of the least of the King's extravagances. Apart from the cost of decorating and furnishing the new rooms in the castle — where the whole of the length of the Corridor alone was furnished with the 'luxury of a drawing room, and full of fine busts and bronzes, and entertaining pictures, portraits and antiquities' — the expenses incurred by the various departments of the household in the first half of 1829 were far in excess of the income. In the Master of the Robes's department alone there was an excess of about £10,000, for the King loved his clothes and could not be persuaded to economize on them. He thought nothing of spending £800 on a cloak or £300 on a plain coat. One of his first acts on being made Prince Regent was to promote himself Field Marshal and when he wore the uniform people noticed that even the seams of the coat were heavily embroidered. It must have cost and weighed, someone said, two hundred pounds. For less formal occasions he had an immense variety of suits and coats, boots and breeches, gloves and hats, some of which he designed himself. He could rarely bring himself to part with any of them and after he was dead, amongst the volumes of love letters (including copies of his own 'descriptive of the most furious passion') amongst the 'five hundred pocket-books of different dates, and in every one of them money', amongst the quantities of women's gloves, the 'vast number of wigs', the trinkets, the dirty handkerchiefs, the faded nosegays, the locks of women's hair 'of all colours and lengths, some having the powder and pomatum yet sticking to them', were found all the coats he had ever had for fifty years, scores of waistcoats, three hundred whips, 'canes without number, every sort of uniform, the costumes of all the orders in Europe, splendid furs, pelisses, etc., hunting coats and breeches', and, among other things, a dozen pairs of new corduroy riding-breeches ordered from his tailor long after he had given up riding.

His pages said that he could remember all these clothes and that he developed an old man's habit of asking for coats and trousers he had worn many years before. He developed, too, the habit of pretending that he had taken part in events or shared feelings which were entirely outside his experience. He once said with a quite passionate sincerity that Lord Chesterfield had told him, 'Sir, you are the fourth Prince of Wales I have known, and I must give Your Royal Highness a piece of advice: stick to your father; as long as you adhere to your father you will be a great and happy man, but if you separate yourself from him, you will be nothing and an unhappy one. And by God, I never forgot that advice and acted upon it all my life.'

In the last years he even liked to pretend that he had fought at Waterloo, won the Battle of Salamanca by leading a splendid charge with his Dragoons, and ridden Fleur-de-Lis for the Goodwood Cup. Often when recalling these stirring events the tears would start to his eyes, and no one was quite sure that he had not persuaded himself that he had actually participated in them.

He had always been excessively emotional and as he grew older he became more and more maudlin, frequently bursting into tears, kissing envelopes and writing letters of grotesque sentimentality, especially when he was drunk.

The death of his favourite brother, the Duke of York, upset him profoundly. Even Charles Greville admitted that he 'showed great feeling about his brother and exceeding kindness in providing for his servants . . . He gave £6,000 to pay immediate expenses and took many of the old servants into his own service.'

He decided that the funeral, which was to be held at Windsor, should be a fitting tribute to the Duke's services. It was, in fact, a disaster. The chapel was bitterly cold and draughty and there was no matting or carpeting in the aisle, where for almost an hour several members of the royal family and most of the Cabinet waited shivering in the gloom. Peel advised old Lord Eldon, the Lord Chancellor, to stand on his cocked hat, which he did. The Dukes of Wellington, Sussex and Montrose all caught severe colds. Canning contracted rheumatic fever. And the Bishop of Lincoln died. 'According to the gossips the common soldiers died at the rate of half a dozen a day.'

And this was not all that the gossips said. But the rumours that were spread concerning the effects of the appalling inefficiency of the King's arrangements were harmless in comparison with those that went about some time later concerning the deceased Duke's younger brother, Ernest Augustus, Duke of Cumberland, the strange death of whose valet Sellis had so distressed George III.

It appeared that a Captain Thomas Garth of Melton Mowbray had filed an affidavit in Chancery maintaining that he had come into possession of certain documents which Sir Herbert Taylor, formerly George III's private secretary, had agreed to buy from him in exchange for an annuity of £3,000 a year and an undertaking to settle all his debts. Taylor, Garth contended, was trying to get these documents removed from the bank where they had been deposited, without fulfilling his part of the bargain. What these documents were was naturally the subject of excited speculation. The most persistent rumour was that they proved that Thomas Garth was the child of an incestuous relationship between the Duke of Cumberland and his sister, Princess Sophia.

Greville did not give credit to this rumour, preferring to believe another story that Garth was the Princess's son by 'some inferior person' in the royal household – the most commonly suggested person being Christopher Papendiek – and that the secret of his birth had been entrusted to General Thomas Garth, one of George III's equerries, whose name he bore. It was Lady Caroline Thynne's more credible belief that General Garth himself was undoubtedly the father. As Mistress of the Robes to Queen Charlotte Lady Caroline was at Windsor when Princess Sophia, being ill, had been removed from the Lower Lodge to Queen's Lodge where she was put in a bedroom beneath General Garth's. 'Nine months from that time she was brought to bed.' The secret of her pregnancy was kept from the old King, who was told she was dropsical and, after the birth, that she had been cured by roast beef. 'This he swallowed and used to tell it to people, all of whom knew the truth, as "a very extraordinary thing".' People had doubted that Garth could be the father as he was so ugly and had a great claret mark on his face but this, Greville decided when he heard the story and believed that it satisfactorily contradicted his misapprehension about Papendiek, was 'no argument at all, for women fall in love with anything'. Certainly, as Lady Caroline knew, Princess Sophia, lonely and passionate, was very much in love with the old General, whom Sir Herbert Taylor had no doubt was the father.

Even if the Duke had been shown to have been his sister's lover, though, the Garth scandal could scarcely have provided gossip more damaging to the royal family. And the King was said to be 'horribly annoyed by the business'. This in addition to the Catholic problem and followed by the suicide of Lord Graves, comptroller of the household to the Duke of Sussex, who cut his throat when he could no longer bear the thought of his wife (the mother of his ten children) having a well-publicized affair with his master's infamous brother, Cumberland, reduced the King to an almost constant state of nervousness and irritation.

He began to sleep very badly and seemed in permanent need of company and reassurance during the night, ringing his bell several times every hour to ask what the time was or to tell a valet to pour him out a glass of water, although there was a jug by his bed. He was frightened that there was something seriously wrong with his bladder, which gave him so much discomfort that he took far more laudanum than he should have done. He had been drinking too much of it, in fact, for years and sometimes, so Mrs Arbuthnot said, passed 'the greater part of the twenty-four hours in a state of stupor'. The Duke of Wellington, Mrs Arbuthnot's informant, said that he had been known to take two hundred drops in a single night. Frequently Ministers called to discuss business with him and found him incapacitated by the drug or by alcohol from doing so.

*

His doctors were far from being in agreement as to how the King should be treated and were on the worst possible terms with each other. Knighton, it was said, detested O'Reilly and distrusted his other colleague, Sir Henry Halford. The King, apparently, did not put much trust in either of them, always sending for Knighton when he was frightened; but Halford prescribed the opium and O'Reilly, although in his patient's opinion 'the damnedest liar in the world', brought him the gossip that he still longed to hear.

The King was a difficult patient, combining a nervous apprehension as to his condition with a refusal to adopt a way of life which might improve it. On occasions he would alarm his doctors by going almost black in the face as he tried to get breath and, afraid that he was going to have a heart attack, they would give him a large glass of brandy, which made him feel so much better he would suddenly decide to go for a long ride in his carriage.

His mode of living during these last months of his life was 'really beyond belief', Mrs Arbuthnot thought:

One day [in the middle of April 1830], at the hour of the servants' dinner, he called the Page in and said, 'Now you are going to dinner. Go downstairs and cut me off just such a piece of beef as you would like to have yourself, cut from the part you like the best yourself, and bring it me up.' The Page accordingly went and fetched him an enormous quantity of roast beef, all of which he ate, and then slept for five hours.

He affected to believe that he would die at any minute, but after saying one day with a sort of reckless cheerfulness, 'You know, I shall

Left, 'State of the Giraffe', a caricature by William Heath, July 1829. The giraffe, a present to the King from the Pasha of Egypt, arrived at Windsor in 1827. Never in robust health she died in August 1829. Lady Conyngham and the King, who had this support made for the sickly animal, were both ridiculed for their devotion to her.

Right, 'Packing up!!!', a caricature by William Heath, 1 July 1830. Lord and Lady Conyngham, with their daughter Elizabeth, are depicted packing up their loot (including the skeleton of the giraffe) after George IV's death.

be dead by Saturday,' he began to discuss the horses he wanted to buy for Ascot races. And when Halford told him that he was, indeed, going to die soon, he refused to accept the dismal verdict and replied that he was sure to recover. On some days, though, he obviously doubted it. On 17 May 1830 Peel visited him and 'in the minds of both men was the thought that it would be their final interview, and all past animosities were put away'. He had been very angry when Peel and the Duke of Wellington had resigned on Lord Liverpool's death thus forcing Canning to form a government which included no sound Tories; and he had been angry, too, when after Canning's death Peel had come into office again as Home Secretary in the Duke of Wellington's government to support the Roman Catholic Relief Bill. But now all this was forgiven, and the two men spoke as friends. The King asked Peel to push his chair to the window and said, with characteristic self-dramatization, that it was the last time he would be able to look out into the garden. 'You are just returned from your father's funeral,' he added, 'you will soon have to pay the like ceremony to me.' Ten days later he made a similar remark to the Duke of Wellington.

There was, indeed, little hope now for his recovery. His legs were scarified to take away the water, but they soon swelled up again. He continued to find it difficult to get his breath; and a Bill had to be passed – for he had begun to grow blind – to enable his signature to be fixed to documents by means of a stamp.

Momentarily he improved. On 9 June he was sitting up in bed talking with Knighton as though he were quite well and young again; and on 12 June the Duke of Wellington found him looking much better and stronger. But he got better only to relapse again. He was so enormously fat now, 'like a feather bed', the Duchess of Gloucester said, and his heart was growing weaker every day. When the Bishop of Chichester knelt by his bed and said the prayer for his recovery

which was to be read in all churches the King said fervently, 'Amen!
Amen! Amen!' and then added the touchingly predictable comment:
'It is in very good taste.'

At about half-past three in the early morning of 26 June he suddenly called out, 'Good God, what is this?' His page, Thomas Bachelor,
ran towards the easy chair in which he had spent the night, his head
resting on his hands across a table, for the palpitations of his heart
prevented him from lying down. 'My boy,' he said, a few moments
later, clutching his doctor's hand. 'My boy, this is death!'

5

WILLIAM IV
– THE RESPECTABLE OLD ADMIRAL

Before the King was buried Lady Conyngham had left the castle,
taking – so everyone in London believed although no one in Windsor
seems actually to have seen her – wagonloads of treasure and, as Mrs
Arbuthnot predicted, no sooner had she gone than she was scarcely
ever 'thought of or heard of more'.

There were many, though, who welcomed the departure of Lady
Conyngham without looking forward to the arrival of her successor.
Queen Adelaide was 'frightful', Charles Greville thought, 'very ugly
with a horrid complexion'. It was not an exceptional verdict. 'The
Queen is even worse than I thought,' a woman told a friend after seeing her for the first time, 'a little insignificant person as ever I saw.
She was dressed, as perhaps you will see by the papers "exceedingly
plain", in bombazine, with a little shabby muslin collar, dyed Leghorn
hat and leather shoes.' The new King had married this unprepossessing daughter of the Duke of Saxe-Meiningen in 1818, seven years after
breaking with Mrs Dorothea Jordan, a motherly actress, who had
borne him ten illegitimate children. These children all came to live at

St George's Hall at the time of the Regency. This water-colour by Charles Wild shows the Hall as it was before being altered by Wyatville.

Windsor with their wives and husbands so that by the summer of 1831 the castle was 'quite full with *toute la bâtardise*'. They were frequently quarrelling amongst themselves and with the King, to whom the sons were constantly appealing for more money and better titles. He gave them all £30,000 in addition to their allowances, but this did not, apparently, prevent one of them, Lord Frederick FitzClarence, sending him a bill for £12,000 and 'flouncing off with 8 or 10 of the King's horses, half a dozen servants and 3 carriages without a word of notice' when the King refused to pay it. Another son, George, created Earl of Munster in 1831, replied that he saw no use in having his picture 'when it was very probable that in less than three years it would be in a pawnbroker's shop', after the King had offered to sit for a portrait for him. A son-in-law, Lord Errol, who had married Elizabeth Fitz-Clarence and was accordingly made a Lord of the Bedchamber, Master of the Buckhounds and Master of the Horse, refused to have his official accounts inspected and, when this was insisted upon, he threatened to resign. The Queen pleaded with him to stay but he 'abused her so violently she threw herself on a sofa in his room in a flood of tears'. At dinner she put a bon-bon on his plate as a peace offering; but he threw it back on to hers.

The King himself did his best to keep out of the family quarrels. He was a good-natured man; and as soon as his brother died 'began immediately to do good-natured things'. One of his first acts was to invite Mrs Fitzherbert to Windsor where he 'treated her with the greatest respect, gave her permission to clothe her servants in the royal livery, placed implicit reliance in all her statements, and having sanctioned an arrangement by which all private papers were to be destroyed — with a few exceptions that were placed under seal at Coutts's banking-house — settled upon her an income of £6,000 a year'.

William IV clearly loved being King and his excitement, enthusiasm and energy during the first few weeks of his reign were touchingly boyish. Without any conception of protocol he walked about London quite alone, nodding, brusquely yet cheerfully, to left and right, and one day in St James's Street the mob followed him and 'one of the common women threw her arms round him and kissed him'. At George IV's funeral at Windsor he strode briskly into St George's Hall, shook Lord Strathavon (Lady Conyngham's son-in-law) heartily by the hand, repeatedly nodding to the other mourners. He talked 'all sorts of nonsense' to Prince George, the young son of his brother the Duke of Cumberland, the 'most mischievous child that ever was born', and then invited himself to dinner with the Duke of Wellington. His 'chief gratification', the Duke of Buckingham said, 'was playing the hospitable host' and he entertained on an average two thousand persons a week. Over a hundred guests were invited to dine in St George's Hall on his first birthday as King and three thousand in the Long Walk; and Charles Arbuthnot, who was one of them, thought it 'the finest thing he ever saw'. The King was in the highest spirits and made a 'very good speech'. He was extremely fond of making speeches, but they were rarely as successful as this one apparently was, for his congenital lack of tact was preposterous.

So far as practical politics were concerned, however, he seemed obligingly ready to follow his Ministers' advice. It did not appear that he had any strong ambitions as a monarch and concerned himself happily with details as his father might more profitably have done. Immediately on his accession he announced, for instance, that he would 'change the uniform of the Guards and put all the cavalry into scarlet except the Blues'. But while he shared his father's passion for the details of military uniforms, he did not seem at all anxious to insist that his ideas even about these should be put into effect. He was quite content to present himself as a bluff, simple, patriotic sailor without dangerous ambitions or aggravating pretensions; and to a large extent he succeeded. The Duke of Wellington, who thought, with good cause, that when, as Duke of Clarence, he had been Lord High Admiral, he had been 'a very bad head for the Navy', now expressed himself as delighted with the King who behaved like a 'respectable old

The Old Gateway and Devil's Tower by Joshua Dolby. This drawing shows work in progress on the south front after George IV's death when Wyatville stayed on at the castle in his apartments in Winchester Tower which the King had given him.

Admiral'. And certainly his people were prepared to welcome him if only for his small virtue of respectability. He had little 'information and strong prejudices', so the *Spectator* wrote of him when he was dead. 'A weak, ignorant, common-place sort of person . . . sufficiently conceited and strong-willed', he was nevertheless 'to the last a popular sovereign'.

To the people of Windsor he seemed a delightful one after George IV. Within a few weeks of his accession he threw the terraces and the drives in the Home Park once more open to the public, who were permitted to go anywhere they liked provided they did not walk immediately under the windows of the private apartments. 'Their majesties are accessible at all hours,' a visitor happily wrote, 'the apartments are open to everybody; there is no seclusion, no mystery, nothing to conceal.' As well as demonstrating that he was less of a selfish recluse than his brother, the new King also showed his people that he was less extravagant. He pruned the castle staff and dismissed the French cooks; he had the recently fitted but uneconomical gas installation pulled out; he replaced the German band by a smaller English one; he pulled down most of the Royal Lodge, leaving only the great saloon that Wyatville had added to Nash's original design as a sad folly to exercise the imagination of the congregation in the nearby Chapel Royal; he sent the expensive animals in the menagerie to the London Zoo; he made over a miscellaneous collection of treasures and objects of art to the nation. His brother had been fond of such knicknackery, he explained, when looking at some pictures, but he couldn't see much in them himself. Aye, they might be pretty. 'Damned expensive taste, though.'

He had no such tastes. Wyatville's work in the castle was completed, and the Waterloo Chamber was built by roofing over an interior court-yard known as Horn Court to house George IV's magnificent collection of paintings — mostly by Lawrence — of distinguished men who had contributed to Napoleon's downfall. But both William IV and Queen Adelaide appeared to take more interest in the model cottages which were going up in the Park than they did in the castle. The Queen visited these cottages on Sunday afternoons and 'when she appeared all the children came running out to her and she talked to them and patted their heads'.

Neither she nor the King liked racing. She took her woolwork to Ascot and he, when asked which horses to enter for a particular race, gaily replied, 'Take the whole fleet. I suppose some of them will win.'

He settled down at Windsor to a life of quiet domesticity not unlike that of his father. He slept in the same room as the Queen, a kind and admirable wife, not at all the frightful creature that Greville had described, and he got up every morning at ten minutes to eight, exactly five minutes after his valet knocked on the door. Immediately he put on his trousers and a flannel dressing-gown and took no notice of anyone until he had been to the lavatory. Despite his brisk start to the day, however, he did not sit down to breakfast until half-past nine, for he dressed extremely slowly, rarely taking less than an hour and a half. After breakfast he read *The Times* and the *Morning Post*, occasionally breaking out with an angry comment such as 'That's a damned lie!' Having finished the papers, he transacted business with his secretary until two o'clock, when he had his luncheon, which usually consisted of cutlets and a couple of glasses of sherry. In the evening while the Queen sat knitting he went to sleep in his chair, 'occasionally waking up for the purpose of saying, "Exactly so, Ma'am"' and then sleeping again. After dinner, while the band played, he went back to sleep once more. He ate moderately and did not drink much, although he did not like people who did not drink at all. And once at dinner in the castle he called across the table to his niece's widower Prince Leopold of Saxe-Coburg, whom he detested, 'What's that you're drinking, sir? Water, sir! God damn it! Why don't you drink wine! I never allow anybody to drink water at my table.'

When this scene took place he was within a few months of his death. He was seventy-one and had aged quickly since he had come to the throne six years before. His early energy had soon wilted and his bon-homie had degenerated into bluster. His Ministers, since the disputes over the Reform Bill, no longer found him tolerant and pliable and he

11

The Thames at Windsor
by J. M. W. Turner

12

The east front
of the Upper Ward
in January 1824
*The competition for the
rebuilding of the castle was
won by Jeffrey Wyatt who
changed his name to
Wyatville in consequence.
Wyatville's drawing shows
the plain front as it was
before his work began.*

13

The proposed alterations
to the east front
of the Upper Ward
*Wyatville's proposals
for new stone mullions,
projecting windows,
battlements and corbels.
His original estimate was for
£122,500 but long before
his work was finished the
cost had risen to well over
£800,000.*

14

Wyatville's design for the dining room
This is the proposed west wall
with carved gilt sideboards beside the fireplace.

in turn shut the doors of the castle against them. When one of his sons told him that he really ought to give a dinner during the Ascot week of 1835, he burst out angrily, 'You know I cannot give a dinner. I cannot give any dinners without inviting the Ministers and I would rather see the Devil than any of them in my house.' As his brother had given offence by refusing to ask certain Whigs to Windsor, so William IV gave offence by only having Tories as his guests there. The sight of Peel in the Royal Stand at Ascot had prompted George IV to remark sardonically that he would 'have as soon expected to see a pig in church' as him at a race. Six years later William IV was making quite as 'extraordinary speeches' at Ascot about Melbourne.

His most extraordinary speech, however, was made in the castle at a dinner party during the late summer of 1836. The circumstances were these: The King had invited his sister-in-law, the Duchess of Kent, and her daughter Princess Victoria to Windsor for the Queen's birthday on 13 August, and he had asked them to stay on at the castle until his own birthday which was to be held privately on 21 August and publicly the following day. The Duchess, ignoring the invitation for the Queen's birthday, said she would come to Windsor on 20 August. The King, having to be in London that day, called at Kensington Palace to discover that his sister-in-law had appropriated a set of seventeen apartments which she had applied for the previous year and been refused.

The King returned to Windsor at ten o'clock and immediately on entering the drawing-room took both Princess Victoria's hands in his own and told her how sorry he was he did not see her more often. Then, turning to her mother and bowing low, he announced that a 'most unwarrantable liberty' had been taken with one of his palaces; he neither understood nor would endure conduct so disrespectful to him.

The following day at dinner he elaborated his complaint. Standing up, with the Duchess of Kent by his side and Princess Victoria opposite him, he declared with mounting anger:

I trust in God that my life may be spared for nine months longer, after which period, in the event of my death, no Regency would take place. I should then have the satisfaction of leaving the royal authority to the personal exercise of that Young Lady [pointing to the Princess], the Heiress presumptive to the Crown, and not in the hands of a person, now near me, who is surrounded by evil advisers and who is herself incompetent to act with propriety in the station in which she would be placed. Amongst many other things I have particularly to complain of the manner in which that young lady has been kept away from my Court; she has been repeatedly kept from my drawing-rooms, at which she ought always to have been present, but I am fully resolved that this will not happen again. I would have her know that I am King, and that I am determined to make my authority respected, and for the future I shall insist and command that the Princess do upon all occasions appear at my Court, as it is her duty to do.

The King ended his alarming speech on a quieter note, referring with avuncular affection to Victoria and her future reign. But the damage was done. The Princess was already in tears; Queen Adelaide appeared in 'deep distress'; and as soon as dinner was over the Duchess of Kent announced her immediate departure.

It seemed doubtful by the end of the year that the King's prayer that he would live long enough for there to be no regency would be answered. And many of those who did not believe that he would die, thought that he might at least go mad. 'His habitual state of excitement,' Charles Greville thought, would 'probably bring on sooner or later the malady of his family.'

The King retained his sanity, however, and he held on to life until Victoria reached her eighteenth birthday. Less than four weeks after that birthday, however, he lay dead in the Blue Room at Windsor.

His thoughts during his last illness were often with his niece. He felt sure she would be 'a good woman and a good Queen'. 'It will touch every sailor's heart to have a girl queen to fight for,' he added with characteristic pride in the service in which his birth and incapacity had denied him fulfilment. 'They'll be tattooing her face on their arms, and I'll be bound they'll all think she was christened after Nelson's ship.'

V

VICTORIANS

1

VICTORIA – THE YOUNG QUEEN

Thomas Creevey was standing outside the castle gate when Victoria rode in as Queen. Her mother was with her and her uncle Leopold, now King of the Belgians, and the 'Boss King very gallantly held his horse in a little to let his Queen niece be first.' 'I was quite delighted with Vicky in every way,' Creevey told Miss Ord. 'She looks infinitely better on horseback than in any other way; she was dressed so nicely too, and her manner *quite perfect.*'

During these first few months of her reign, there was scarcely anyone who did not agree with Creevey that the little Queen was delightful. From the very hour when Lord Conyngham, as Master of the Household, and the Archbishop of Canterbury, having ridden through the night from Windsor to Kensington Palace, told her that she was Queen and knelt before her to kiss her hand, she had behaved with a quiet grace and simple dignity. Later on that morning she received the Privy Council, and acted 'with every sort of good taste and feeling'. A little bewildered, occasionally looking at Lord Melbourne for instruction when she had any doubt what to do, 'which hardly ever occurred', she remained calm, self-possessed, graceful and modest. Her voice was soft and, if a little high and thin, beautifully clear.

Those who knew her best were well aware, however, that behind her attractive manner was a spirit far tougher than could at first be imagined. She was uncompromisingly truthful and direct, obstinately accurate and tenacious, capable and conscientious, nervous yet insensitive. She had many firmly held prejudices. She attached great importance to the observation of forms and precedents and had a respect for detail which she never lost. On going down to Windsor to offer her sympathy to the Queen Dowager on King William's death, she realized that the flag on the Round Tower would be flying at half-mast. She suggested to Lord Melbourne who was with her that a message should be sent on ahead of them that the flag should not be raised in honour of her arrival. Melbourne confessed that he 'had never thought of the flag or knew anything about it'.

Her life at Windsor was energetic and she was as happy as she had ever been. She worked quite hard, allowing herself to be guided by Lord Melbourne, while anxious to understand the complexities of government herself. But she spent many hours every day enjoying herself and was often still dancing at three o'clock in the morning singing the tune or nodding her head in time with the music.

She had not liked the castle at first. It always, so she wrote to her 'dearest, best Uncle', appeared very melancholy to her; but soon she grew to love it and to feel a deep respect for what her Private Secretary was later to describe as its 'dignified feudalism'.

Sometimes she got up early, but more often, and always after a late night, she would lie in bed, feeling vaguely guilty, before having breakfast in her room. For three or four hours every morning she devoted herself to business, reading all the dispatches and having 'every matter of interest and importance in every department laid before her'. Between eleven and twelve o'clock Lord Melbourne came to see her and they would talk about business or gossip; and after luncheon she would go riding in the Great Park, 'the greater part of the time at full gallop', accompanied by several equerries and ladies-in-waiting. Later in the afternoon there was music and singing and if there were any children staying in the castle — 'and she is so fond of them,' Creevey said, 'that she generally contrives to have some there' – the Queen would play and romp with them. On Sunday evenings, after having been twice to church during the day, the ladies would accompany the Queen for a stroll on the Terrace and around the great parterre, watched by crowds of men and women and Eton boys whom the gentlemen of the household tapped out of the way as she got close to them. The band played; the standard on the Round Tower flapped in the wind or drooped against the white pole; and the fountain splashed its water high into the air.

At half-past seven the guests assembled for dinner and the men were told by the lord-in-waiting whom to take in with them. A little before eight o'clock the Queen came into the room, preceded by the gentlemen of the household and followed by her mother and her ladies. She spoke a few words to every woman who was there, bowed to every man, and then went immediately into dinner, with the man of the highest rank in the room or a foreign ambassador on her right, and Lord Melbourne on her left.

The men were not permitted to remain long after the ladies had retired and were usually back in the drawing-room drinking coffee within a quarter of an hour. The Queen, who did not sit down until they had returned, spoke a few words of a 'trivial nature, all however very civil and cordial in manner and expression', to each of them.

Charles Greville recorded this as a typical conversation the Queen once had with him:

'Have you been riding today, Mr Greville?'
'No, Madam, I have not.'
'It was a fine day.'
'Yes, Madam, a very fine day.'
'It was rather cold, though.'
'It *was* rather cold, Madam.'
'Your sister, Lady Frances Egerton, rides, I think, doesn't she?'
'She does ride sometimes, Madam.'
A pause.
'Has Your Majesty been riding today?'
'Oh, yes, a very long ride.'
'Has Your Majesty got a nice horse?'
'Oh, yes, a very nice horse.'

When the series of little conversations was over, the band struck up again, chairs were brought up to the Duchess of Kent's whist table, and the Queen sat down with Melbourne at a large round table with those guests who were not playing cards, to indulge in two hours of further and often as wearying conversation.

Melbourne was nearly always there. At first it was through a sense of duty, but he was not a man 'to carry out a duty so rigorously, if it went against his inclinations. As a matter of fact, all his inclinations were in its favour; and what had begun as a duty very soon turned into an intense pleasure'.

Men who had known him well in the past were amazed at the change in him. 'Never was such a revolution seen in anybody's occupations and habits.' Instead of sprawling about in his chair, talking, laughing and swearing, as he had been used to do at Holland House, he sat bolt upright and his conversation was 'carefully guarded and regulated by the strictest propriety'. He was clearly extremely fond of his young Queen, 'passionately fond of her as he might be of his daughter if he had one', Greville observed, 'and the more because he is a man with capacity for loving without having anything in the world to love'. People even made jokes about an early marriage.

His influence for good could not, though, be denied. The Queen needed such a man. She was, after all, very young and her lonely up-bringing had given her a curiously naïve outlook on the world. She was often shrewd but her judgements were never tentative, never in doubt. It was not merely that she was incapable of dissembling or lying, but that she was incapable of understanding that there were degrees of reprehensibility. A thing was right or it was wrong; a person was good or bad; and once her mind was made up she had absolute confidence in her opinion.

There were occasions when the Queen's strength of character and innate prejudices were too powerful to be restrained or guided by the elderly, handsome and distinguished man she so obviously worshipped. The most notorious of these occasions in her early career was one which temporarily threatened all the goodwill that had surrounded her from the day of her accession. The origins of this sad affair went back to the days of her frustrating childhood.

*

The atmosphere at Kensington Palace was stifling and clouded with intrigue. The Duchess of Kent, 'a short, stout, foolish woman, rustling self-importantly about in velvet and ostrich plumes', was intoxicated by the thought that she was mother of the future Queen. She distrusted nearly all her late husband's relations and, as William IV had so vehemently complained, rarely permitted Victoria to see them. Her brother Leopold was allowed to exercise a deeper influence, but even he was not entirely to be trusted. Victoria was consequently rarely left alone. Her nights she spent in her mother's bedroom; her days were carefully regulated by Baroness Lehzen, the strict, narrow-minded, vigilant daughter of a Hanoverian clergyman who was her 'Lady Attendant', in fact her governess.

Victoria was rather frightened of this plain, yellow-skinned woman with her rasping voice and her passion for caraway seeds, just as she was frightened of her mother, who once made her pin a sprig of holly to the neck of her dress to make her sit erect at table; but she also, as she later admitted herself, adored the Baroness and the Baroness in turn adored her pupil, who had been in her care from the age of five. She protected her jealously from those who hoped to profit by their closeness to her and in particular from the Duchess of Kent's confidential secretary, the equivocal, pompous and scheming Sir John Conroy, formerly the Duke's equerry. Few people liked Conroy but

Louise Lehzen hated him, and Victoria shared her hatred. It was said that the Princess had once discovered her mother in his arms and that they were lovers; and it was also believed, with better cause, that they had plotted together to have Victoria's coming of age delayed so that the Duchess might become Regent with Conroy as her principal adviser. What at least was certain was that soon after she became Queen, Victoria dismissed Conroy with an annuity and broke the close bonds that had formerly tied her to her mother.

Immediately upon her accession she gave orders that her bed should be removed at once from the Duchess's room; she had her meals by herself; and she recorded with pride and relief in her journal, underlining the important words, that on the day of William IV's death she saw the Lord Chamberlain, the Archbishop of Canterbury and the Prime Minister 'of course quite alone'. The Duchess came with her to Windsor, but she was never allowed to regain control over her daughter's life or household, all the details of which the Queen now regulated herself with the help of Melbourne and Baroness Lehzen.

There remained, however, one unwelcome link with the past and that was the Duchess of Kent's lady-in-waiting, Lady Flora Hastings. Lady Flora returned to the castle at the beginning of 1839 from a holiday in Scotland, and it was rumoured that she had shared a carriage as far as London with the detested Conroy whose plots, hatched at Kensington Palace, she had apparently helped to further. A month or so after her return Lady Flora's stomach began to swell and when they discovered that the court physician, Sir James Clark, shared their suspicions, neither the Queen nor Baroness Lehzen had any doubt that Lady Flora was pregnant and that, as the Queen wrote in her journal, the horrid cause of the pregnancy was that 'monster and demon incarnate' whose name she forbore to mention. Lady Flora was asked to submit to a medical examination which revealed that she was not pregnant at all. Her distended stomach was due to an enlarged liver. Melbourne with characteristic sound sense had advised against taking any action which would complicate what might turn out to be an extremely awkward situation. He was constantly, if often by implication, advising the Queen to be more tolerant, to curb the excesses of her youthful morality, not to expect perfection in anyone; and, although he was anxious that nothing should be done to compromise the dignity of the Crown or Court, Melbourne was also anxious that the Queen should not appear unduly censorious. But there was always this difficulty of making her see that 'you cannot always go straight forward, that you must go round about sometimes'. By insisting that Lady Flora should be medically examined, by refusing to do more in the face of Lady Flora's brother's angry protests than apologize coldly and in private, the Queen appeared not merely censorious but vindictive.

The matter might have died quietly down had not the justifiably indignant Hastings family published their correspondence with the Court, a correspondence which the newspapers and disaffected politicians made the most of. Eventually the Duke of Wellington, who loved 'being consulted and mixed up in messes', lent his great reputation to a pacification of the whole affair. But the damage had been done. 'In the space of a week or two, the Queen's early popularity had vanished.'

At Ascot that year she was hissed as she drove down the course; and as she came out on to the balcony a man shouted out 'Mrs Melbourne'. Always deeply distressed and furiously indignant when she was criticized, she complained to Melbourne that this sort of disrespect to the Sovereign ought to be stopped by law. 'Those two abominable women', the Duchess of Montrose and Lady Sarah Ingestre who had expressed their disapproval of her conduct in a most humiliating way, 'ought to be flogged'. Then in the summer, Lady Flora became seriously ill. The Queen at first refused to believe that she might be dying, but Melbourne persuaded her that she was and that she ought to visit her. Reluctantly she consented and the sight of the sick woman's haggard, fevered face upset her profoundly. 'Poor Lady Flora! Poor Lady Flora!' she kept repeating and ten days later when Lady Flora died, the Queen burst into a flood of tears. She sent a carriage to follow the funeral procession to the station. And the police had to guard it from being wrecked.

In this same year the Queen's troubles were further increased by what became known as the Bedchamber Plot, an affair which confirmed the distrust with which most Tory politicians regarded her.

In May 1839 the Whig government was clearly collapsing and the Queen was faced with the dreaded possibility of losing Lord Melbourne. She begged him 'not to forsake her'; but he told her that there was no avoiding it and advised her to send for the Duke of Wellington who said, in his turn, that he was too old and suggested she asked Sir Robert Peel instead. The Queen disliked Peel. She found him uncouth, cold and clumsy, without grace or charm, and she was determined not to have him as her Prime Minister if she could possibly retain her beloved Melbourne. Peel's insistence that she should replace some of her ladies — who being chosen by Melbourne were all the wives or daughters of Whigs — by others with a Tory background, gave her her opportunity. She adamantly refused to change any of her ladies; she had become devoted to them. 'The Queen maintains *all* her Ladies,' she insisted. And she did maintain them. Melbourne, who had advised her to give way to Peel, realized she would never do so and agreed, with a pleasure clouded by apprehension, to stay in office.

The delighted Queen gave a ball for the Grand Duke Alexander of Russia the night she brought the Bedchamber Plot to this dangerously triumphant conclusion, and she danced happily till a quarter past three in the morning. The Red Drawing Room at Windsor shone with the glittering light of hundreds of candles and the Queen's eyes sparkled with excitement as the handsome figures in their splendid uniforms swirled around her dancing the Mazurka and a new German dance, the *Gross Vater*. The young Grand Duke was delightful. Indeed, she confessed in her diary, she was a little in love with him. She was 'talking jokingly', of course; but a young person like her, who hated 'a Sunday face', 'must *sometimes* have *young* people to laugh with'. She said as much to Lord Melbourne. 'Nothing so natural,' he replied and there were tears in his eyes.

Later on that year another handsome young man came to Windsor and after two days in his company she had decided that she was in love, not 'jokingly' this time but truly and deeply. It was providential that she was so, for an early marriage and an heir was essential if the country were to be saved from the danger of the Duke of Cumberland inheriting the Crown.

Prince Albert of Saxe-Coburg-Gotha, her uncle Leopold's nephew and her own cousin, was 'fascinating' and '*beautiful*'. On the fourth day she made up her mind to marry him; and on the fifth day, having decided, as she told her aunt Gloucester later, that Albert 'would never have presumed to take such a liberty to propose to the Queen of England', she sent for him to come to her little blue boudoir and there, trembling as she spoke, she told him that he had gained her whole heart and that he would make her intensely happy if he would make the sacrifice of sharing his life with her.

He accepted her proposal graciously, but his letters reveal his reluctance to abandon the quiet, studious life he preferred for the frivolities and superficiality of an unintellectual court. He danced well but he hated late nights; he enjoyed serious conversation but he detested gossip.

Although he was far more attracted by the Queen than Lytton Strachey suggests, he wrote of marriage as if he were going into battle. 'I will not let my courage fail,' he assured his tutor in that stilted, portentous style which characterized most of his writings. 'With firm resolution and true zeal on my part, I cannot fail to continue noble, manly and princely in all things.' 'Oh, the future,' he sighed to his grandmother. 'Life has its thorns in every position,' he told his stepmother, 'and the consciousness of having used one's powers and endeavours for an object so great as that of promoting the good of so many, will surely be sufficient to support me.'

The sentiments may have a sadly priggish and sanctimonious ring for a young man of twenty, but they were unquestionably sincere. Prince Albert was an honest and good, a profoundly dutiful and a devoutly conscientious man. And it was, indeed, these almost oppressive virtues, unrelieved by any frailty except a certain hesitancy and deviousness, a bigoted outlook on religion and sex, an occasional nervous irritability and a tendency to 'allow himself opinions', as Duke Ernest of Coburg said of him, 'which are wont to arise from contempt of mankind in the abstract', which led to his being accepted by Englishmen with ill-concealed reluctance. He clothed his shyness with a veneer of stiff formality. He seemed, on occasions, excessively critical and condemnatory, even harsh. His fine features and clear blue eyes were often overcast by a disquieting expression, distant and lugubrious.

One evening at Windsor shortly before his wedding he was playing a letter game with Melbourne who was given the word 'pleasure' to guess. Offering the Prime Minister a hint, the Prince said forlornly, 'It is not a *common* thing.'

*

The honeymoon took place at Windsor and Charles Greville thought it 'a very curious affair'. Very early on the first morning the bridegroom and his wife were up and dressed and walking in the garden, and Greville remarked to Lady Palmerston that this was not the way to provide the country with a Prince of Wales. Lady Palmerston, for her part, was much irritated by the whole business. The honeymoon was practically public. An immense party of guests was staying in the castle, where a dance was given three days after the wedding, to which, incidentally, scarcely any Tories had been invited. Lady Palmerston was much vexed that the Queen, whose 'prejudices and antipathies were deep and strong' and whose disposition was 'very inflexible', should have nobody about her to tell her that this was 'not becoming and would appear indelicate. But she has nobody that dares tell her, or she will not endure to hear such truths.'

A detail of colour plate 15 showing the miniature of Prince Albert on Queen Victoria's right forearm.

She had not yet fallen as completely as she was later to do under the Prince's benign yet overwhelming influence; and, although she wished him to be made King Consort by Act of Parliament or, at least, accorded the first place of precedence in the country after herself, she did not intend to forget that *she* was Queen and must maintain her position and dignity. She did not want him to take any part in political business, allowing him to do little more than 'help with the blotting paper', as she herself ingenuously put it in her journal, and she organized his official life to such an extent that she chose all the officers of his household, including his confidential secretary. He protested mildly at first and then almost despairingly, but the Queen calmly and firmly assured him that he could 'perfectly rely on her'. And he gave way. He was a patient as well as an unselfish man.

He had his own way, however, with regard to London, which the Queen had loved and from which he always longed to escape. Within six months he had succeeded in transforming the Queen's tastes to accord with his own. She who had once delighted in court ceremonies, etiquette and trivial formalities – as the Prince long before their marriage had complained to a friend – who enjoyed staying up late at night, sleeping late into the day, and who took not the slightest interest in nature, now began to share his love of the country and of a peaceful life. She eventually agreed that to come to the castle from London was like being 'freed from some dungeon'.

The Prince himself was delighted with Windsor. 'I feel as if in Paradise in this fine fresh air,' he told his brother, and there was so much to do that interested him. He set to work to improve the estate with an industry which no one could but admire. He planted trees, laid out new paths, supervised the stables, reorganized the Home, Norfolk and Flemish Farms – which extended in all to nearly two thousand acres – until they were making a profit. He saved the remains of George IV's Royal Lodge and the fishing temple at Virginia Water from destruction. Inside the castle he inspected with an expert eye the treasures of centuries which hung on the walls, which stood scarcely noticed on out of the way tables or lay disregarded on cupboard shelves; and he soon had librarians and indexers at work sorting out the vast muddle of the Queen's papers.

He was helped and encouraged in this work by Baron Stockmar, a shrewd little doctor who had been his Uncle Leopold's confidential adviser and his own tutor. Gladstone thought that Stockmar was a 'mischievous old prig' and there were many others who believed his influence over the Prince and the Queen was, in some curious and undefined way, far-reaching and sinister. In fact, he was moody, sardonic, hypochondriacal, inflexibly and obsessively moral, loyal and tenacious. He liked to think of himself as an indispensable adviser; and at Windsor, where he stayed for months on end, he was as familiar a sight as that other old family friend who shared his middle-class German background, Baroness Lehzen. Permitted to ignore many of the rules of court etiquette, he could be seen in the morning walking

The Visit of King Louis Philippe to Windsor in October 1844. The King is being invested as a Knight of the Garter in the presence of Prince Albert and other Knights who include Adolphus, Duke of Cambridge.

about the castle in his dressing-gown and slippers and in the evening
going in to dine without decorations and wearing ordinary trousers
instead of the regulation court breeches. After dinner, he was allowed
to go straight through the drawing-room back to his own apartments.
Here in his studiously thorough way he conducted his voluminous
correspondence and prepared his immense memoranda, indulging his
'harmless foible of thinking that he directed and controlled his old
pupil'.

*

If Stockmar's foible was harmless and his advice generally beneficial,
it was impossible to view the prejudices and activities of Baroness
Lehzen in the same light. She had always been more anxious to stir up

trouble between Victoria and her mother than to settle their differences, and once the Prince Consort had succeeded in ending the estrangement between his wife and the Duchess of Kent, the Queen began to learn that 'dear Lehzen' had not always taken her part for the right reasons. The more successful the marriage between Victoria and Albert promised to be, the more jealous and interfering the Baroness became; and no one could have expected her not to be, for she felt unwanted and lonely, cut out of a life over which she had formerly held such a dominating influence.

As the Queen's personal private secretary during the early years of her reign, with unquestionable authority in all the affairs of the household, she had formed one of what Roger Fulford has aptly described as a 'cosy triumvirate' and had been even more concerned than her fellow members, Victoria and Melbourne, to exclude from this triumvirate 'a new-comer who was certain to ask questions and to raise objections'.

The Distribution of Gifts on New Year's Day in the Riding School, 1846 by Joseph Nash. £10,000 was voted for the work on the building in 1838. The final design was made for Victoria in 1839, the year before Wyatville's death. Shortly before he died he handed over its execution to his assistant, Henry Ashton.

Before the Prince brought his more far-seeing mind to bear on the affairs of the household she had not only been in the habit of padding about the castle, giving orders and making inspections, but she had also been largely responsible for the explosively provocative appointments to its senior posts, all of which were held by Whigs, and so many of them by Pagets that newspapers had referred to the castle as the Paget Club House. Lord Conyngham, the husband of a Paget, was allowed to remain as Lord Chamberlain after he had obtained a court appointment for his mistress who, on at least one occasion, was discovered in her lover's arms; and the Lord Steward, another Paget — and one, incidentally, who was particularly antagonistic to the Prince — also established his mistress at Court.

The Prince, who confessed to his secretary that 'he had never feared temptation with regard to women because he had no inclinations in that respect and that the species of vice disgusted him', naturally found such appointments not only inexcusable on moral grounds, but unforgivable on political grounds as endangering the position of the monarchy. And when Baroness Lehzen spent £15,000 of the Queen's money on behalf of the Whig Party, the Prince was 'alarmed and horrified' and protested to Melbourne. The Baroness, however, was undeterred. She replied to the Prince's exasperated attempt to dismiss her from Court that 'he had not the power' to turn her out of the Queen's house.

Prince Albert had won the battle in the end, though, and by the summer of 1841 the moon was, in his own words, 'on the wane'. He had not had the courage to approach the Queen directly about the Baroness, but eventually he succeeded in making her accept the advisability of her departure. In October 1842 Baroness Lehzen left Windsor never to return. After she had gone the Prince told the Queen the history of his quarrels with her. 'I blame myself for my blindness,' the Queen wrote contritely in her diary. 'I shudder to think what my beloved Albert had to go through.'

*

Soon after Baroness Lehzen left the castle, the Prince began to consider the complete reorganization of the household, the archaic administration of which Baron Stockmar had outlined in one of his memoranda.

In this memorandum the Baron explained the difficulties of running the castle when its daily life was ruled by three separate departments — those of the Lord Steward, the Lord Chamberlain, and the Master of the Horse — which changed with every Ministry. The heads of these departments no longer lived at Court but delegated their authority to 'servants very inferior in rank', none of whom was sure how far they might trespass upon the customary preserves of another department and all of whom went through an elaborate procedure before anything important was done.

When guests arrived no one was prepared to show them to or from their apartments. There was often, in fact, no one to be found who

knew what or where these apartments were, so that it frequently
happened that visitors to the castle were unable to find the drawing-
room and at night if they happened to forget the right entrance from
the corridors they wandered for an hour helpless and unassisted. Once
a visitor got lost on his way to bed and was forced to spend the night
on a sofa in the State gallery adjoining the Waterloo gallery where a
housemaid found him and supposing him to be drunk fetched a police-
man. And when Guizot got lost one night, 'he spent nearly an hour
wandering about the corridors to try and identify his bedroom'. At
length he opened a door which he imagined led to it and came upon
the Queen having her hair brushed by a maid. Even when a man could
be found to perform an unexpected duty, there was frequently an
argument as to whether the duty could properly be performed by his
department. On a celebrated occasion Stockmar complained to the Master of the Household that the dining-room was always cold. 'But you
see,' that official replied, 'properly speaking, it is not our fault; for the
Lord Steward lays the fire only, and the Lord Chamberlain lights it.'

It distressed the practical, methodical and somewhat parsimonious
minds of Stockmar and Prince Albert to discover how ill organized the
household was; and they set about reforming it. They had no cause to
complain of the way the specialists amongst the 445 persons under
the authority of the Lord Chamberlain (£2,000 a year) performed
their duties. The Rat Killer (£80 a year), the Chimney Sweep (£111),
the Chemist and Druggist to the Person (£50), the four Physicians to
the Person (£214 each), the two Sergeant Surgeons (£283 each), the
Physician Surgeon and Apothecary to the Household (£200, £400 and
£414 respectively), the Dentist (£100), the Poet Laureate (£72), the
Principal Painter (£59) all performed their duties, no doubt, with more
or less distinction. But housemaids who were paid by the year when
they only worked for half of it, candles (still an official perquisite)
newly installed every day in the public rooms, an under-butler who
received £1 15s. 0d. a week for 'Red Room Wine' — a legacy from the
days when officers on guard in George III's time were allowed this sum
for wine served in a room hung in red — were extravagances which
could no longer be tolerated. They were all stopped on Prince Albert's
orders; and the running of the household was made more efficient by
making the Master of the Household responsible for the coordination
of the activities of all the separate departments involved.

*

Naturally the activities of the Prince Consort did nothing to make him
better liked. Caricatures of him were drawn depicting him ferreting for
candle-ends at Windsor where, it was said, he had given instructions
that the servants must provide themselves not only with their own
soap but with their own tea, mops and brushes. Servants in the royal
service had grown accustomed to their perquisites, official and assumed,
and guests did not take kindly to being allowed only two candles in
their rooms and on ringing for more being told by the maid, as Madame

Titiens was when she was summoned to Windsor to sing to the Queen, 'that the allowance to each room was just two candles and no more. "But," added the maid considerately, "there is no regulation which would prevent you cutting those two candles in halves and making four." '

In the town of Windsor the Prince was, it seems, particularly unpopular. His profits on the royal farms were said to be the result of unfair competition; his improvements of the parks and his diversion of footpaths were said to have been done without regard to the feelings and, indeed, the rights of local people; his reverence for the Game Laws was said to be absolute and anachronistic; and when a firm of architects prepared a fantastic scheme for removing the town and placing it a more suitable distance from the castle as a preliminary step in overcoming royal objections to the Great Western Railway line being brought farther south-west from Slough (Stephenson's *North Star* did the journey from there to Paddington in less than half an hour in 1838) it was all said to be his idea.

To the Prince Consort, though, the fulfilment of duty was more important than the attainment of popularity. And he could never be popular. He was so serious, so high-minded, so aloofly reserved. He was also so German. By blood the Queen was, too, for she had only the merest trace of British blood, derived from the Electress Sophia, grand-daughter of James I, the mother of George I and her own great-great-great-grandmother; but her husband was German by birth, education and temperament. And it was clear that he wanted to remain so, that he resisted Anglicization as if it were in some way degrading, that he did not much care for English people. In the way

The Upper Ward in the mid-1840s by Joseph Nash. The Tsar Nicholas I, the Prince Consort and the Duke of Wellington can all be recognised in the cavalcade. The figures were by John Doyle.

he talked, in the way he wore his clothes, in the way he rode a horse and shook hands, there was something unmistakably, and, so it seemed, determinedly, even arrogantly foreign. His English was slow to improve and he usually spoke German with his wife. When shaking hands he kept his elbow tucked well into his side in the German manner. His clothes were almost aggressively strange, and although the 'black velvet jacket without a cravat' that he wore on his honeymoon seemed 'youthfully manly and perfect' to his bride, and although the long boots of scarlet leather he wore out shooting at Windsor were described by her as 'very picturesque', they appeared to others in a different light. He was, it had to be admitted, a good shot; but his liking for a *battue*, conducted on the lines of a military operation in which hundreds of animals were killed, his insistence on breaking off for a hot luncheon, and the evident difficulty he experienced in concealing his 'chagrin if he shot badly, combined to give the impression that he was not a sportsman in the English sense'. If he had always shot badly much might have been forgiven him; but his skill with a gun, like his enterprise when hunting with the Belvoir, and his graceful accomplishments as a tennis player, a swimmer and a fearless and vigorous ice-hockey player, all seemed vaguely suspect.

With women he was especially ill at ease and they found it difficult to forgive him because he was so obviously unmoved by their charm. In the Park at Windsor he would ride by with his equerry or walk across their path with his adored greyhound Eos and he would scarcely glance at them. In the drawing-room his dignity was frigid.

Formal as the Court had been – despite the extra-curricular activities of some of its senior officers – before the Queen's marriage, it became and remained far more so afterwards. No man was thenceforward permitted to sit in the Queen's presence except at dinner; none of her maids of honour was allowed to sit in the Prince Consort's presence, or to speak to him unless first addressed. When presented to the Queen a gentleman was expected to go down on one knee and raise his right arm, with the back of the hand uppermost. The Queen would then lay her hand on his, and the gentleman would 'barely touch' it with his lips. He must not speak. After rising he must bow, first to the Queen and then to the Prince Consort. Ladies on approaching the Sovereign's presence had to drop their trains – these were to be at least three-and-a-quarter yards in length – which were spread out for them by attendants armed with wands. And although the Queen no longer sat on a raised throne so that those presented to her had to walk backwards down the steps without falling over their skirts, they still had to retreat several paces backwards holding their trains over their arms.

The Queen, who ultimately became even more inflexible than the Prince regarding the procedure to be observed at presentations, was inflexible, too, over the clothes to be worn. Married ladies wore lappets; unmarried ladies wore veils; both wore a headdress of three white feathers. A Mrs Sebastian Gassiot who, being unable to fasten her plumes in the usual way because ill-health had obliged her 'to have all

her hair cut quite short', wanted to know whether she might appear
in a 'Dolly Varden cap with the plumes and lappets fastened to it',
was told that the Queen, who had been 'much amused' by the request,
had replied to it — 'decidedly no'.

Gentlemen, if they were not entitled to wear a uniform, had to
appear in court dress with a claret-coloured coat, knee breeches, long
white stockings, buckled shoes and sword, although later on in her
reign old men were allowed to wear breeches which came down to the
ankle and buttoned there. They were meant to 'give the same impression as stockings'.

The problem facing American ministers abroad was settled by
William Marcy, Secretary of State, who ruled that they should appear
'in the simple dress of an American citizen'. At that time the American
ambassador in London was James Buchanan, who later became
President. Sir Edward Cust, the Queen's Master of Ceremonies, told
Buchanan that although the Queen would no doubt receive him whatever he wore, an ordinary suit would be disagreeable to her, so he
appeared in a black coat and pantaloons, white waistcoat and cravat.
The Queen greeted him with an 'arch but benevolent smile'.

If the Queen's views on court dress called forth a good deal of
satirical comment in the Press, her views on the uses and scope of the
Court Circular aroused much more. Every day, in the most ponderous
and humourless way, her activities and those of her family were
recorded under this heading in the newspapers. Every time the Queen
left Windsor for 'the Paddington Terminus of the Great Western Railway', every time she and the Prince 'promenaded in the pleasure
grounds adjacent to the Castle', every time he went 'shooting in the
royal preserves', every time she invited an honoured guest to 'partake
of a collation', the facts were recorded and detailed until Thackeray
promised to subscribe to any daily paper which came out without such
'trash — were it the *Morning Herald* itself'. Once 'Her Majesty was most
graciously pleased during her stay at Windsor to enjoy most excellent
health and spirits'. And later 'Her Majesty, attended by Viscountess
Jocelyn, went riding in the Park on two ponies'.

Visitors to Windsor Castle frequently complained of the lack of
'sociability which makes the agreeableness of an English country
house'. There was no room in which the guests could 'assemble, sit,
lounge, and talk as they pleased'. The billiard room was so inaccessible
it might as well have been in the town of Windsor; the library, 'although well stocked with books', was cold, and unfurnished, 'offering
none of the comforts of a habitable room'. If the 'most agreeable people
in the world' were invited one hardly saw them as the 'chacun chez soi
system' was the fashion of the place.

At dinner, when the guests met for the first time during the day, a
military band usually 'covered the talk', as Lord Macaulay discovered
on a visit in 1851, 'with a succession of sonorous tunes'. He found
himself next to a 'foreign woman who could hardly speak English
intelligibly'. And this was not at all uncommon. Lord Ashley found

that the band was very necessary to fill up the long 'pauses of conversation'. Even during Ascot races when a splendid banquet was given in St George's Hall, which appeared 'very magnificent, blazing with gold plate and light', it was, Charles Greville thought, despite the splendour, all 'very tiresome'.

After dinner there was sometimes a concert by the castle band or by a distinguished musician invited to Windsor for this purpose. Occasionally there was an opera, the performers and orchestra being brought down to Windsor by special train and sent back afterwards. The performance was given in the Waterloo gallery where the acoustics were not very good and where Francisco Tamagno, not having arrived in time to try out his voice there, once let himself go with such force that the Queen, who was as usual sitting in the front row, almost had her cap blown off. Occasionally, too, there was a play — after the Prince's

A performance of 'Macbeth' in the Rubens Room on 4 February 1853. This room was formerly known as the King's Drawing Room. The actress Ellen Keen performs before Queen Victoria, Prince Albert and six of their children.

death the Queen did not enter a public theatre again, believing that for a widow it was not seemly — with a cast brought down from the West End. More often the play was performed, rather nervously, by members of the household or by the royal children, and sometimes there was a presentation of tableaux in which all the members of the royal family joined and this was 'very wearying for the audience, who had to sit for two and a half hours with very long intervals between the tableaux'.

But boring as these performances usually were, it was better to have something to do after dinner, Charles Greville decided, having sat through a series of declamations by Rachel in French which he could not understand, for otherwise there was nothing at all with which to occupy the evening. And getting through the evening was always the 'great difficulty in Royal society'.

The Prince Consort, himself, confessed that he got bored in the evenings and told his brother that he sometimes wished he were back at Coburg 'in a small house' instead of living the life that his sense of duty had imposed upon him. He was constantly disappointed that he had not been able to fulfil his ambition and bring scientific and literary people about the Court, to make it a more general reflection of the life of the country.

There were times, though, when he seemed relaxed and content. Children were born and he watched them grow with fond concern. 'He romps with them so delightfully,' the Queen wrote, 'and manages them so beautifully and firmly.' And when they had gone to bed there were evenings when he could enjoy himself with his games of double chess and when he evidently derived deep pleasure from his organ which he played with 'such master skill', so a lady-in-waiting said, 'modulating so learnedly, winding through every kind of bass and chord'. There were times, too, when he could indulge his taste for interior decoration by changing the appearance of a room in the castle, re-hanging the Gainsboroughs and the Winterhalters, finding new places for the prints and etchings long since forgotten in the library drawers.

Sometimes the Prince was even cheerful. His humour was generally limited to making puns and inventing riddles, and catching the unwary out on April Fool's Day. But he was far from being as incapable of laughter as many of his contemporaries supposed. He was even capable of laughing at himself and had a large collection of caricatures, some of which lampooned him mercilessly. One evening after dinner he showed the Queen and her ladies some caricatures, 'running from one to the other, and standing over us to see how we laughed,' the widowed Lady Lyttelton told her daughter, 'and laughing so loud himself as to be quite noisy and boyish. But' — and there was so often this *'but'* — 'his voice! It is sadly disenchanting.'

The Queen without doubt still worshipped him. He was, she wrote in her journal, her 'inestimable husband and friend', her 'all in all'. She could not disguise her pleasure at his 'utter indifference to the attraction of all ladies', nor could she disguise her jealousy of 'his talking much even to men', for she was so afraid that he might develop other interests in which she could not join. But there was no fear of this. He was in that sense as in so many others a perfect husband for her. From the beginning he set himself the task of forming her mind, drawing out her natural talents and powers which had been only partially developed by her education, selflessly guiding her in the creation of a new English monarchical tradition. He taught her to bear with more understanding and less resentment the actions and opinions of those she took to be her enemies, and he was so wise and unselfish, wary and discreet, that she was soon not only trusting him absolutely, allowing him to step on to the very throne of England, but expressing her belief that women were not fit to govern. People began to refer to her, noticing the change, as Queen Albertine. She could disregard the scorn. To her it seemed a compliment. 'It is you,' she said to him, 'who have entirely formed me.' And she was proud and happy that it was so.

The conversation at dinner on informal occasions began to be less trivial. 'Many bits of information, and naval matters, and scientific subjects come up, and are talked of very pleasantly,' Lady Lyttelton said. 'The Prince, of course, encourages such subjects.' He was always a 'nice neighbour', she thought, and Baron Stockmar was always 'comfortable and easy'. Indeed, dinner at the castle was far less of an ordeal now. Sometimes when the Duke of Wellington came it was rather exhausting to have to sit next to him for he was so fearfully deaf and shouted so. *'Very good-looking man,'* he once bawled in Lady Lyttelton's ear, referring to the Tsar Nicholas I who sat immediately opposite and understood English perfectly. 'Always was so – scarcely altered since I saw him last – rather browner – no other change – very handsome man now – *don't you think so?'* And she felt compelled to scream out her answer, 'Yes, very handsome, indeed!' But usually it was just 'a great joke' to hear him talking 'as loud as thunder' about some 'matter of such serious and critical and difficult State importance that it ought only to have been alluded to in cabinet' and to see the Queen blushing 'over and over' and at last succeeding in 'screaming out upon some other subject'.

After dinner it was sometimes almost gay in the drawing-room now that Baroness Lehzen had gone. Occasionally the Prince, who nearly always left the dining-table before the other men, sang a duet with the Queen; and one evening the whole Court 'took to playing spillikins and puzzling with alphabets'; another evening they 'learnt a new round game', and they 'all grew quite noisy over it' – it was called *main jaune* and they liked it better than *mouche*. When they played *vingt-et-un* or Pope Joan the stakes were never high, and it was rather tiresome always to have to remember to carry new coins so that court etiquette should not be broken by passing used money to the Sovereign, but the maids of honour, all wearing their badge of the Queen's picture surrounded with brilliants on a red bow, looked so cheerful when they were gambling and a haul of even threepence excited them. Quite often there was a children's dance or a children's charade and the little Prince of Wales did his 'highland fling, a sort of difficult and athletic hornpipe'. And then there were the balls when the reels and Scottish jigs, the 'wildest and merriest dances', were performed with such spirit and grace. And one evening they danced the reel 'con

The reception of the Emperor and Empress of the French on 16 April 1855. The State Entrance was built in 1362. The Queen's Audience Chamber and the Queen's Presence Chamber above the Hall were built by Hugh May in the seventeenth century. Queen Victoria and the Emperor Napoleon III lead the procession, followed by Prince Albert and the Empress Eugénie.

amore: it was very amusing and made the Queen laugh heartily'. And on another evening the minuet broke down because the band could never learn the tune, so they danced 'quadrilles and Sir Roger de Coverley; and then the Queen issued her commands that every one should dance the country dance who could dance at all! The obedience was like the effect of a magical horn . . . Lord Aberdeen who looked more like a scarecrow than ever, quite as stiff as timber, and Sir Robert Peel, so mincing with his legs and feet, and his countenance full of the funniest attempt to look unconcerned and "matter of course", while he was evidently, very naturally, both shy and cross.'

At Christmas, which was always spent at Windsor, the chandeliers were taken down in the Queen's private sitting-room and big Christmas trees hung with candles and toffees took their place; and the dining-room tables were piled high with food and on the sideboard stood an immense baron of beef; and in the Oak Room there was another Christmas tree surrounded by presents for the members of the Household, and on each present was a card written by the Queen. Everything, so the Prince told his brother, was 'totally German and *gemütlich*'. Sometimes the lake at Frogmore would freeze over, and the family would walk down to the ice and the Prince would skate 'so picturesquely before them, the snowflakes from the trees caught in his hair'.

*

The years passed and the Queen's devotion to her husband deepened. 'She is certainly an odd woman,' Charles Greville noted in his diary with more than a hint of scorn. 'Her devotion and submission seem to know no bounds.' She hated to be away from the Prince. Even to part from him for a day when he went shooting at Windsor caused her unhappiness, and when he spent four days in Germany without her, she complained that his prolonged absence was '*very* trying'. 'Four days absence!' Greville commented derisively, 'Her Majesty thinks nothing of taking her Ladies from their husbands and families for a month together.'

She delighted in being alone with the Prince and was never more contented than when she was at Osborne, the small estate on the Isle of Wight which they had bought soon after their marriage so that they could have a place to do with as they liked, or when at Balmoral, the Scottish castle in the Highlands that they both loved, and when she could forget the Chartists and all those other tiresome people at home and abroad who were trying to disturb the settled and satisfactory structure of the world.

She would watch him as he sat at his desk, growing bald now and, despite his nervous energy, rather fat, writing with his sharp quill pen, drafting letters for her, thinking, planning, putting his sound common sense to a hundred different uses.

They were both called at seven o'clock by a wardrobe-maid and he got up almost immediately and went to his desk in his dressing-gown. He felt the cold and wore a wig indoors and he usually had a fire lit, although the Queen disapproved of this except in winter. He dressed before breakfast, often putting on one of those gaily coloured waistcoats that his mother-in-law gave him at Christmas and always wearing the ribbon of the Garter under it. At breakfast he read *The Times* and did not like to be disturbed, and sometimes he showed his irritation if his children or the Queen interrupted his concentration.

Usually he was patient with the Queen, though. He was tolerant of her sometimes cloying admiration, for, after all, he did love her; he was tolerant, too, of her moods of gloomy depression, her self-indulgent lamentations when someone she loved died, her outbursts of irritation, her sudden and (except to him) engaging bouts of giggling. And there were those, of course, who thought that he was frightened of her.

At Windsor when the clocks struck eleven and it was time to go to bed, the Queen's voice could be heard: 'Tell Lord Alfred to let the Prince know that it is eleven o'clock. Tell him the Prince should merely be told the hour. The Prince wishes to be told, I know. He does not see the clock.' And the Prince obeyed his summons.

Greville believed, from what Lord Clarendon told him of conversations he had had with Baron Stockmar on the subject of the children's strict upbringing, that the 'Prince could do nothing; that he was completely cowed, and the Queen so excitable that the Prince lived in perpetual terror of bringing on the hereditary malady'. That he did not approve of the 'aggressive system' which the Queen adopted towards her children, but that he had 'always been embarrassed by the alarm he felt lest the Queen's mind should be excited by any opposition to her will'.

Certainly the Queen was a selfish and sadly unimaginative, almost — despite her consciousness of her own inadequacies — an unfeeling mother, determined that her daughters should marry men who would not upset the rhythm of her life and that her sons should be treated with the most rigid severity, for they would have no one else to be strict with them unless their parents were. When they were small, their governess said she was *'exigeante'* and was always complaining that they were making insufficient progress or were too naughty. And as they grew up she often spoke slightingly of them, wishing, for instance, that the Princess Royal were better looking, or that the Prince of Wales was more like his father. This was his trouble, of course, and everyone else's. No one compared well with the Prince. And she, for her part, needed no one else in her life, neither children nor intimate friends. She believed with an 'instinctive certainty' that God would *never* part them and that He would allow them to grow old together. But when on the evening of 1 December 1861 she came to

Interior of Prince Albert's Dairy. This dairy in the Home Park was designed by John Thomas under Prince Albert's direction and was built in 1858. The ceramic decorations of the creamery were probably not completed until the early 1860s. The white against dark blue profile portraits in relief of the Queen and Prince and all their children (not visible in this photograph) are reminiscent of the work of the Della Robbia family.

bed and found him shivering with cold and unable to sleep, she felt at once that he was seriously ill.

He got up the next morning, however, and lay on a sofa while the Queen read to him. Sir James Clark was called and reassured her that he was suffering from a 'feverish sort of influenza'. 'I think that everything so far is satisfactory,' he said. But he had been wrong about Lady Flora Hastings and he was wrong now. Dr William Jenner was asked for his opinion and he diagnosed typhoid fever.

For months the Prince, worn out by work and worry, had been suffering from a growing lassitude. 'I am tired, I am tired,' he had complained continuously as he looked out of the castle windows across the Park to the stark shapes of the leafless chestnuts. That year the Duchess of Kent had died at Frogmore and the Queen recorded with her sure eye for every vivid evocative detail, how a cock crowed and a dog barked in the distance and how a large watch in a tortoiseshell-case struck each quarter of an hour, bringing back all the recollections of her childhood, for she used to hear it at night at Kensington. The Prince 'melted into tears . . . unusual for him' when they realized that the faint breathing had stopped and he clasped the Queen in his arms and led her into the sitting-room where a 'little canary bird which *she* was so fond of' was singing.

'I do not cling to life,' the Prince had told the Queen. 'If I had a severe illness, I should give up at once.'

For a fortnight in December 1861 he lay dying in the castle; and the castle itself was, no doubt, the cause of his death.

Work had begun only fifteen years before on an adequate system of drainage, but only the main drains had been constructed and 'nothing had been done', so the Lord Chamberlain reported, 'to improve the drains in connexion with the various water closets, sinks, etc., within the Castle. The noxious effluvia which escapes from the old drains and the numerous cesspools still remaining, is frequently so exceedingly offensive as to render many parts of the Castle almost uninhabitable.'

The Queen had suffered from typhoid fever many years before, the Prince of Wales was later to have an almost fatal attack, and now the Prince Consort was dying of it, and he knew that he was.

There was something else, though, the Queen thought, apart from the castle drains, which was responsible for her husband's illness. A fortnight before that evening when she had come to bed to find him shivering feverishly, he had had a telegram to tell him that one of his favourite cousins, King Pedro of Portugal, had died of typhoid fever in Lisbon. The following day he was told something which, in the Queen's words, broke her Angel's heart: the Prince of Wales, at the age of nineteen, had got into trouble over a woman. The Prince Consort's reactions might seem abnormal, but he could not accept such information with a normal mind. Obsessively concerned with the reputation of monarchy, he was at the same time incapable of viewing sexual behaviour outside marriage with anything but horror and disgust.

The Queen did not doubt that worry over their son was hurrying her husband to his grave. She refused to ask the Prince of Wales to come to Windsor, although she could not but be sure that Albert was dying; and eventually he had to be summoned to the castle by his sister without their mother's knowledge.

*

The Blue Room. This is where the Prince Consort died on 14 December 1861.

Early on the morning of 14 December the Queen went into her husband's room, the Blue Room, in which her uncles George IV and William IV had both died. 'It was a bright morning, the sun just rising and shining brightly,' she remembered. 'The room had the sad look of night-watching, the candles burnt down to their sockets, the doctors looked anxious. I went in, and never can I forget how beautiful my darling looked.'

She never did forget. At first she 'thought she was going mad' with grief. During his illness, while she watched over him as he lay on his bed moaning when she kissed him as if he felt that she was leaving him, she had not once cried; but every hour or so she had gone into the next room and given way to 'a terrible burst of misery'. Nor when she knew that he was dead had she cried out, but had kissed him on the forehead and, dropping to her knees, had 'called him by every endearing name', before being helped from the room. But now she kept tapping her forehead and repeating 'My reason, my reason.' Dr Jenner prescribed the comforting presence of her four-year-old daughter Beatrice, who was brought down to her bedroom every morning as soon as she woke up; but the close warmth of the child did little to alleviate her mother's loneliness, and a change of scene seemed essential. The Queen took her uncle's advice and, so as not to be at Windsor while the funeral was taking place in St George's Chapel, she left the castle for Osborne, wearing the widow's clothes she never discarded.

She was only forty-two, but it was as if she were already an old woman. The Prince had said of her that she lived 'much in the past and in the future, perhaps more than in the present'. When he died she abandoned herself to the past and to her memories of him with a passionate intensity. It was selfish and hysterical, but it was predictable. She could not forget him: no one else must. Everyone at Court had to wear mourning on all social occasions until the end of 1862; and after 1864, although her ladies were allowed to wear grey, violet, lilac or white, the lady-in-waiting was obliged to continue to wear mourning as deep as the Queen's own. Even the castle servants had to wear 'a black crape band upon their left arm for at least eight years'.

She gave orders that at Windsor and elsewhere her husband's rooms were to remain exactly as he had left them, and she had cards fixed to the doors, not only of his rooms but of her own boudoir, which informed the curious that everything within had been arranged by the Prince. No clothes, no papers were to be touched. Lytton Strachey recorded, on the evidence of 'private information' – 'gossip' a lord-in-waiting, Lord Ribblesdale called it, 'which even in my time (the 1880s) nobody believed', although it was in fact quite true – that each evening at Windsor a manservant placed a jug of hot water in his dressing-room and laid out fresh clothes on his bed. It has also been recorded that before she signed a document of State she would look up at the Prince's marble effigy and ask him softly if he approved, and that the glass from which he had taken his last dose of medicine was kept by his bedside in the Blue Room and that it remained there for forty years. And almost every day she strewed fresh flowers on his bed and took more to St George's Chapel.

It was expected that he would be buried at Windsor in the chapel which Henry VII had begun in 1494 as a tombhouse for himself and Henry VI and which Wolsey, who had been a canon at Windsor between 1511 and 1514, had also hoped to occupy when he was dead. The Queen had its walls lined with marble and its roof crowned with copper, and on the sarcophagus the wings of four bronze angels supported the Prince's marble effigy. The tombhouse was renamed the Albert Memorial Chapel.

She had never intended, however, that he should be buried there, but, in accordance with the 'Prince's own inclinations', in a more pastoral setting. And so, a year after his death, his body was removed from St George's Chapel, where it had lain in the entrance to the royal vault, and taken to a mausoleum at Frogmore, near the mausoleum where his mother-in-law the Duchess of Kent lay buried. And it was to Frogmore that the Queen herself was to be taken when the century was past.

The Royal Mausoleum by H. Ward, 1871. It was in accordance with the Prince Consort's 'own inclinations' that a year after his death his body was removed from St George's Chapel to a more pastoral setting at Frogmore. The Queen, too, was buried here.

2

VICTORIA
– THE WIDOW AT WINDSOR

The Queen lived on as a widow for forty years. In the beginning she shut herself away with her family and household, seeing her Cabinet Ministers as rarely as she could. When she came to Windsor or left it, the railway station had to be cleared of other passengers as if she were in *purdah*. She had only been able to tolerate her duties as Queen, the ceremonial functions of monarchy, she explained, because of the support of her husband. Now that he was gone they could not expect her to carry on as before.

When the Prince of Wales was married in St George's Chapel in March 1863 to Princess Alexandra, daughter of Prince Christian of Schleswig-Holstein-Sonderburg-Glucksburg and niece of the King of Denmark, the Queen looked down upon the tiaras from the high oak closet on the north side of the altar that Henry VIII had built so that Catherine of Aragon could watch the ceremonies of the Order of the Garter. She was wearing the black streamers of widowhood and a long white veil, and her only concession to the happy splendour of the occasion was a badge of the Order of the Garter that her 'beloved one had worn'. She had 'felt very low and nervous *before*', Lady Augusta Bruce recorded. 'All seemed so lost without him to organize and arrange everything . . . Her expression was profoundly melancholy.' When the organ played the first anthem, to 'his' music, and Jenny Lind sang in the chorale she sat 'as if transfixed'. She looked across at the new East Window and reredos that the Deans and Canons had erected in his memory (in place of Benjamin West's Resurrection which Fanny Burney has found so 'earthly') and she suffered 'indescribably'. 'Not a gleam of joy at her son's marriage illumined her desolation.'

Yet the wedding was, in Disraeli's opinion, 'a fine affair, a thing to remember'; and Bishop Wilberforce thought it 'the most moving sight'

A photograph taken on the day of the wedding of the Prince of Wales to Princess Alexandra of Denmark. The Queen sits beneath the bust of the Prince Consort with (from the left) Princess Louise, Princess and Prince of Wales, Princess Beatrice, Prince Leopold, Alice, Princess Louis of Hesse, Princess Helena and Prince Louis of Hesse.

he ever saw. The only unpleasant moments were when the bridegroom's four-year-old nephew, the future Kaiser Wilhelm II, tried to throw the cairngorm from the head of his dirk across the choir and, his uncles Prince Alfred and Prince Leopold restraining him, he 'showed his displeasure by biting them hard on the legs'; and when the Eton boys, who had been given a holiday, rushed at the bridal carriage on its way to the railway station.

Nothing stood before us [one of these excited boys, Lord Randolph Churchill, told his father]. The policemen charged in a body, but were knocked down. I got right down to the door of the carriage where the Prince of Wales was, wildly shouting 'Hurrah!' He bowed to me, I am perfectly certain; but I shrieked louder. I am sure, if the Princess did not possess very strong nerves, she would have been frightened; but all she did was to smile blandly.

The Queen, meanwhile, was performing her duty to her nine hundred guests; and as soon as she had done so, she went down the path to Frogmore to give way to her tears alone in the Prince Consort's mausoleum.

As the years passed and she showed little inclination to come out of her lugubrious seclusion, her people began to grumble and the newspapers took up their complaint.

There were malicious rumours, too, about her relationship with one of her Scottish servants, the gillie John Brown, who had been sent down from Balmoral to Osborne with her favourite pony when she refused to leave her rooms in the early agonies of her bereavement, as it was hoped that the sight of them would tempt her to take some exercise. Brown, faithful, honest and blunt, had already been a servant for twelve years then and the Queen, so obviously in need of a link with her dead husband that it was said in London that Brown acted as a medium at seances, became excessively fond of him, allowing him to say things to her which she would not have permitted in anyone else. He put whisky in her picnic hamper, he criticized her clothes, he even, on occasions, called her 'woman'. He was appallingly disrespectful not only to her but to the members of her household and her Ministers whom he would slap on the back. Gladstone detested this 'moor-cock turned peacock' as Ivor Brown has aptly described him, but Disraeli was astute enough to come to terms with him. It was as well to do so, for Brown, in the Queen's own words, was 'groom, footman, page and maid'. He came to Windsor when she came, sleeping in a room not far from hers, and she grew to depend upon him 'in a manner both touching and ludicrous'. She was undoubtedly attracted by him as a man, but no one close to them seems to have believed that their relationship was anything more than that of employer and devoted, if tiresome and objectionable, retainer. The lives that kings and queens are constrained to lead makes them liable, of course, to particularly close relationships with servants who do not have the

Queen Victoria in her carriage. Followed by servants and her dog, the Queen's carriage approaches the Castle down the Long Walk.

same sort of ambitions that courtiers and politicians have; and Queen Victoria was peculiarly susceptible to such influences. She was always indulgent with her servants — except with housemaids who put things back in their wrong places — and she could never bring herself to feel the indignation of her informants when told of the pilfering and tippling that went on below stairs at Windsor. When a drunken footman fell over and dropped a lighted lamp in the castle, her only recorded comment was, 'Poor man!'

With Scottish servants she was especially indulgent — for most things Scottish she had a high regard, and one of her favourite statues of Albert was one which portrayed him in the dress of a Highlander — and with Brown she was so indulgent that stories of a criminally irresponsible liaison were widely accepted as true.

When Brown died in 1883 she erected a monument to his memory; she had numerous statuettes of him made; and every Sunday at Windsor she had placed on her luncheon table where she could see them two silver salt cellars, in the shape of shells supported by mermaids, which he had given her. She would have written a third journal of her life in the Highlands, which would have been all about John Brown, had not the Dean of Windsor, Randall Davidson, advised her strongly against it. She was very cross and Davidson felt obliged to offer his resignation, but in the end she agreed that volume 3 should not be written and Davidson ultimately became Archbishop of Canterbury.

The damage, however, had already been done. Queen Albertine, formerly Mrs Melbourne, was now — and the insinuation was far more damaging in late nineteenth-century society — Mrs Brown.

*

A republican feeling had already grown up in England. Charles Bradlaugh, the Radical atheist, made speeches condemning the royal family; numerous republican clubs were inaugurated all over the country; G. O. Trevelyan in a widely read pamphlet entitled *What does she do with it?* condemned the Queen's parsimony and her hoarding of money; and Charles Dilke, who estimated the cost of the royal family to the nation at £1,000,000 a year, suggested in a loudly cheered and much praised speech at Newcastle that this enormous expenditure was 'chiefly not waste but mischief'.

It was felt, too, that despite the great cost of maintaining the royal family, foreign rulers and other important people were not being received during their visits in the way that they ought to have been received.

Before the Prince's death, in a single year (in 1841) altogether 113,000 people had dinner at Windsor. But since he had died the Queen seemed to have given up entertaining almost entirely. Queen Emma of the Sandwich Islands who came to England in 1865 was asked, for instance, to come to Windsor at half-past three in the afternoon so that the Queen would not have to have luncheon with her.

Comparisons were made with the splendid receptions formerly given to the Tsar Nicholas I, the King of Saxony, Prince William of Prussia, King Louis Philippe, the King of Sardinia, Napoleon III and the Empress Eugénie, all of which had been very popular in the country: 'The Queen was being magnificent in her entertainment of the Kings of the earth (and that is what a Queen should be).' People could feel

The Crimson Drawing Room in the 1860s. On either side of the fireplace hang portraits of the Duke and Duchess of Kent and the Prince and Princess of Wales. At the far end of the room the Queen's private band played after dinner.

proud that in the magnificent Waterloo banqueting hall at Windsor, their Queen, 'the little *Hausfrau*', in Lytton Strachey's evocative words, 'who had spent the day before walking out with her children, inspecting her livestock, practising scales at the piano, and filling up her journal with adoring descriptions of her husband, suddenly shone forth, without art, without effort, by a spontaneous and natural transition, the very culmination of Majesty'.

It had not mattered that the Tsar, according to Greville, had been 'excessively disgusted with the dullness of the Court' at Windsor, nor that the suite of Louis Philippe seemed grave and bored, nor that the King of Sardinia appeared to be 'frightful in his person, a great, strong, burly, athletic man, brusque in his manners, unrefined in his conversation, very loose in his conduct, very eccentric in his habits', the only Knight of the Garter that the Duchess of Sutherland had ever seen 'who looked as if he would have the best of it with the dragon'. Nor had it mattered that the Queen had put up her face to be kissed 'for ever so long before the King of Sardinia consented to touch it'. It had not even mattered that when he was installed as a Knight of the Garter, he had put forward one leg, then the other until 'at last he said to the Queen in his loud, short voice, "*laquelle?*". She nearly let fall the Garter from laughing, the Prince was in fits and all the K.G.s at the table began to titter.'

Nor had it been of much consequence that the Prince Consort did not — as was well known — approve of the morals of Napoleon III who 'struck everybody', so Charles Greville said, as a 'mean and diminutive figure' of vulgar appearance. And it had only been a momentary embarrassment when the Prince seemed to take 'longer than usual' to tie the Garter buckle round the leg of the Emperor, who afterwards put his wrong arm through the ribbon. For the visits were all, on the whole, as successful as such visits could ever hope to be. Indeed, the success of Napoleon III's visit had been 'complete'. Elaborate preparations had been 'put in hand', as Raymond Mortimer explains in his introduction to the Queen's own subsequently published account of the visit; 'new carpets and silks were bought for the suite to be occupied by the imperial couple; the furniture was regilded; the Waterloo Chamber was tactfully renamed.' The Queen had decided that the Emperor was entrancing, 'so very quiet, good natured and unassuming and natural'. And with the King of Sardinia she had been 'wonderfully cordial and attentive' and had got up at four o'clock in the morning to see him depart.

Of course, it was often difficult for a woman of the Queen's temperament to tolerate the eccentricities of some of these visiting monarchs without the support of her husband.

When the Tsar had come to Windsor his first action was to send to the stables for a bundle of straw on which to sleep, and he had spent a large part of the next day making eyes at all the pretty women he saw. And when King Louis Philippe came to the castle — the first time a French King had visited England since 1356, when John II had been brought there after the battle of Poitiers – he was preceded by an alarming letter from his daughter who said that he must on no account be allowed to come down to breakfast as he would certainly eat something if he did and this was dangerous before he had his chicken broth a little later on, that he must have a hard bed with a horse-hair mattress, laid, if possible, on a plank, and that he must never be allowed to ride the horses which he was having sent over from France. These instructions did not worry her unduly, however, for Albert was there. But now that he was there no longer, the arrangements that had to be made for such potentates as the Sultan of Turkey and the Shah of Persia were excessively tiresome and worrying to her. A report about the Shah's behaviour and entourage that reached Windsor from Berlin was, for instance, peculiarly distressing: 'His Majesty generally dines alone, and when so, prefers to have his meals on the carpet. For that purpose a moveable carpet should be kept ready whereupon *his* servants will put the dishes etc. brought to the door by the English servants . . . The Shah does not like to have cut up his meats. Rice, lamb, mutton, fowls are favourite dishes. The cuisine should be somewhat *relevée*.' According to the British ambassador in Berlin nobody had ever dared venture to tell the Shah that he should not put his arm round the Queen's chair at dinner, 'or put his fingers into dishes, or take food out of his mouth again to look at it after it has been chewed, or fling it under the table if it does not suit his taste', and that he should not make such embarrassing attempts to console himself for the absence of his harem.

The Queen could not perhaps be blamed then for being so 'fidgety', as her Secretary, Sir Henry Ponsonby, described her, before the Shah's visit to Windsor and for asking crossly why he was called 'Imperial'. 'Because he is the Shah in Shah,' Ponsonby replied. 'Well, that's no reason!' she snapped; and the title was removed from the programme. But she *could* be blamed, it was generally agreed, for twice changing her mind about the date of the Military Review to be held in his honour in the Park, and for declining to come down from Balmoral a single day early for the Sultan's visit when, as the Prime Minister put it, English influence was just now paramount at Constantinople and might well be damaged if the Sultan were received less royally and graciously at Windsor than in Paris or Berlin. And she *could* be blamed for refusing to return the hospitality of the Tsar, who had entertained the Prince of Wales for three weeks, because she was 'UTTERLY *incapable* of entertaining any Royal personage as she would wish to do, except those who are very nearly related to her, and for whom she need not alter her mode of life'.

Eventually she gave in, though. Having made her vehement protests, she entertained the Tsar, just as, after overcoming her gloomy and hypochondriacal apprehension, she consented to put herself out for the Sultan and the Shah. Indeed, she quite enjoyed their visits. The Sultan was so obviously delighted with Windsor and with the Order of the Garter which the Prince of Wales persuaded his mother to give him, although a Moslem. And the Shah turned out to be a far less formidable person than she had feared, 'fairly tall and not fat', with a 'fine countenance and very animated'. She received him in full state at Windsor, wearing her large pearls, and she sat next to him in the middle of the White Drawing Room, surrounded by Persian and English princes and princesses, conscious of the absurd figure she must have cut and feeling 'very shy'. But he behaved most decorously and was so impressively attired with huge rubies as buttons in his diamond-studded coat, and epaulettes of diamonds and emeralds. She invested him with the Garter and, having kissed her hand, he gave her two Orders in return and the Grand Vizier helped to save her hat from falling off.

At luncheon in the Oak Room, bagpipers marched up and down and the Shah told her that he had had her *Leaves from the Journal of a Life in the Highlands* translated into Persian so that he could read it. He had little to eat but fruit, so that he had no opportunity of trans-gressing western decorum as he had on another occasion when he threw an unwanted quail bone under the table, and he drank quantities of iced water and afterwards he went for a rest attended by his pipe-bearer and cup-bearer. When he appeared again he had taken the aigrette of diamonds out of his astrakhan hat and put on his spectacles. The Queen was so pleased with him that she conducted him all over the castle herself, and when he left it he showed the crowd a miniature of Her Majesty 'set in diamonds, which she had given him, and kissed it with reverence'.

*

These days of pleasure were rare now. The Queen had outgrown the worst of her grief; but there was always this insistent consciousness of bereavement and widowhood.

Her general mode of life was still severe as well as withdrawn. And it continued to be severe after the Prince of Wales's recovery from typhoid fever in 1871 and her own survival of attempts on her life in 1872, after the hectoring, rough affection of the faithful John Brown and the amusing society of the chivalrous Disraeli – so welcome a relief from the critical Gladstone and the rudely self-opinionated although ultimately acceptable Palmerston – and after the profoundly bene-ficial effect of the publication of her warm and human *Highland Journals*, had all contributed to restore to the Queen her lost popularity and to bring her out from the black shrouds of her self-enforced seclusion.

It was still an austere life, for she remained for ever conscious of her widowhood and the influence of the long-dead Prince. She might smile sometimes, even laugh; she began once more to record incidents in her diary that had amused her; her letters became more cheerful; she brought herself to play nostalgic tunes on her piano, and she began to dance again – she was still dancing ('like a pot' a German prince whose English was not strong enough for the compliment informed her) at

Windsor when she was seventy — she told funny stories about herself and was fond of relating how one clear and starlit night she had opened her bedroom window to look out into the dark sky and a sentry at the foot of the castle wall, thinking she must be a housemaid, 'began to address her in most affectionate and endearing terms. The Queen at once drew her curtains but was simply delighted at what had happened.' She was still capable of exercising an undoubted charm, which a Dean of Windsor described as 'irresistible'.

There was no relaxation, though, in the prudery that the memory of Albert's strict moral sense had emphasized. At meal-times she would suddenly change the conversation if it took an unsuitable turn, and when she overheard what she believed to be excessive eagerness in conversation or a lack of delicacy in laughter at the other end of the table she would ask what the subject of discussion was, and if she did not think it was a proper one she would indicate her disapproval and thereafter the meal continued in embarrassing silence. This was not, however, always considered a disadvantage, for at least it ensured that the members of the household could keep their eyes on their plates and concentrate on eating rather than on whispered exchanges with a neighbour. This was important, as the Queen ate quickly and the servants, according to Lord Ribblesdale, had 'a menial trick of depriving us of our plates as soon as she had finished'. The lords-in-waiting, being 'mostly of the deferential breed', did not complain and were, therefore, all the more astounded when one evening a guest did complain. This was Lord Hartington who was in the middle of enjoying some mutton and green peas.

The Queen could dispose of peas with marvellous skill and dexterity [Lord Ribblesdale said], and had got into conversation with Lord Hartington, thus delaying his own operations . . .
Well, anyhow, in the full current of their conversation the mutton was taken away from him. He stopped in the middle of a sentence in time to arrest the scarlet-clad marauder: 'Here bring that back!'

The members of the household held their breath, but when Lord Ribblesdale looked up at the Queen he saw that she was both amused and pleased. 'I knew this,' he said, 'by one of the rare smiles, as different as possible to the civil variety which, overtired, uninterested or thinking about something else, she contributed to the conventional observations of her visitors.'

Lord Ribblesdale had to admit, though, that for the most part the Queen's own observations were conventional in the extreme. 'One way or another,' he wrote in his memoirs, 'I must have dined a great many times at the Queen's dinner party, and I personally never heard her say anything at dinner which I remembered next morning. Her manners were not affable; she spoke very little at meals; and she ate fast and very seldom laughed. To the dishes she rejected she made a peevish *moue* with crumpled brow more eloquent than words.'

She refused few dishes, though, for she had an excellent appetite. She preferred plain food, such as boiled chicken and roast beef, haggis

Queen Victoria at breakfast in 1895. Attended by her Indian servants, the Queen had breakfast in the Oak Dining Room. At the table on this occasion are Princess Beatrice, her husband Prince Henry of Battenberg and their children, Prince Leopold, Prince Alexander and Princess Victoria Eugenia.

and potatoes, to anything more exotic; but she liked a good helping and she liked her brown Windsor soup made no longer simply, with ham and calves' feet as served to her children in the nursery, but including game, madeira wine and shell-fish; and she loved her puddings, her cranberry tarts and cream, her chocolate cakes and chocolate biscuits, her 'stodgy trifle of jam and sponge cakes'.

During the meal conversation was 'carried on in whispers', noted the young and beautiful American heiress, Consuelo Vanderbilt, who had married the Duke of Marlborough, for the Queen's stern personality imposed restraint. She demanded impeccable discretion in conduct as well as in conversation. She found it difficult to forget – and the Prince perhaps had found it impossible to forgive – the conduct of Palmerston, who, 'always enterprising and audacious with women', had once, years before, at Windsor gone into the room of one of her ladies in the unfulfilled hope of making love with her. George Anson, the Prince's secretary, putting a slightly different interpretation on Palmerston's visit, recorded that he had been accustomed to sleeping with another lady in that bedroom and 'probably from force of habit floundered in'. To satisfy the Queen, people whose birth or duties brought them into her presence must not merely be innocent, they must never have appeared to be guilty.

They must also conform to those rules of conduct she established for her household. It was well known, for instance, that she did not approve of any of its younger members, of either sex, getting married. The maids of honour, in fact, had never been allowed to receive any man, even a brother, in their own rooms, and they had had to entertain them as best they could in the waiting-room downstairs. When Sir James Reid, her Resident Physician and a particular favourite of hers, being both a Scot and a German scholar, had the audacity to become engaged to one of her maids of honour, Susan Baring, Lord Revelstoke's daughter and Maurice Baring's sister, the Queen was so cross she refused to see Reid for three days and only forgave him when he amused her by promising 'never to do it again'.

It was also well known that there must be no smoking in any room she might enter. Nor were her secretaries allowed to smoke when handling papers she might have to touch. Before she was persuaded – apparently by John Brown – that a little tobacco smoke was 'no bad thing to have about a hoose', cards were framed and hung upon the walls of the castle calling attention to the prohibition against smoking; and visitors to Windsor waited until the Queen went to bed and they could go along to the billiard-room, the only place where smoking was tolerated. Once Count Hatzfeldt, who could not be bothered to make the long journey to the billiard-room, yet 'could not live without a cigar', was reduced to lying on his bedroom floor and blowing the smoke up the chimney. The King of Saxony was less discreet and profoundly shocked the Court by having the audacity to walk up the grand staircase with a cigar in his mouth. Courtiers who smoked secretly took to carrying peppermints in their pockets, for there was no telling when a summons to the Queen might come; and even to be in church was no excuse for being late in answering it.

The duties of a courtier were rendered even more tiresome by the rule that all communications with the Queen had to be in writing and the letters, which had to be sealed with an official seal, had also to be couched in the most formal terms. As the Queen's eyesight became very bad during the last years of her life it was necessary to make each word big and unmistakably legible, and Frederick Ponsonby, who was appointed Assistant Private Secretary in 1895, was constrained to buy some copy-books published for girls' schools and 'some special ink like boot varnish' and to develop a completely new handwriting. It was unfortunately so large and black, though, that it showed through on the other side of the paper and he was compelled to write on one side only, and, as the Queen kept all the important papers in a case in her room, this did not suit her, for in a short time they became so bulky. He was told to revert to his former method. He ordered a much thicker paper which could carry the writing on both sides; but this did not suit the Queen either. He went back to ordinary paper and ordinary ink, and was told to write blacker because she couldn't read his writing. Ponsonby 'grasped that it was hopeless' and consulted Sir James Reid who told him that explanations would be useless.

It was not only, as Reid knew, that the Queen would not have accepted the explanation, but that she might well have been cross with Reid and Ponsonby for bringing the unpalatable fact of her failing sight into discussion. Ponsonby himself had had experience of this problem. While his father was alive and acting as Private Secretary, Frederick Ponsonby was serving in the Army in India and the Queen had sent him a telegram asking him to go and see the father of her favourite Indian servant whom she had recently promoted from Khidmutgar to Munshi, destroying all photographs of him handing dishes to her and giving him permission to enter the billiard-room and even the dining-room as though he were one of her secretaries. The Munshi was (like John Brown) a man whom the rest of the household found disconcertingly pretentious. He went everywhere with the Queen, giving her daily lessons in Hindustani, and he was soon an object of jealousy and hatred. His father, so he said, was a Surgeon-General in the Indian Army. Ponsonby did as he was asked, sought the man out in India and discovered that he was, in fact, an apothecary in the gaol at Agra. Ponsonby told the Queen this when he came to Windsor to take up his household appointment and for a year she did not ask him to dinner.

Thereafter he acted with extreme caution in his dealings with her. One of his duties was to write out the details of certain public occasions to enable her to enter them accurately in her diary; and when in 1897 she reviewed the Colonial troops and it was reported in the newspapers that she had spoken to the Indian officers in Hindustani, which he knew she had not done, he did not know whether to add this item or not. He decided to do so, but when the Queen had Ponsonby's account read out to her she commented 'That's not true. I did not speak in Hindustani but in English.' Should that part be crossed out? she was asked. 'No,' she said, 'you can leave it, for I could have done so had I wished.'

More and more imperious, cantankerous and forthright as she became old, she let it be known that she did not want anyone to meet her in the Park when she went out for a drive in her pony chair. The very sight of this carriage was enough to make men jump out of sight behind trees and bushes, and once when the Chancellor of the Exchequer found himself in danger with no suitable cover in sight — for he was six feet four inches tall — he was advised to turn back. New servants were not permitted to look her in the face, for, although she loved to have her photograph taken, she hated to be stared at by strangers, and when receiving orders they had to look at the ground by her feet. If she by chance met one of them in a corridor of the castle as she passed by in her wheel-chair or hobbled along with the help of a stick and an Indian attendant, she would look straight ahead as if he were not there.

Her closest attendants in these years were her Indians — 'rather second-rate servants', Aga Khan thought them. When they were not required to serve her with food, they stood motionless behind her chair, dressed in scarlet and gold in winter, in white in summer, their hands clasped in front of their sashes, their beards so startlingly black against the pale, spotless cloth. As the Queen disliked changes in her household, most of its members were very old — some of them were over eighty — and consequently the few young ones did not enjoy their evenings much. 'As no one had the least knowledge of whist, I cannot say it was amusing,' Frederick Ponsonby commented sadly. 'Lord Stafford, who was an equerry, had always been told that the danger of card-playing was that unscrupulous people looked over one's hand, and therefore held his hands so tightly under his chin that it took him nearly two whole minutes to find a card. Of course no smoking was allowed.'

The Queen, perhaps, understood little of their boredom. She did not often see them, except at dinner, and spent most of her free time with her ladies and with her youngest daughter Beatrice, Princess Henry of Battenberg — whose husband and four children lived with the Queen — and with those numerous relatives who came frequently to visit her.

It was an honour to come, for she was Europe's matriarch. Understanding this and that the strange, often irritable, old 'Widow at Windsor' in her shapeless but expensive black clothes, her widow's cap occasionally enlivened by diamond stars at a dinner-party, her several lockets containing strands of hair or miniature portraits of her innumerable relations, knowing that this little woman was the ruler of an immense Empire (with which Disraeli had so skilfully identified her), her own people, too, felt proud that she belonged to them. She might have some curious ideas and many outrageously provocative opinions. She might be 'Coburgised from head to foot' and take the part of foolish foreign royalties with extraordinary zeal; she might believe that education ruined the health of the 'higher classes uselessly' and rendered 'the working classes unfitted for good servants and labourers', that the campaign for women's suffrage was 'a mad, wicked folly', and that Lady Amberley who supported it 'ought to get a good whipping'. But she was an admired and respected institution

Princess Beatrice reading a newspaper to Queen Victoria in 1895.

as well as a reactionary, and she had, after all, been on the greatest throne in the world for more than half a century.

Young relatives who came to see her at the castle in these last years found a solemn but benevolent old lady, demanding yet kind, impatient of humbug but often surprisingly tolerant. She felt more at ease with these young relatives, particularly with her grandchildren, than she had ever felt with her own children, and would allow them liberties that surprised those who believed her to be so uncompromisingly severe. She liked to have them near her when she was watching a game of tennis or a display by an Indian servant of acrobatic riding;

and she liked to bring performing bears to the castle for them and Punch and Judy shows; and once Buffalo Bill and his troupe came to put on their show below the East Terrace. And another day a man with a barrel organ and a monkey was summoned to the quadrangle for the Little Princess Ena who had seen them in the town, and the 'Queen was much amused when the monkey climbed the portico and tried to find a way into the castle through the dining-room windows'.

'She wore a white tulle cap, black satin dress and shiny black boots with elastic sides,' one of her forty grandchildren remembered. 'What fascinated me about "Gangan" was her habit of taking breakfast in little revolving huts mounted on turntables, so that they could be faced away from the wind.' She would ride to the huts in her carriage to be served with steaming hot porridge by her Khidmutgars and then she would send for her Private Secretary and begin the business of the day.

The Queen was still even now often shy with young people and would sometimes giggle apprehensively or give a diffident little shrug of her shoulders as she cross-examined them. But the affection of those who succeeded in penetrating beyond the crust of her nervous reserve was undoubtedly genuine. 'Grandmama so kind and dear as usual,' Princess Victoria of Prussia told her mother, describing in her letters home the quiet summer days at Windsor, the green grass in the Park — 'no one knows what grass is until they come to England' — and the rhododendrons — 'like a dream' — the Queen making a speech, 'so well and without hesitation' as she gives away new colours to a regiment in the courtyard, the drives to Frogmore and the picnic teas with the nurses in their long, rustling dresses running after children down the slopes, the Queen working so conscientiously at her papers in the shade of an immense cedar tree, the games of tennis on the courts below the East Terrace, the Eton boys rowing on the river in the evening and Uncle Bertie, charming and pleasingly raffish, coming to dinner and talking of a different world.

Queen Victoria's world was already dying, and she clung with characteristic tenacity to her memories of the past, remembering with distressing accuracy the anniversaries of the deaths of nearly all the members of her family and refusing to perform any public duties which interfered with their proper observance. It was characteristic of her attitude, for instance, that she refused to have her Jubilee on 20 May as planned because her 'Uncle William IV had died that day'.

The four rooms she used at Windsor contained almost two hundred and fifty pictures as well as the many photographs that were carried from Balmoral and Osborne every time she moved. They covered the green silk walls of her bedroom and the rich crimson flock of her sitting-room; they stood on her desk and on tables by the heavy damask curtains; and her servants often found her looking round at them as she played patience in the evenings by the light of the wax candles in the huge chandeliers. In the daytime, too, she was often to be seen pottering about amongst her treasures, picking them over with her chubby, heavily beringed fingers, looking at bundles of letters, sheets

The Queen's funeral procession, 1901.
The cortège passes through the cobbled streets of Windsor followed by King Edward VII and the Kaiser.

of music, paper weights, ink stands, old penknives, dead flowers, turning the pages of her ever-expanding inventories or of her birthday book, full of the signatures of her visitors, that she took with her wherever she went so that it was sometimes mistaken for a Bible.

The century drew close to its ending and the Boer War began and she went to the barracks at Windsor to inspect the troops before they embarked for South Africa. Thirty-five years before she had inspected others of her soldiers before they sailed for the Crimea and they were wearing scarlet then. Their uniforms were khaki now and it seemed a curiously symbolic change as well as a practical one. In May 1900 Mafeking was relieved and the boys from Eton gathered in the upper quadrangle of the castle to sing patriotic songs to her and she leant out of her window and said 'Thank you, thank you', repeating the words many times. And as she listened to the last song, the Eton boys were astonished to see an Indian servant appear at her side and hand her a Scotch and soda.

She was sleeping badly now, and her eyesight and rheumatic pains were getting worse. But she went on working until the end, although she could hardly see the papers she signed.

She died in January 1901, like a great three-decker ship sinking, the Duke of Argyll said, now rallying, now failing. For two and a half hours the Kaiser, kneeling down by the bed, supported her with his arm; but the last coherent word she spoke was 'Bertie'.

A few moments later Bertie was King and the Edwardian Age had begun and, as if to herald its beginning, the Kaiser, the King of the Belgians, and the King of Portugal, while waiting for the funeral of the Queen to start, stood by a fireplace in a corridor in the castle, smoking cigars.

VI

EDWARDIANS

1

EDWARD VII — 'A VERY BAD BOY'

There is no position in the world more difficult to fill than that of Heir-Apparent to the throne. It is beset by more than all the temptations of actual royalty, while the weight of counteracting responsibility is much less directly felt. It must be with a feeling akin to hopelessness, that a man in that position offers up the familiar prayer, 'Lead us not into temptation'.

As the readers of *The Times* knew very well when they read this comment, the new King, as Prince of Wales, had succumbed to temptation often enough. It was, though, as was generally admitted, not altogether his fault. His upbringing as a boy at Windsor had not been as severe, perhaps, as that of the Prince Regent and his brothers; but it was quite as severe as any education a boy in his position might expect to have in the middle of the nineteenth century. And after his father's death, his mother, who could never forget what she took to be the Prince of Wales's responsibility for her widowhood, had been determined that her eldest son should not exercise any power or influence or enjoy any privileges that might have been exercised or

The Prince of Wales in June 1857.

enjoyed by her husband, and had continued a regime that she believed her 'Angel' would have approved.

He was a far from clever boy and although he had a good memory and an alert mind he did not take kindly to his lessons. Even English came with difficulty to him, and in his bilingual nursery he preferred to speak German and never in after life lost the faint traces of a German accent. His lessons were drawn up by his father and mother, with the help and advice of Baron Stockmar, into a regular and demanding curriculum. As soon as he was seven, half an hour had to be devoted every day to each of the following subjects: writing, music, drawing, geography, calculating, and religion, and a full hour had to be spent in learning French, English, and German. But the longer he spent with his books, the less profit he seemed to derive from them.

He was considered not only rather stupid but, despite his cheerful and lively nature, lazy and obstinate. As his tutor, a kind and tolerant Eton master with the inappropriate name of Birch, was unsuccessful with him, it was decided that his father should administer a sound whipping. This proved useless and a phrenologist was consulted who reported upon the Prince's 'nervous excitability, extreme obstinacy and passionate nature'. His next tutor, a severe barrister named Gibbs whose strict moral sense was more to Baron Stockmar's liking than the tolerance of Henry Birch, had no more success with the Prince than his predecessor had had. 'A very bad boy,' he wrote in his diary, making a sad entry which had regrettably been paralleled on several earlier pages. 'The P. of W. has been like a person half silly. I could not gain his attention. He was very rude, particularly in the afternoon, throwing stones in my face. During his lesson in the morning he was running first in one place, then in another. He made faces, and spat. Dr Becher complained of his great naughtiness. There was a great deal of bad words.'

The Queen did not disguise her opinion of her eldest son. 'With the Prince of Wales,' she told Major Howard Elphinstone, a member of her household, 'one had to contend with an unhappy temper, incapacity of concentrating his mind and defective mental qualities.'

He was certainly always longing to escape from the schoolroom, but while 'sport and amusement of a sober kind were permitted to him' (provided they were 'strictly rationed and supervised') he was kept aloof from companions of his own age, lest they lead him astray, as his great-uncles had been led astray. Freedom in any relation in life was, in fact, to be 'sternly denied him'. On the rare occasions when suitable companions were summoned to the castle to play games with him, they dreaded the invitation, for the Prince was likely to spend most of the time bullying them. He was, in any case, never very successful with his outdoor pursuits even when he was not fighting.

He rode hard, he played fives in the courts at Eton, he practised his croquet shots, he went out with the royal buckhounds at Windsor, and shot regularly from his thirteenth year over the Windsor coverts, but he never managed to become as good a shot as his father (although sometimes he appeared to be so since he never fired at a difficult bird), and he never became more than an average performer at any ball game. It was obvious that he enjoyed games as a boy only as a means of escape from his lessons and his early wish to become a soldier, despite the difficulty he had had restraining his tears when as a little boy he had watched the military reviews in the Park and heard the boom of the cannon, seemed to stem more from his interest in uniforms and his desire for travel and independence than in any taste for military glory.

The Prince Consort, however, persisted in trying to make a scholar out of him. He was provided with appropriately accomplished friends who were in no sense companionable; he was brought into touch with scientists, historians, professors and bishops who could impart nothing to him; he was sent to Edinburgh University as well as to Oxford and Cambridge without obtaining much benefit from his short courses at any of them except a softening of his German accent. His father, who felt that the only use for Oxford was that it was 'a place for study', wrote to him and trusted that he understood that 'the Balls etc., etc., which he visited were not visited by him for his own amusement but to give pleasure to others'. There was something profoundly pathetic in these repeated entreaties made to him by his father in his determination to raise his son's mind and character up to the level of his own; and there is something quite as pathetic in the son's inability to profit by them or even to attend to them, for in the admiration and respect he felt for his father there was a depth of love he did not fully recognize until it was too late to show him that it existed.

He had been able to share few of his father's interests. Music — except French and Viennese light operas — meant little to him; painting and literature bored him. As a child he had enjoyed the Christmas plays in the castle when Charles Kean had been the director of performances; but his happiest memories were of conjurers — Papa knew how all the tricks were done, he proudly confided to a guest — of circuses, and the antics of Wombwell's menagerie which he had seen perform in the quadrangle. And in later life he preferred light plays and musical comedies which did not exert undue strain upon his limited intellectual strength or upon his somewhat narrow imaginative faculties. When he was given a book he would say how much he was looking forward to reading it, but he rarely got beyond the first few pages and often did not attempt even those. Clothes and decorations interested him, of course, and his collection of uniforms and helmets, of the robes of various Orders of Chivalry and Masonic regalia was immense. His insistence on all the regulations concerning dress was in later life to be such a 'conspicuous foible' that he would 'rebuke with a freezing inattentiveness or a biting scorn the least neglect of sartorial convention'. One of his secretaries — who said that he 'adored uniforms and decorations' and that if there was one thing he liked doing 'it was presenting medals' — has recalled several occasions upon which he was excessively put out when people appeared in his presence in the wrong clothes or wearing their orders the wrong way round.

The Prince and Princess of Wales in 1888.

An English girl who came to an official luncheon in Algiers wearing 'flannels' and a squash hat, a groom-in-waiting who intended going to a wedding in a black waistcoat — 'My dear fellow, where is your *white* waistcoat? Is it possible you are going to a *wedding* in a *black* waistcoat?' — an unconcerned Lord Rosebery who went aboard the royal yacht wearing a Yacht Squadron mess jacket and a white tie and at Windsor came to a banquet in evening clothes instead of uniform — 'I see you belong to the American Embassy' — a careless Lord Haldane whose hat 'looked as though it had been inherited from Goethe', all upset him profoundly. To see a decoration worn incorrectly caused him even greater pain, and he once sent Benjamin Constant a Garter ribbon to show him that the colour he had painted it in a portrait of Queen Victoria was the wrong shade of blue.

Edward himself never made a mistake and was always faultlessly attired. Today his overcoats might be considered a trifle too tight and his large tie-pin faintly vulgar, but they did not offend his fashionable contemporaries, whose ambition was to dress as he did and know as much about clothes as he did. He even had a special dress for visiting picture galleries: country clothes being too informal and a frock coat too formal, he went in a short black coat and a top hat. And he even knew what the answer was when the Russian ambassador asked him if it would be proper for him to attend race-meetings when he was in mourning: 'To Newmarket, yes, because it means a bowler hat, but not to the Derby because of the top hat.'

Like his father he did not often linger at the dinner-table, but this was not because he did not enjoy male conversation and ribald stories, drinking brandy and smoking cigars, but because he preferred the company of women; and it was, in fact, his reputation as a *donnaiuolo* that lay behind much of the solemnly censorious and understandably apprehensive comment that surrounded his accession.

*

While his mother had been living out the last years of her life at Balmoral, Osborne and Windsor, the Prince of Wales had been entertaining her subjects with the reports of his adventures at Marlborough House in Pall Mall, at his country estate, Sandringham, in Norfolk which had been bought for him in 1861 for £220,000, and at various other places up and down the country and abroad where his activities as a gambler, *bon viveur* and *paillard*, a patron of cockpits, of racecourses, casinos and brothels were assiduously discussed with some exaggeration and a great deal of conjecture.

Partly no doubt from an unwillingness to share the power and privileges of her position but also because she had so little faith in his capacity, the Queen continued to try to keep him excluded from even the feeling of responsibility. He succeeded in learning much of affairs of State from her Ministers and from foreign ambassadors, of course, but he did not obtain a key to Cabinet boxes until seven or eight years before she died. 'He had no intellectual grasp, no balance or stability:

he seemed to think that the correct wearing of an order or decoration was of greater moment than the merit that had won it. It was ludicrous, absolutely laughable, to imagine that, while his mind was still so unformed, his judgement, his views on great issues could be of value; and with his unguarded tongue, secret negotiations and lines of policy would soon be known to the Rothschilds who were such friends of his.'

It might have been gratifying to the Queen, perhaps, that he was an arbiter of fashion, had the fields in which he gave the lead not been those in which she would have been happier to see him less at home. There was little harm, no doubt, in the fashions he set. He had always followed her advice, given many years ago, never to be *'extravagant'* or *'slang'*. The waistcoat did possibly look better with its bottom button undone, even if the fashion was inspired, as were others, by his own comfort; and the soft felt hat he brought back from Homburg was perhaps acceptable despite its rakishly curling brim; and, after all, he could not be blamed for the new way of shaking hands with the elbow held stiffly to the side, for he had been obliged to shake hands like that because of the rheumatism in his elbow; and neither he nor his wife could be blamed for the 'Alexandra limp' which became such a fashionable way of walking when the Princess of Wales developed a limp after an attack of rheumatic fever. But the bad habit of smoking cigarettes, and the even worse habit of smoking cigars directly after dinner, were entirely his responsibility. And he had even invented a 'Cocktail' of whisky, Angostura bitters, maraschino, champagne, pineapple, lemon peel and powdered sugar, which was, she must have felt sure, reprehensible in every way.

Then there were the scandals over the Tranby Croft baccarat case and the Mordaunt divorce and all the stories about his gay and irresponsible life and – despite an income of more than £100,000 a year – his constant debts, which fixed the Queen's determination to contradict the rumours that she might abdicate.

It was too late now to wonder whether it had been wise to bring him up so strictly and under so careful a surveillance until his marriage, and then allow him his freedom as a rich young man of twenty-two. Hearing about his activities at 'Mott's' and the 'Cremona', his visits to young women from *cinq à sept*, his wild parties at the houses of his extravagant friends and his enjoyment of all the careless pleasures of the mid-Victorian 'epidemic of *nostalgie de la boue*', there were many who agreed with the Queen that, when her son succeeded her, the monarchy would enter a phase as dangerous as the one that her uncles had precipitated.

It was all very well for the Prince to show that he was regal as well as *roué*, or coldly to inform a man who had gone too far by calling across the billiard-table after a bad shot, 'Pull yourself together, Wales,' that his carriage was at the door; but it is not always easy to understand that it was not so much that he was pompous as because he had a passionate belief that royalty must be accorded a special respect.

15

Queen Victoria
in the early years of her marriage
A portrait by Herbert I. Smith.

16 (overleaf)

King Louis Philippe leading Queen Victoria
into dinner in St George's Hall on 11 October 1844
A water colour by Joseph Nash. The decorative scheme is by Wyatville
whose idea it was to place the shields
of former Knights of the Garter in the panels of the wooden ceiling.

17

The interior of
the mausoleum at Frogmore
By W. Brewer.
Queen Victoria is seen mourning
by the Prince Consort's tomb.

Nor was it always easy to understand that when brandy was poured over Christopher Sykes's head this was not only to indulge in his regrettable pleasure in practical jokes – they must never be played on him – but also to make his friends laugh with him at Sykes's complaisantly lugubrious, inimitably long-suffering, 'As your Royal Highness pleases'. And it was all very well for him to show, with such evident expectations of compliment, how fond and proud of his beautiful wife he was, and how well he had demonstrated that he was, in at least one sense, a family man by ensuring that she had several healthy children, when every one of his mother's subjects knew that being a proud and virile husband was only one of the requirements of an heir to the throne.

2

EDWARD VII
– 'L'ONCLE DE L'EUROPE'

The Prince of Wales was already in his sixtieth year when his mother died; his beard was grey; he had become very portly; and, although a lotion was vigorously applied to his scalp twice a day, he was nearly bald. The death of his eldest son – the lethargic and dissipated Prince Eddie – in 1891 had been a profound shock to him; and his heavy smoking had exacerbated his bronchitic tendency.

While making no secret of his disappointment that his honours had come to him so late in life, he nevertheless undertook his duties as King with his habitual energy and a deep consciousness of the importance of his vocation. He was anxious to learn quickly. Lord Esher, the Deputy Constable and Lieutenant-Governor of Windsor Castle, who was later to exercise so much influence over him, described how he would ask question after question, interrupt the answers with his quick, 'Yes . . . yes . . . yes', give orders, scribble notes on bits of paper in his scarcely legible writing, and then stand in front of the fire with one of his immense cigars between his teeth, 'looking wonderfully like Henry VIII, only better tempered'. The impression he gave Lord Esher was 'that of a man, who, after long years of pent-up action, had suddenly been freed from restraint and revelled in his liberty'. He insisted on having all his letters 'brought to him unopened, about 400 a day', and sorted them by himself. 'He tried at first to open them all but found that impossible.'

When he came to the castle for the first time as King with what Sir Sidney Lee called his 'charming circle of cavaliers' it was much as though, so one of his grandsons was given to understand, 'a Viennese hussar had suddenly burst into an English vicarage'. Soon motor cars were rattling unsteadily through the arches, and his own Daimler and Mercedes were garaged in the converted coach houses; plumbers were installing new bathrooms and ventilation; telephone engineers were trailing their equipment over the carpeted corridors, extending a system first introduced in 1896; and inventory clerks were listing the muddled accumulations of half a century: the thousands of mementoes, the innumerable photographs, the ornaments and pieces of bric-à-brac, the elephant tusks and boxes of armour and statuettes of gillies, the ornamental dinner services, the gold plate and horse harnesses, the treasures of a distant childhood, the quantities of marble busts, the silver dishes for roasted chestnuts in the form of table napkins, and the countless relics of a dead age which lay, stored in improbable places or exposed to unwilling view, amidst the remains of George IV's magnificent collections.

The King strode through the castle, supervising all the redecorations, for the new Queen had little interest in such things, 'with a pot hat on, and his stick and his dog . . . as if he were out for a walk'. He went to the library one day 'and ransacked every kind of bookcase and picture cupboard. He got rid of an enormous number of rubbishy old coloured photographs and things'. 'I do not know much about Arrt,' he would say, rolling his r's, 'but I think I know something about Arr-r-angement.'

He rearranged and repainted almost everything; but he felt compelled to leave the heavy carpets and curtains untouched for they were, although so unbecoming, as good as new.

The ceremonious Lord Esher was doubtful at first that all the changes were for the better. 'It may be my imagination,' he confided to his journal, 'but sanctity of the throne has disappeared. The King is kind and debonair, and not undignified – but too *human*!' All the atmosphere of the castle had changed. The Indians wandered about 'like uneasy spirits, no longer immobile and statuesque'. In the evening the King came unannounced into the Green Drawing Room with his daughters and his sister, and 'the quiet impressive entrance of the Queen into the corridor' was 'as obsolete as Queen Elizabeth'. The dinner was 'like an ordinary party. None of the "hush" of the Queen's dinners. Afterwards we left "arm-in-arm" as we entered.' Later the etiquette 'stiffened up very much' but it was never as formal as before,

Edward VII's sitting-room. Above the fireplace is Landseer's painting of his mother and father who are depicted by a window overlooking the East Terrace after Prince Albert's return from shooting.

and Esher could not help but 'regret the mystery and awe of the old Court'.

All the old members of Queen Victoria's household and all her servants were permitted to retain their places and salaries for six months, however, including the Indians who continued to occupy their rooms in King John's Tower. But before their departure, secretaries, equerries and servants who had been with the King as Prince of Wales were found employment too, for Edward VII was determined to change immediately the whole ambience of the Court.

*

Queen Victoria, who considered that the English aristocracy, 'apart from a righteous remnant', had 'no other aim in life save pleasure-seeking or dissipation', had frequently reproached her son for his appalling taste in friends, not only for the numbers of apparently idle aristocrats amongst them but also by the terms of familiarity upon which he lived with other socially unacceptable people who, after her death, entered the rooms at Windsor and altered their whole atmosphere. Tradesmen, financiers, Jews and actresses were accepted into a Court where unhealthy prejudices about race and colour were not tolerated, where intelligence and wit and money and a knowledge of fashionable scandals were more dearly prized than Coburg blood. In addition to Americans, of whom he had always been fond – although he could not bear their clothes – and in addition to men in public life like Lord Fisher whose personality and views he admired, parties at

Windsor often included such apparently disparate guests as the Marquis de Soveral (the clever, ugly and loquacious Portuguese diplomatist — 'a sort of Cyrano,' Lord Esher called him, 'very ugly but hypersmart' — whose monocle and fierce black moustache interfered in no way with his easy charm), Sir Ernest Cassel, son of a Cologne banker, reserved but masterful, rich and generous, Sir Thomas Lipton, also rich and far less reserved, Eduardo de Martino, a Neapolitan who had served in the Italian Navy and had been a Marine Painter-in-Ordinary to Queen Victoria and was now 'a sort of Court Jester, a butt for the King's jokes' to which he would reply with 'quaint remarks in very bad English', Sir Felix Semon, a nose and throat specialist of German descent, who was a witty *raconteur* and an excellent bridge player, and the Sassoon brothers, rich and charming descendants of Jews from the Middle East.

It seemed, then, entirely appropriate that at a magnificent ball held in the Waterloo Chamber at Windsor in 1903, the first ball held in the

Queen Alexandra's sitting-room. 'A clutter such as I never saw', commented one of her visitors.

castle for half a century, Prince Adolphus of Teck and Princess Victoria should fall flat on their backs, when the Prince's spurs caught in the 'awfully long gown' of Mrs George Keppel, the King's vivacious mistress.

*

King Edward was fond of his wife and children but a quiet family life bored him and he liked to fill Windsor with rich, amusing and worldly guests and to make the castle as much like a rich man's country house as possible. 'He always was accessible and friendly,' the American Duchess of Marlborough said, 'and knew how to discard ceremony.' But he never allowed behaviour or conversation at Windsor which he thought might detract from his dignity. Even if it were obviously inadvertent, a *faux pas* was inexcusable; and one poor woman had her name struck off the court list for falling over in front of the King and Queen because she could not manage her train.

Abroad the King enjoyed a reputation for gay familiarity. He would cheerfully tolerate La Goulue who shouted at him one night in Paris when she caught sight of him in the middle of her 'quadrille in delirium', 'Allo, Wales. *Est-ce que tu vas payer mon champagne?*' He smiled at the black-stockinged leg thrust out at him through an expanse of billowing petticoats, and he bought her a bottle. But when an Englishwoman, who he felt should have known better than to have been so arch with him, offered him a cup of tea at a charity fair at the Albert Hall and, having taken a sip of it herself, said that the charge had consequently gone up from its already very high price to five guineas, he looked at her with cold distaste, gave her the five guineas and said sharply, 'Will you please give me a clean cup.'

The Queen, too, carefree as she usually was, insisted on being treated with the formal respect which the King liked her to receive. Lord Ormathwaite confessed that he could never forget his first waiting at Windsor.

We were standing about the drawing room after dinner listening to one of the Guards' bands which happened to be playing some of the loudest passages from Lohengrin [he wrote in his memoirs]. Quite forgetting that Queen Alexandra [who was already rather deaf] always heard best when the noise was loudest, I said incautiously to my neighbour: 'Are we never going to sit down tonight?'
To my horror the Queen turned round and I realized that my remark had been overheard and nearly died of shame.

The King insisted that his women guests should wear tiaras at dinner every night at Windsor and that the men should wear court costume and their decorations. Nor did he permit any woman to go to bed before the Queen went, which was rarely before midnight, or any man to go before he went, which was between one o'clock and half past. Everyone had to spend the evening doing something which appeared to him enjoyable and this was as much a duty for his guests as for his household. One evening he went on a tour of inspection, counting the number of men in the drawing-rooms and, finding one short, he rang for a page and told him to go and fetch back the absentee who, he imagined, was one of the younger guests. It turned out to be General Sir Dighton Probyn, v.c., the seventy-five-year-old Keeper of the Privy Purse, who had gone to bed because he was not feeling well. The King 'was very much amused at this, but Sir Dighton was not'.

But although an exacting host and an exacting master, King Edward was far more considerate with members of his household than his mother had been, 'always thinking of small acts of kindness and often, without being asked, suggesting to some married man that he should go away and spend the week with his family'. He was considerate with his domestic servants, too. He often gave them orders himself in his sharp, intimidating voice, but he made sure they were well looked after and had comfortable quarters. A French visitor to Windsor noticed how pleasant their rooms had been made since the Queen's death and how many bathrooms they had.

As well as being considerate the King was also very businesslike. All the departments of the household were modernized and the abuses that had grown up in the day of his mother, who hated all change, were swept away. The economies did not go far enough for Henry Labouchère, the fiery Radical proprietor of *Truth*, but there could be no doubt that the household was a much more efficient organization than it had ever been since Prince Albert's death; nor could there be any doubt that the castle was a much more pleasant place in which to spend the night than it had been for years. 'The whole arrangements here are extraordinarily comfortable,' Lord Haldane told his mother at the beginning of 1905. 'They could not be more so.'

The Lord Chamberlain's office was also reorganized and the old afternoon receptions or 'Drawing-rooms' became the new evening 'Presentation Courts', while the times of levées, which had previously prevented those who attended them from having any luncheon, were altered to a convenient hour.

Being very businesslike, the King liked everyone to be punctual, and the Queen, who was usually late for everything — even, so it was said, for her own coronation — tried him sorely. She was rarely less than twenty minutes late for dinner at Windsor and the King would wait for her with the face of a Christian martyr'. He had long since accepted her unpunctuality 'as inevitable and never attempted to remonstrate with her'.

He would get extremely cross with anyone else who kept him waiting, however, and once when Herbert Asquith was late in arriving to join a party in the castle courtyard, the King 'looked first at his watch and then at the castle clock, and fussed crossly about the yard'. He had told Asquith and his wife to join himself and the Queen at four o'clock 'to motor first to the gardens and then to Virginia Water for tea'. But Asquith was late. Once before he had forgotten about an invitation to Windsor altogether and had gone abroad on holiday instead. It looked as though he had forgotten this appointment, too. The King 'angrily turned to his gentlemen-in-waiting, Harry Stonor and Seymour Fortescue, and demanded, "What have you done? Where have you looked for him? Did you not give him my command?" ' Mrs Asquith suggested that they should start without him, but the King snapped 'Certainly not!' So she went to the Queen and said that she 'feared there had been a scandal at Court and that Herbert must have eloped with one of the maids of honour'. She begged the Queen to save her blushes 'by commanding the King to proceed, at which she walked up to him with her amazing grace, and her charming way, tapping him firmly on the arm pointed with a sweeping gesture to his motor and invited Gracie Raincliffe [the Countess of Londesborough] and Alice Keppel to accompany him; at which they all drove off.'

The Queen could manage him better than anyone else. She was a delightful and remarkable woman, possessively devoted to her children and loyal to her wayward husband. She was ill-educated, without intellectual curiosity or any artistic taste except a liking for music, which in her later years she could not hear any more. Gay and lively, beautiful, graceful, recklessly generous and painfully insensitive, with large deep blue sympathetic eyes and a delightful accent, she had an 'almost childish interest in everything', a lively sense of the ridiculous — which included, it has unfortunately to be admitted, her husband's fondness for practical jokes — and a refreshing irreverence for convention. She once appeared, to the King's appalled consternation, wearing 'the famous Koh-i-noor as well as the fabulous Cullinan diamonds', with her Garter star on the wrong side because, so she said, it clashed with her other jewels.

Sir Frederick Ponsonby has described her curious views on golf. The King, who was very fond of the game, had a course made at Windsor in the grounds below the East Terrace, but the Queen seemed to confuse the game with hockey and was 'under the impression that one had to prevent the opponent putting the ball in the hole. This usually ended by a scrimmage on the green. She also thought that the person who got into the hole first won it, and she asked me to hurry up and run between my strokes. It was very good fun, and we all laughed.'

The Queen's hockey-golf was, of course, very hard on the balls, which she managed, when playing with her daughter Victoria, to batter into crooked pyramids. The King, finding a pair of these curious shapes on the first tee one afternoon, thought that his opponent was 'trying to be funny', and was extremely cross until he learned that his wife was responsible.

Although extremely indulgent with the Queen's caprices, the King was capable of outbursts of alarming anger if anyone else irritated him. He would swear furiously if his golfing partner played badly; and once, playing croquet with Frederick Ponsonby, Harry Chaplin, his old Oxford friend, and the beautiful Madame Letellier, he got so cross with Ponsonby (who kept knocking the King's ball to the other end of the ground because he did not like the game and did not want to be asked to play again) that Madame Letellier begged him 'with tears in her eyes not to make the King so angry'. At bridge, though he did not play at all well, he did not hesitate to criticize all his partner's mistakes and he would say crossly 'This is becoming a very expensive evening.' But the anger generally died down as quickly as it had risen, and then would come that 'kindly and merry laugh, and he lit another enormous cigar which made him cough'.

It was 'usual with the King after he had let himself go and cursed someone,' one of his equerries said, 'to smooth matters by being especially nice to them afterwards'. 'If the King assailed you, as he sometimes assailed me,' Lord Esher said, 'it was almost certain that within an hour or two he would send for you, or dispatch a few lines on a slip of paper, on some wholly different subject, in the friendliest manner, with no allusion to what had passed.'

For despite a peppery temper, a caustic tongue, moods in which he indulged his taste for what the Duchess of Teck called 'odious chaffing', and despite a domineering manner that made even his best friends frightened of him sometimes, he was an essentially and obviously warm-hearted man. 'He was naturally and genuinely kind-hearted,' Winston Churchill decided, remembering an occasion when, as a young subaltern, he had kept the King waiting twenty minutes for supper, been reprimanded severely and then, almost immediately, forgiven. Lord Esher found him the 'kindest and most considerate' master and friend that a man could have. 'Jealousy was a word he could not understand . . . If he gave his confidence it was given absolutely.' Esher had, of course, as Lord Mersey said, 'a flatterer's tongue', but these compliments were not undeserved.

In many respects, though, King Edward's was a childish nature. He rarely dissembled; he refused to try to understand problems that did not interest him; he worked quite hard at being a King but this was mainly, perhaps, because he enjoyed the work. 'It's all so interesting,' he once explained to Lord Redesdale when settling down at midnight to great boxfuls of papers. He never grew tired of giving presents and decorations. He was sulky when he lost a bet and paid his debt as though he were making a presentation. He was fecklessly and unconsciously extravagant and thought nothing of bringing an immense cast of West End actors and actresses to perform for a few friends at Windsor or of asking an expensive veterinary surgeon to come out to Marienbad at a fee of £200 when his adored dog Caesar was ill.

Caesar, a curiously scruffy fox terrier, was as devoted to the King as he to him and would jump up at his legs whenever he saw him and the King would pat him and say, 'Do you like your old master then?' The little dog walked proudly round Biarritz and Paris and through the corridors at Windsor bearing on his collar the legend: 'I am Caesar, the King's dog'. If he was ill, the King decided, of course he must have the best man sent from England to look after him. It did not occur to the King that he was being extravagant — he had a generous mind, not a sensitive one. He did not much care what the provident thought of him. His actions were governed more by instinct than by calculation. He indulged himself certainly, but his concern with the allevia-

Above, Edward VII's dog, Caesar. This beloved terrier wore a collar on which was inscribed the legend, 'I belong to the King'. Much indulged by his master, who took him abroad with him, he was allowed to sleep in an easy chair by the King's bed.

Above right, Edward VII's bathroom. A bowl for the King's dog can be seen at the foot of the wardrobe.

tion of pain, the care of the sick, and his interest in cancer research, went far deeper than the superficialities of royal patronage. He was prepared to spend £200 on his terrier but he was also prepared to spend £30,000 on giving dinner to the London poor. He was 'good old Teddy!' to them. Not many of them objected to his cigars and his racehorses or to the genial and generous, witty but discreet Mrs Keppel, whose pretty face smiling under her enormous hats was so often at his side. He was a popular king because he was so obviously a human one. 'He is loved,' Lord Granville said, 'because he has all the faults of which the Englishman is accused.'

*

Englishmen saw much more of him than they had seen of his mother. His restlessness ensured that he was often abroad, and every year he felt in need of a cure at a watering-place to offset the effects of his *gourmandise*. But when he was at home he was constantly on the move, going with perfect regularity to all the principal race meetings and visiting the country houses of his numerous friends, who can be seen with him in a hundred different photographs staring fixedly, be-whiskered, self-confident and strangely menacing into the camera's lens.

He was accompanied to these country houses by a large train of servants, including his own footman to wait upon him at meals, and his Austrian valet, Meidinger, to get him out of bed early in the morning. But although he was so coddled and so practised a guest, he was not always an easy one. He liked to know who all his fellow guests would be, and was known not only to cross off names he did not like on the list submitted to him by his hosts, but also to add other names to them. He was superstitious and hated to sit down to dinner when there were thirteen at table — he once comforted himself with the knowledge that on one occasion when he had appeared to tempt providence in this way he had not in fact done so because one of the thirteen guests (Princess Frederick Charles of Hesse) was pregnant — and it was even said that he disliked having two knives laid in front of him at once in case they became crossed. He preferred, as a dedicated *gourmet*, to leave his mind free to concentrate on his food and to leave conversation to the intervals between the courses. He was not a 'great talker', Sir Sidney Lee said, nor did he compare as a raconteur with most of his friends. He was a pleasant enough neighbour, though. He was a good listener and liked to be told gossip by pretty women.

He had an excellent appetite like his mother, and, although he did not drink much, he could 'eat with impunity a wonderful quantity and mixture of dishes'. He could enjoy several dozen oysters at a sitting and he set the good example of eating them with brown bread and butter. He loved lamb and chicken and turkey and trout and eggs in aspic and strawberries; and with his dessert he always liked to drink champagne, preferably Duminy *extra sec*, 1883, decanted — another fashion set — into a glass jug from which he helped himself.

He did not eat much before luncheon but at Windsor, when he had a morning's work ahead of him, he would have a 'true country breakfast'; and after luncheon (which was served at half-past two) and before dinner (the time of which varied according to the evening's arrangements) he was ready for a good tea at five o'clock with sandwiches, cake and biscuits. Dinner was served in the State dining-room and afterwards the King liked to play bridge in the White Drawing Room, or to walk about ensuring that all his guests were enjoying themselves, or to watch, with one of his immense Corona y Corona cigars in his mouth, the impromptu dancing in the Crimson Drawing Room where the band played every night.

This was the life he loved, and the rich were the people whose company was essential to his happiness. He never got on very well with the professional classes or the gentry, whose lack of wealth kept them from Court, or with intellectuals. He did not always succeed with women, and Margot Asquith decided after a week-end at Windsor that 'if you don't keep a firm grasp on yourself on the rare occasions when you are with Kings and Princes, you notice little, enjoy nothing and lose your individuality. Royal persons are divorced from the opinions of people that count, and are almost always condemned to take safe and commonplace views. To them clever men are "prigs"; clever women "too advanced"; Liberals are "socialists"; the uninteresting "pleasant"; the interesting "intriguers"; and the imaginative "mad".'

The King always found it difficult to carry on a conversation with a man or woman who did not share at least some of his tastes. On one occasion, finding a conversation with a bishop appallingly heavy-going, he switched in despair from one subject to another without arousing the least response. At length, catching sight of a photograph of himself on a side table, he thought he would try that. What did the bishop think of the likeness? 'Yes, yes,' the bishop replied, having put on his spectacles, 'yes, yes, poor old Buller!'

It was rarely, though, that he had such little success. He had the good manners, rare in kings, to display an apparently absorbed interest in the people to whom he was talking, and he took the trouble — as all of his successors on the throne were also to do — to find out all he could about them, storing the information in an exceptionally retentive memory. Above all he was, when he wished to be, captivatingly charming. Had he not been so he would never have become *l'Oncle de l'Europe*.

It took more than charm, of course, to become that, to make Europeans believe, as millions of them did believe, that he was 'the arbiter of their fate', 'Edward the Peacemaker'. It took moral courage and

A royal gathering at Windsor in 1907 showing, from left to right, Queen Victoria Eugenia of Spain, King Edward VII, the Kaiserin, Kaiser Wilhelm II, Queen Alexandra, Queen Amelia of Portugal, King Alphonso XIII of Spain, Queen Maud of Norway.

common sense and his sort of intuitive tact. It took an ability to make men realize that there was a purposeful seriousness behind the gaiety, that the *milieux* of Lily Langtry and the Professional Beauties, of Lady Warwick and the Palais Royal, of Yvette Guilbert and the Moulin Rouge, of Harry Chaplin and the Turf Club were not the only interests he had. He could persuade Gambetta that although he had no real power it was far from being a waste of time to talk to him. And by becoming a distinguished European figure he could help to bring about the dream of his youth, an *entente cordiale* with France.

As he moved about Europe from Paris to Hamburg, Carlsbad to Cannes, to Biarritz and Marienbad, setting fashions and earning the sort of popular adulation that made women collect cigar stubs that had touched his lips and enabled men to sell bones that had been left on his plate, he gained a personal though sometimes overrated influence in European affairs that his conceited and jealous nephew the Kaiser Wilhelm II was never able to rival, except through the power of Germany.

When he returned to England he was able at Windsor to impress his guests by a return of hospitality on a scale that had been unknown there since the 1850s. Visiting emperors, kings and presidents were dazzled by its splendour. King Alfonso might hold his stomach with hunger 'as he waited for luncheon, at the awful hour of half-past two, while King Edward displayed the treasures of his ancestral house to the Master of the Escurial'. And the genial, red-faced President Loubet might become exhausted by his long walks down the halls and galleries, but neither he nor the Spanish King could fail to be impressed by what they saw. Even the disliked and distrusted Kaiser was overwhelmed when he found himself the principal guest at a magnificent luncheon in the castle with twenty-three other royalties.

The Kaiser's visit took place in the autumn of 1907 and the King was showing signs of increasing ill-health. His bronchitis was now a matter of serious concern, yet he would not give up smoking and sometimes the paroxysms of his breathlessness and coughing were alarming. He was more and more subject to fits of almost savage ill-temper, and although he quickly recovered and quickly apologized with a laugh 'like the sound of tearing linen', it was clear that his physical health and emotional stability were being affected. He was subject now to long moods of depression in which he saw republicanism as an irresistible force and his efforts to compose the quarrels of Europe leading to tragic failure. He had done his best to show his sympathy with social reform by identifying the monarchy with the awakening conscience of his people; but he had no time for socialists and never succeeded in understanding their ideals. He was 'a strong Conservative', Sir Charles Dilke said of him, 'and a still stronger Jingo', and he feared that 'continental socialism' was threatening all that he held most dear. He had been careful never to flout the Constitution, as his mother had done, but he went to his death believing that his son would be the last king of England.

VII

WINDSORS

1

GEORGE V

The new King, George V, appeared to have few qualifications for his office and his consciousness of his own inadequacies seemed justified. He had lived in the shadow of a domineering father whom he had unquestioningly admired, whose advice he had always sought and followed, and whose word he had accepted as law.

As Duke of York and later, after his brother's death, as Prince of Wales, he had lived in his father's grounds at Sandringham in a small house, York Cottage, which others described as a 'glum little villa' but which seemed perfectly adequate to him. He lived there as a young Norfolk squire 'to whom money was no object, and business duties but an interlude of no grievous length'. He was not well educated, having gone to sea at an early age after the Reverend John Neale Dalton, his tutor, had advised his parents that neither he nor his brother would be able to keep up to the standard of their contemporaries at a public school; and he had no deeper intellectual curiosity or more fully formed artistic tastes than his father had had.

He had been perfectly happy leading a regular, quiet, even placid country life, helping with the management of the estate, shooting — he was a fast and very accurate shot — dabbling in gardening, watching his children have their bath, and then playing a game of billiards with an equerry or reading aloud to his wife. He liked babies and animals, and he loved his wife and his mother — at the age of twenty-five he was still signing his letters to 'darling Motherdear', 'your loving little Georgy'. In fact he was the epitome of the contented family man.

He wanted little else from life. He 'preferred recognition to surprise', as Sir Harold Nicolson said, 'the familiar to the strange'. He could not talk easily to many of his father's friends, particularly the beautiful and witty women and the foreign men, for he was conscious that his mind though shrewd enough was far from subtle. He did not altogether trust foreigners, anyway, and he detested travelling abroad.

He liked to have a down-to-earth conversation, blunt and direct; and once he had settled down to talk he was nearly always voluble as well as noisy, often indiscreet and sometimes so emphatic that he would bang on the table with his fist. His humour was predictably broad and simple and, like most men who compensate for an innate diffidence by a boisterous gusto, he enjoyed practical jokes, provided they were limited to the family circle.

He confounded all his critics, though, by proving an exceptionally skilful king. He never pretended to understand the complexities of the more abstruse political or diplomatic questions of his day, but he worked hard and conscientiously to grasp the fundamental problems that faced his governments, never contenting himself with summaries as his father had done, and reading his papers, as he read his books, with a slow, thorough, tenacious mind. Had that mind been more subtle and devious he could never have achieved the success he did achieve in establishing the central position and constitutional importance of the monarchy.

King George V and Queen Mary digging potatoes in 1917. The King showed Lady Curzon his potato patch one morning. Did he do all the work himself, she asked him. 'Of course I do,' he told her, indignant at her doubt. 'I dug it all — just look at my hands.'

He was a Conservative at heart, but when a Labour Ministry came into power and a member of his entourage, 'whose roots were firmly planted in the Edwardian age', attempted to commiserate with him on his having to deal with these 'tiresome' people, he turned his back on the would-be sympathizer and would not answer him. He had shown in the Navy that he was not only intensely loyal and balanced but also quite without snobbishness or pretension, and he showed these qualities as a king. It helped him, of course, to be so English, to be quite without the German accent of all his Hanoverian predecessors, to have married a girl who, despite her German origins, had been brought up in England and seemed as English as himself, to combine with his father's interest in yachting and shooting and other sports considered to be more or less those of a gentleman, an interest in football and in cup-tie finals at the Crystal Palace.

Being 'a very homely person', he at first preferred Sandringham and Balmoral to Windsor, which he associated with ceremonial and large-scale entertainment; and he did all he could to make the castle as domestic as possible. He also did all he could to ensure that nothing was changed, insisting that the Blue Room, which was his sitting-room, should remain exactly as his father had furnished it, every object from the red leather chairs to the pictures on the walls to be left in precisely the same position as he had always remembered them.

Once when the arrangement of the furniture was changed by a new housemaid who 'put everything back wrong', the King flew into one of his sudden rages. He rang for the housekeeper, who watched apprehensively as the slight, bearded figure of her master strode up and down across the carpet, asking furiously and repeatedly why the girl should have done such a terrible thing.

Although nothing in his sitting-room was changed thereafter, much else in the castle was; for the new Queen was a museum director *manquée*. She was frequently to be found walking about the castle giving orders for the removal or replacement of pieces of furniture, objects of art or of vertu, and of souvenirs and relics in the lace room. She was interested more in royal iconography than in art, and her reputation as an infallible connoisseur is certainly unjustified; but she did train herself to be something of an expert on antique furniture and china and was a determined, indeed an avaricious, collector, diligently pursuing items dispersed from the royal homes by Queen Victoria, who had allowed members of her family to borrow freely from them, and even soliciting gifts from owners by no means willing to part with them. She kept details of her private possessions and those of her husband and his family in little notebooks, and delighted in conducting guests round the Windsor collections of which she liked to think of herself as 'custodian for the nation'.

A traditionalist like her husband, she had never been able to accustom herself to the activities of her father-in-law's friends. *'Je n'aime pas leurs "goings-on",'* she confessed to her old governess; and she told Lady Airlie that Edwardian society suffered from a 'surfeit of gold plate and orchids'. Yet she was always far more sympathetic towards those whose tastes differed from her own, particularly the young, than the King could ever bring himself to be, and she was never aggressively censorious. Open-minded and curious, she once asked a member of the household to teach her some of the new dance-steps of the period; but the lesson was interrupted by the King 'who expressed himself so violently' that she never attempted to repeat the experiment.

She was 'almost Victorian in her attitude to her husband', Lady Airlie thought. 'She had more originality of mind than he, and their views on current topics often differed widely, but when he contradicted her she never argued with him.' Even the style of her clothes was dictated more by her husband's taste than her own, for she believed that everyone, herself included, should bow to his will. Once she thought that she would like to shorten her skirts in accordance with current fashion, as she had attractive legs and ankles, and she accepted the offer of one of her ladies who suggested that she act as a guinea-pig to test the reactions of the King. The King did not at all approve of the lady-in-waiting's appearance, and the Queen's idea of becoming fashionable was immediately abandoned. Also, because her husband did not like them, she gave up wearing picture hats in the summer when these came into fashion after the First World War. She remained, in fact, with her long, voluminous skirts, as if rooted in the past; and the distressing toques that covered her grey hair, and the folds of pale blue and mauve brocade and the silk and lace that concealed her stately bosom, were accepted as essential and entirely appropriate parts of the *persona* that she had become.

The King himself never forsook the fashions of his youth, continuing throughout his life to wear stiff collars, hard hats and cloth-topped boots — all, incidentally, like his every other possession, of the most expensive quality. Even in the mid-1930s he was still wearing trousers with side creases, and his letters to his obsessively dress-conscious eldest son are full of scornful criticisms of what he took to be laxness in some detail of dress that he had noticed in a photograph. Anyone who did not observe the conventions in dressing was a 'cad'; and the picture of his own son wearing 'a turned down collar in white uniform, with a collar and black tie' was acutely painful. 'Anything more un-smart' he never saw.

The sight of visitors to Windsor Castle walking about the grounds carelessly or outlandishly dressed always irritated the King, and one Easter Bank Holiday the Queen was obliged to call on him 'peremptorily to be silent' when she was embarrassed beyond endurance by the loud comments and criticisms — 'Good God, *look* at those short skirts, *look* at that bobbed hair!' — which he delivered from an open window while looking down upon the visitors who passed along the Terrace below.

To his children the King appeared as a stern, demanding and intimi-dating figure. The bluff, quarter-deck, insistently jovial manner in which he addressed them in his less severe moments was both aggra-vating and embarrassing to sensitive children. Neither the eldest son

King George V and Queen Mary in the Royal Box at Ascot in 1931.

David nor his younger brother, who in the words of his biographer was 'easily rebuffed and prone to take his weaknesses and mistakes too seriously' ever felt completely at ease in his company. Nor did his favourite child, Mary, who blushed scarlet whenever he teased her, which was often. He was emotional and susceptible himself, yet he did not have the imagination to understand how these same characteristics affected the personalities and attitudes of his children.

He could never overcome his obstinate prejudices against the activities and attitudes of those whom he thought of with perplexed distaste as the 'Younger Generation'. He was constantly shocked by them. New ways of dancing, American drinks and jazz, Soviet Russia, painted finger-nails, going away for the week-end, girls who smoked in public or rode horses astride, men who rode in jodhpurs and polo-neck sweaters, all excited a wrath which he did not hesitate to advertise in front of his servants and household in the most pungently acrimonious or disdainful terms. If his favourite expression was 'keep your hair on', picked up in his Navy days and never abandoned, he was almost as often heard to say, 'Well we never did *that* in the olden days.'

With such a man at its head it was not to be expected, of course, that life in the castle could be remotely gay. Meals were prompt and quickly served and usually very simple. The King hated exotic food and once when the Prince of Wales ordered him an avocado pear for a special treat he was horrified. 'What', he asked, 'in heaven's name is this?' After dinner was over – it rarely took more than half an hour – and the Queen had been followed out by the ladies, each of whom curtseyed to the King who bowed in return, he would remain talking to his male guests, whose company he preferred, drinking port.

If there were no guests, and often there were not, the King would spend the evening by the fire with the Queen, looking at his stamps, or reading – biographies mostly, or books of adventure by John Buchan or Charles Kingsley, and 'he could enjoy a good detective story'. He had enjoyed a game of whist occasionally, too, as a young man, but when bridge took its place he found the new game too difficult and took up poker instead. He did not often play, however, and when he did it was only for small stakes. Nor did he enjoy the wireless much, although he would occasionally listen to the news. He preferred the gramophone because he liked to have the same record, often a Gilbert and Sullivan song, put on time after time 'innocently regardless of the tastes of his audience. Indeed, he was suspicious of the "highbrow" (a word which had once puzzled him when he had believed that it was spelt "eyebrow")' – he was always a bad speller and never became adept at either punctuation or syntax. Sometimes in later years there was a film. He liked adventure films best, such as *Lives of a Bengal Lancer*, or English comedies, particularly Tom Walls's. He went to bed at 11.10 p.m. precisely.

The longer he lived, the more deeply his people became aware of the admirable qualities of his personality, so stable, so honest, so old-fashioned and reassuring in an almost hysterical world.

In 1932, when he eventually overcame his reluctance to use a new invention and made his first broadcast, his bluff yet kindly voice enchanted them. Already the war had made them think of him as the Father of his People; now he was far less remote a figure. At his Jubilee in 1935 the unmistakably enthusiastic acclamations made him realize, as if for the first time, how really loved he and his wife had become. 'I'd no idea they felt like that about me,' he said on his return from a visit to the East End during which he had been vociferously cheered. 'I am beginning to think they must really like me for myself.' He made a speech afterwards, and at the end his voice failed him when he made a reference to the Queen. He had known it would and when preparing the draft had told his Secretary to put that part at the end. 'I can't trust myself to speak of the Queen when I think of all I owe her.'

Of the King's devotion to her no one could doubt, and he felt sure, listening to the continuous cheers that so pleased and astonished him that Jubilee Day in 1935, that they were cheering her as much as him. For he, after all, as he told the Archbishop of Canterbury, was 'a very ordinary fellow'. That was his triumph, of course. He *was* an ordinary fellow and yet he was the King; and there were few Englishmen who did not feel moved when he died.

2

EDWARD VIII

The Prince of Wales had been told of his father's illness while out shooting with friends in the Great Park. A few years before he had moved into a 'grace and favour' house six miles from the castle – Fort Belvedere, 'a castellated conglomeration', as the Prince himself described it, which, begun by William, Duke of Cumberland, had been enlarged by Wyatville on George IV's instructions. And it was while modernizing the house and clearing its tangled grounds that the Prince had discovered the 'true charm of Windsor Castle'.

Until then it had seemed more of a 'museum than the residence for the Sovereign', but now that he had come to live nearby and grew to know it better he began to 'revere it not only for its treasures but also for its tranquillity'. He had spent part of his boyhood at Frogmore when his father was Prince of Wales and had enjoyed riding in the Great Park, going for trips with his mother in a big electric launch upriver to Maidenhead and downstream to Staines, exploring the roof of the castle – 'all the more desirable because it was forbidden ground' – playing hide-and-seek amongst the marble busts in George IV's long corridor, wheeling his brothers about on the tall ladders in the library. Although Frogmore itself, with its single bathroom on the ground floor, its innumerable marble busts and memorials to the dead, was more of a family necropolis than a house, this did not worry the royal children as they pedalled furiously on their bicycles around the rhododendrons, past the mausoleums where their great-great-grandmother, the Duchess of Kent, and their great-grandparents lay buried.

When their father returned from his shooting in the north, the carefree games were played with more restraint. His children were once more, as his eldest son David, the future Edward VIII, put it, 'on parade'. Stockings were pulled up over the knees to the thighs, starched Eton collars encircled their necks, the pockets of their sailor suits were sewn up so they could not put their hands in them. A lanyard a fraction of an inch out of place or a sporran slightly awry would earn a parental reprimand of terrifying vehemence.

David grew up young for his years and perpetually conscious of the gulf that separated his father from himself. He tried to be obedient, he did his best to carry out his duties conscientiously, but there was always the shadow of his father behind him, demanding, anxious and critical. There was cause, of course, for the father's concern; but frequent chastening served only to make his son 'secretive, stubborn and more self-willed than ever . . . he came to look upon his father, the Archbishop and some of the older Ministers as a critical and unsympathetic company, designed to frustrate his natural eagerness. He therefore made his own life as he wished.'

Restless, impatient, impulsive, frustrated, emotional, affectionate, unstable and indiscreet, he earned as Prince of Wales much popularity and some respect. He had far more charm than talent, far more capacity for feeling than for thought. His sudden enthusiasms, his discordant ambitions, were likely to die as quickly as they had been born. His longing to fight in the war, his insistence on learning to fly, his reckless steeplechasing, his carefree friends, can all be seen as a revolt against his upbringing or as a reflection of his passionate wish to be accepted as an ordinary human being.

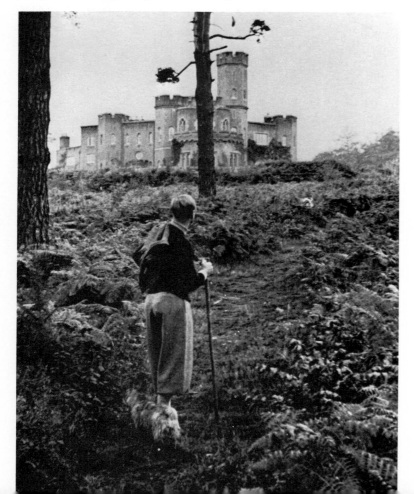

The Prince of Wales in the 1930s in the grounds of Fort Belvedere.

It was his tragedy that he never entirely succeeded in reconciling, as his grandfather had been ultimately able to do, his love of life with his position and responsibilities.

He became irritable and morose. His servants, to whom he had always behaved with exceptional consideration, began to find him thoughtless and even petty. For days on end he would not attempt to do any work before noon, and frequently men summoned for interview would be sent away without having seen him. Often excited and even exhilarated, he rarely seemed happy. The only place where he appeared to be content was at Fort Belvedere, on which he had spent so much time and energy. And it was at Fort Belvedere that the Prince entertained, at several week-end parties during the last months of his father's life, Mr and Mrs Ernest Simpson.

He had first met Wallis Simpson, a handsome, well-dressed, ambitious, intelligent, good-natured but independent and determined woman with a pronounced Baltimore accent, at Melton Mowbray in 1931. Both she and her husband had been married before and were then living in London in a flat in Bryanston Square where the Prince was soon a regular visitor. By the time of George V's death it had been widely suggested abroad, although not yet by English papers, that the Prince was in love with Mrs Simpson and wanted to make her his Queen. His widowed mother, of course, was horrified. Her life had been ruled by 'one single abstract passion' — her passion for the British Monarchy; and her son's determination not to put his duty as King before his love for a woman caused her, so she confessed, a deeper distress and humiliation than any other event in the whole of her life.

He was King for less than a year. He did not neglect his duties, but without any political crisis to inspire him and without any encouragement from his Ministers to devote himself personally, as he would have liked, to the problems of the poor and the unemployed, he spent many weeks of his short reign on holiday. 'He has it in him,' Lord Wigram, who had been Lord Stamfordham's successor as George V's private secretary, told Aga Khan, 'to be the greatest King in the history of our country.' But the King did not feel he could achieve this distinction, or any sort of distinction, 'without the support of the woman he loved'.

She was more important to him than anything and he would not put her out of his life just because he had become a king.

On 10 December 1936 the King announced his decision to abdicate. The following evening he left Fort Belvedere for the Royal Lodge, where his three brothers and his sister and mother were waiting to dine with him. While they were still at dinner his friend Walter Monckton came to drive him to the castle. 'The great quadrangle was dark and deserted as we entered,' he wrote later. 'I mounted the Gothic staircase to my old rooms in the Augusta Tower.' Here Sir John Reith, Director of the B.B.C., met him and asked him to read a paragraph from a newspaper to test his voice. Then Reith announced in his deep voice, 'This is Windsor Castle. His Royal Highness, Prince Edward.'

Prince Edward's voice, 'thick and tired', read the message, short, sincere and pathetic, which Winston Churchill, who had parted from him with tears in his eyes that afternoon at Fort Belvedere, had helped him write.

When the broadcast was over he left immediately for the Royal Lodge where his brothers were waiting to say good-bye to him. 'Dickie, this is absolutely terrible,' the eldest of them had said earlier to Lord Louis Mountbatten. 'I never wanted this to happen; I'm quite unprepared for it. David had been trained for this all his life. I've never even seen a State Paper. I'm only a naval officer; it's the only thing I know about.'

But the naval officer had already become a king, and as Prince Edward left the Royal Lodge that night, he bowed to him in the doorway, and their youngest brother, the Duke of Kent, 'shook his head and cried almost fiercely, "It isn't possible! It isn't happening!"'

3

GEORGE VI

The Duke of Windsor regarded George V's life as a 'stubborn rearguard action against the acceptance of the march of his own times'. The views of his brother, the Duke of York, who now succeeded him as George VI, were much more sympathetic to those of their father. George VI's opinions were more progressive than George V's had been, but he was far from being a revolutionary or an iconoclast; and he had always been prepared to listen to his father's advice: 'very different to dear David'. If change were to come, he believed that it must come slowly and moderately. He was to be a faithfully constitutional monarch, but his own tastes and beliefs were always to remain innately and fundamentally conservative.

The regime of his childhood had had as marked an effect upon him as upon his brother, but the effect was ultimately a quite different one.

Forced to write with his right hand when he was naturally inclined to be left-handed; obliged to wear splints for part of the day and even, for a time, in bed at night to straighten his knock-kneed legs; wanting desperately to satisfy his father but frequently being made to understand that he did not, he became liable to outbursts of anger and to moods of silent depression. By the time he was eight he had developed the stammer which, despite his determined and life-long struggle against it, was never entirely overcome. Yet he never broke out into open defiance or rebellion, for it was his nature to accept discipline, to understand and eventually to share his father's views on behaviour, duty and restraint.

As a shy naval cadet at Osborne, and later at Dartmouth, he was conscientious, patient, painstaking and thorough. He was neither a clever nor an entertaining boy, and he played games with more diligence than skill. But of his application and his courage there could be no doubt.

His character, as it developed, grew more and more to resemble his father's. It was seen that they shared the same ideals; that they had similar faults and similar prejudices; that they were equally emotional. And as the son's self-confidence increased, he became capable of the father's abrupt displays of cantankerous criticism, sometimes made more wounding by the persistent and disdainful sarcasm. He was not at ease, as his father had never been at ease, with clever and brightly amusing or highly imaginative people. He preferred the company of sailors whose experiences he had shared, of men in positions of high responsibility whom he could question about their work, of men like gardeners whose interests were his interests and whose conversation was unlikely to stray into territory where he might lose himself. He was, in fact — again like his father — an unambitious, conservative country gentleman at heart and a king *malgré lui*. When he married in 1923, characteristically he chose a wife whose name was unfamiliar to most of his countrymen.

Modest, appealing and kind, Lady Elizabeth Bowes-Lyon was, though, more than a characteristic choice: she was an ideal one. More responsive and less shy than her husband, instinctively gracious and unemphatically good-looking, 'pretty and engaging and natural' as her mother-in-law said, she had no personal enemies. George V adored his son's 'dear little wife' and could even find it in his heart to forgive her when she was late for a meal. 'You are not late, my dear,' he was once, to the astonishment of everyone present, heard to say in reply to her apology. 'I think we must have sat down two minutes too early.'

The King, too, loved his wife and he was devoted to his two pretty daughters. He found it difficult to relax, however, for he was a man with an exhausting regard for the particularities of life, and eventually, as Sir John Wheeler-Bennett has said, he 'wore himself out with his care for detail'. He could become excessively angry over trifling annoyances and, although his anger soon cooled, as his father's had done,

The Duke of York (later George VI) out shooting in 1920.

his servants dreaded arousing it and being confronted by the King when they had offended him and having to listen to his angry voice and to see the muscles twitching in his cheek.

His sporting life was almost his only relaxation; and in this life shooting provided his greatest pleasure. The pattern of 'royal sport', as his great-grandfather and grandfather had known it, was already almost destroyed when he became King. The grandeur and stage-management of the *grand battue* and the wholesale slaughter of driven birds, followed by a fine luncheon served by numerous retainers in a tent, had had to give way to a more exacting and less comfortable sport in which men had to shoot instead of simply firing their guns. And this was the sort of shooting that appealed to the King's nature.

The qualities that made his fellow sportsmen revere him were the qualities that caused him to meet the challenge of the war with such effect. While Mr Churchill, in his own phrase, was answering the call to provide the lion with a roar, the King set an example, on a necessarily more muted note, which was felt to be at once unselfish and inspiring. It became his habit to come up from Windsor each morning to work at Buckingham Palace or to inspect the damage done in recent air raids. And one morning the Palace was bombed while the King and Queen were in it. 'I'm glad we've been bombed,' the Queen said; 'it makes me feel I can look the East End in the face.' She and her husband continued their tours of inspection as long as the raids lasted so that, as Mr Churchill told them with understandable enthusiasm, the throne and the people were drawn 'more closely together than was ever before recorded' and Their Majesties were 'more beloved by all classes and conditions than all the princes of the past'.

It was clear when the war ended, however, that the King's health, which had never been strong, had been irreparably damaged. He

George VI and Queen Elizabeth with Princesses Elizabeth and Margaret in the gardens of the Royal Lodge in 1946.

had never hesitated to do whatever his Ministers had suggested he should do, and his scrupulous, not to say obsessive, regard for detail had made his activities far more exhausting than they need have been.

King George VI would never, of course, have risen to greatness through his own merits, which he well knew were limited. He had ascended the throne reluctantly and with trepidation. Never having been allowed by his father to be initiated even into the everyday working of government, he had 'stood appalled at the volume and the nature of the business which emerged day by day from those leather-clad dispatch boxes which inexorably dog the life of every British Sovereign', Sir John Wheeler-Bennett has written. 'He was, moreover, more than ever conscious of his own physical disability and of what he believed to be his inferiority in comparison with his brother.'

This belief in his own inferiority never completely left him; and in his later years his nervousness in the presence of strangers was sometimes masked by an almost aggressively domineering manner wholly alien to his true nature.

His career may not have had any deep political or constitutional significance, his personality may not have been striking, but, despite his limitations and his frailties, Roger Fulford may well be right in believing that his character 'is likely to command both the attention and admiration of historians'.

4

ELIZABETH II

Princess Elizabeth was fourteen when she came to Windsor in 1940 to spend the rest of her childhood there.

Already the castle had taken on the aspect of a fortress. Air-raid shelters had been built and the dungeons had been made bomb-proof, flower-beds had been turned into vegetable gardens, anti-aircraft guns had been sited at the foot of the castle slopes, black-out material hung in folds above hundreds of windows, stores contained food sufficient for several weeks of isolation, evacuees from London arrived to occupy houses in the Park and troops practised their drill in the quadrangle and were instructed in their duties as escort in case it became necessary to take the Princesses away to a place of greater safety. Queen Mary thought it sounded 'so depressing' that she decided to remain at Badminton; so the two young girls were usually the only members of the royal family at Windsor during the daytime throughout most of the war. Occasionally their lessons would be interrupted by fire practice, or an hour of instruction in the art of bomb disposal, or a run across the East Terrace towards the cover of the slit trenches in the park. At week-ends sometimes their parents would spend a day with them and they would go for a walk together; and their father, wearing the civilian clothes he never wore in London, would look less tired and tense. Each Christmas they helped to write a pantomime which was performed by themselves and the children of the household and staff in the Waterloo Chamber, from which all the portraits had been removed; and one year they took part in a nativity play performed by the children of the Windsor tenants, and the King, overcome with emotion, confessed that he 'wept through most of it'.

Princess Elizabeth was a happy, though serious and well-mannered child, less lively and more obedient than her sister Margaret Rose. She showed no marked intellectual capacity, nor any evidence of a strong or original imagination. Her mother, who had planned and directed her education, and who had herself taught her to read, had not, indeed, placed any particular emphasis on strictly intellectual disciplines or upon the development of a creative imagination. She had been content to see her daughter's academic studies play no greater part in her upbringing than other pursuits which she considered of equal or of greater importance. To spend as long as possible in the open air, to enjoy to the full the pleasures of the country, to be able to dance and draw and appreciate music, to 'acquire good manners and perfect deportment, and to cultivate all the distinctively feminine graces' were all activities and aspirations which the Duchess believed more essential to her daughters' education than mere book-learning. So that when it became apparent that Princess Elizabeth 'would never progress beyond the simplest elements of mathematics', for example, 'it did not worry the Duchess at all.'

But although she never did master mathematics, Princess Elizabeth's academic attainments were not otherwise unduly disappointing. She showed no precocious enthusiasm for study; there were subjects — German was one of them — in which she could make no headway; but she had a good memory and a careful, orderly and conscientious mind. That it was a mind more receptive than creative was considered no disadvantage in a girl who one day soon might be Queen.

As Queen her conscientiousness has been undeniable. Even during the Ascot meeting the red leather-covered dispatch boxes arrive daily at Windsor station, except on Monday, and their contents must be examined and approved. It is not difficult for her to be conscientious, though, for she enjoys her work and the satisfaction of being so privileged a spectator of the secret movements within the corridors of power.

She gets up early and after breakfast she looks at the newspapers which have been previously read by the private secretaries who have marked or cut out items likely to be of importance or interest to her. She reads these items with close attention. If Parliament is sitting she then reads the report on the previous day's proceedings, which it is the duty of the Vice-Chamberlain of the household to write for her.

There is then her correspondence to attend to. She receives an immense number of letters every day, most of them from complete strangers, and all of them are answered 'even those from manifest lunatics'. Those from friends and, when she has time, those from acquaintances, she answers herself in her own hand, addressing the envelopes also, which accordingly have to be delivered by messenger or sent by registered post to avoid giving temptation to an inquisitive Post Office worker. After the letters have been answered, the work on the dispatch boxes begins and when this has been done, she may — if she has no outside engagements — receive the first of her visitors or sit for one of those portraits which are constantly required by her subjects at home and abroad. Frequently an artist is staying at the castle painting a picture commissioned for an embassy, a high commissioner's office, a governor-general's house, a service headquarters or a

Elizabeth II, the Duke of Edinburgh, Prince Andrew and Prince Edward.

charitable institution under royal patronage; frequently a photographer arrives to satisfy the demand of an apparently insatiable public appetite for new pictures of the Queen; and frequently a dressmaker calls in an endeavour to ensure that Her Majesty's clothes are as discreetly fashionable and as varied as they are expected to be.

Her working days at Windsor are as carefully planned as those on which her public duties are performed. Having an orderly mind and a taste for regularity, she dislikes the unexpected. 'She is a planner,' one of her less fulsome biographers has written of her, 'a hard worker, sometimes a worrier . . . she is conscientious, perhaps even over-conscientious.'

Her conception of the privileges, duties and responsibilities of queenship, as well as the inhibitions of an essentially shy and reserved nature, have made it difficult for her to make many intimate friendships or to feel at ease with people whom she does not know well. She has not, after all, had much opportunity of learning how to live or behave with people outside her own family or household. Parties with the children of the Windsor staff and tenants, afternoons with Girl Guides, even an N.C.O.'s course at the Mechanical Training Centre at Aldershot at the end of the war when she was granted an honorary commission in the Auxiliary Territorial Service, cannot have taught her much about the lives and reactions, attitudes and behaviour of people who would have treated her as an ordinary woman rather than as a special Princess.

Sensitive to criticism, real, implied or imagined, she can appear both haughty and censorious when she is in fact merely unsure of herself or of her effect on others. She sets extremely high standards for her own conduct and expects high standards in those whose work brings them into contact with her. She has almost as inflexible notions of what is good and what is bad as her great-great-grandmother Queen Victoria had; and she is as capable as she was — and, for that matter, as her great-grandfather Edward VII, her grandfather George V and her father all were — of outbursts of sudden anger and moods of sulky irritation. She cannot, of course, be expected to have as much sympathy, understanding, consideration and tolerance as her more recklessly enthusiastic champions claim for her; but she does possess all these virtues in some degree and of her courage, determination, constancy, balance and sincerity there can be no doubt or argument. She is not a clever or a quick-witted woman; she does not pretend to any deep love of art; she prefers watching television to reading books, and gets her knowledge of the world from people; her vision is sometimes impeded by an inordinate regard for detail. And yet, despite these limitations, she is a highly successful queen, her success being due as much to her own character as to the British view of monarchy itself or to the help which she has received from her husband.

When he was a schoolboy Prince Philip's headmaster remarked upon his 'most noticeable' qualities of leadership, though these, he added, were 'marred at times by impatience and intolerance'. These

Windsor Castle, by the Duke of Edinburgh.

qualities and these limitations are still evident in his character now; and yet the limitations can be interpreted as virtues in the kind of public personality he has created for himself. He has an obvious 'enthusiasm for all that is energetic, progressive and masculine in the nation's life and work, especially in industry, technology and sport'. He is outspoken, so self-confident that he is sometimes accused of arrogance, intelligent, adventurous and virile. He can be both rude and irritable, for he has no patience with people who do not interest him and with things which he believes should not interest others. A man of high and varied talents and of formidable vigour, he is at once a stimulus and a provocation.

'When he asks questions,' his cousin the former Queen of Yugoslavia has written of him, 'and he asks questions everywhere, they are no longer the discreet, harmless little inquiries so long murmured by royalty, but questions both pointed and pertinent.' They are also frequently and intentionally challenging, and an evasive or muddled answer may well be greeted with ill-concealed disdain. It can be said, though, that he has some right to show this disdain, for he takes the trouble to discover what questions will be most difficult to answer and most worthwhile considering. And although his emphatic opinions sometimes lead him to make assertions which are highly controversial, he usually briefs himself thoroughly and, having done so, he has the capacity to acquit himself well.

'Good God,' George V exclaimed when his eldest son told him he had accepted an invitation to talk to the British Association, 'you evidently don't seem to realize, my dear boy, what you've taken on. Don't you know who these people are . . . Your audience will represent the most formidable brains in the country. The last member of the family, indeed the only one, who ever felt equal to the task was your great-grandfather, the Prince Consort, *and he was an intellectual.*'

The Duke of Edinburgh would not, of course, care to consider himself an intellectual, but *his* address to the British Association was remarkably successful, and indicated well the sort of leadership which he, apparently, would like to see the monarchy give. This leadership, he is given the credit of believing, cannot be achieved if the royal family is overwhelmed by the kind of adulation that began to threaten its whole existence at the time of the Queen's coronation. And the steps, short and hesitant though they be, towards a more acceptable presentation of the monarchy are supposed to have been taken along a path mapped out in accordance with his suggestions.

The monarchy remains, however, as the Duke himself has been happy to admit, an essentially 'old-fashioned institution'. And Windsor Castle remains a symbol of its strength and permanence, its ancient traditions and history.

Of that history there are mementoes everywhere at Windsor; and it is impossible not to be moved by them – the stone figures of Edward III and the Black Prince in their niches beside the high arched window of the State Entrance, the exquisite iron gates in St George's Chapel behind which Edward IV lies buried, the oriel above them that Henry VIII built for Catherine of Aragon whose pomegranate badge it bears, the windows of so many periods overlooking the North Terrace where Queen Elizabeth I took her hurried walks, the French banner in the Queen's Guard Chamber still rendered annually by the Dukes of Marlborough as token rent for the royal park of Woodstock and the palace of Blenheim.

Each object, each picture, each room calls forth the past from its shadow. And seen again is Queen Anne sitting at the oriel window where she was given the news of the first Duke of Marlborough's great victory in 1704; and George III's good-looking daughters running across the garden of Queen's Lodge in their full, white dresses and their enormous hats; and their father trotting down Castle Hill with Colonel Goldsworthy panting after him; and their mother sitting in her room, worrying and frowning and sniffing snuff; and their eldest brother crying in his cups; and their other brother making his rambling speeches and going to sleep in his chair; and Queen Victoria dancing under the chandeliers and looking up happily into her husband's blue and anxious eyes, and hobbling, years later, down the long corridors in her black clothes and shiny black boots; and her eldest son marching up the stairs with Caesar at his heels, his hat on his head, a huge cigar in his mouth; and George V looking out of a window and criticizing the behaviour of the young in his loud, alarming voice; and the Prince of Wales, in his starched Eton collar, wheeling his brothers about on the steps of the library; and George VI, pale and drawn, watching his daughters act in a play with tears in his tired eyes. And behind them all and around them all is the Castle itself, warmed by the sun and washed by the rain, massive and immutable throughout the passing years.

Windsor Castle today.

BIBLIOGRAPHY

AGA KHAN, *The Memoirs of Aga Khan* (1954)

AIRLIE, Mabel, Countess of, *Thatched with Gold*, Ed. Jennifer Ellis (1962)

ALLEN, W. Gore, *King William IV* (1960)

ANSTIS, John, *Register of the Order of the Garter* (1724)

APPLEBY, John T., *Henry II* (1962)

APPLEBY, John T., *John, King of England* (1959)

D'ARBLAY: Charlotte Barrett (Ed.), *Diary and Letters of Madame D'Arblay, 1778–1840* (1904)

ARBUTHNOT: Francis Bamford, and the Duke of Wellington (Eds.), *The Journal of Mrs Arbuthnot* (1950)

ARTHUR, Sir George, *King George V* (1934)

ARTHUR, Sir George, *Queen Mary* (1935)

ASHMOLE, Elias, *The Institution, Laws and Ceremonies of the Most Noble Order of the Garter* (1672)

ASQUITH, Cynthia, *The Family Life of Her Majesty Queen Elizabeth* (n.d.)

ASQUITH, Cyril, and Spender, J. A., *The Life of Herbert Henry Asquith* (1932)

AUCKLAND, William Eden, 1st Baron Auckland, *Journal and Correspondence* (1861–2)

BABEES BOOK: F. J. Furnivall (Ed.), *The Babees Book* (1868)

BAGLEY, J. J., *Henry VIII* (1962)

BALSAN, Consuelo Vanderbilt, *The Glitter and the Gold* (1953)

BARLOW, Frank, *The Feudal Kingdom of England* (1961)

BECKINGSDALE, B. W., *Elizabeth I* (1963)

BELL, G. K. A., *Randall Davidson* (1955)

BELLOC, Hilaire, *Charles I* (1933)

BELTZ, G. F., *Memorials of the Order of the Garter* (1841)

BENSON, E. F., *King Edward VII* (1933)

BENSON, E. F., *Queen Victoria* (1935)

BLACK, Sister Catherine, *King's Nurse, Beggar's Nurse* (n.d.)

BLOOMFIELD, Georgiana, Baroness, *Reminiscences of Court and Diplomatic Life* (1883)

BOLITHO, Hector, *Albert the Good* (1932)

BOLITHO, Hector, *George VI* (1937)

BOLITHO, Hector, *King Edward VIII* (1937)

BOLITHO, Hector, *My Restless Years* (1962)

BOLITHO, Hector, *The Reign of Queen Victoria* (1949)

BOLITHO, Hector, *The Romance of Windsor Castle* (1947)

BOORDE, Andrew, *Scoggins Jests* (1626)

BOSWELL, James, *The Life of Samuel Johnson* (Everyman's Library, 1920)

BRAMSTON, *The Autobiography of Sir John Bramston* (1845)

BRETT, A. C. A., *Charles II and His Court* (1910)

BROOKE, Christopher, *The Saxon and Norman Kings* (1963)

BROWN, Ivor, *Balmoral* (1955)

BROWN, *The Diary of Miss Margaretta Brown* (Extracts printed in *Etoniana* and in *Report of the Society of the Friends of St George*, 1960, by Olwen Hedley in 'Court and Chapel 1760–1873')

BRYANT, Sir Arthur, *Charles II* (1955)

BRYANT, Sir Arthur, *George V* (1936)

BUCKINGHAM, Richard, Duke of Buckingham and Chandos, *Memoirs of the Courts and Cabinets of George III* (1853–5)

BUCKINGHAM, Richard, Duke of Buckingham and Chandos, *Memoirs of the Courts and Cabinets of William IV and Victoria* (1861)

BULSTRODE, Sir Richard, *Memoirs and Recollections* (1721)

BURNET, Osmond Airy (Ed.), *Burnet's History of My Own Times* (1897)

BURNEY: Madame D'Arblay, *The Life of Charles Burney* (1832)

BURTON, *The Diary of Thomas Burton* (1828)

BURY, Lady Charlotte, *Diary of a Lady-in-Waiting* (1908)

BUXTON, Aubrey, *The King in His Country* (1955)

CAVENDISH, Mary Charlotte, *The Biography of Queen Mary* (1930)

CECIL, Lord David, *Melbourne* (Reprint Society, 1955)

CHAMBERS, E. K., *The Elizabethan Stage* (1923)

CHAMBERS, R. W. (Ed.), *A 15th Century Courtesy Book* (1914)

CHAPMAN, Hester W., *The Last Tudor King* (Cape, 1961)

CHATEAUBRIAND, *Mémoires D'outre Tombe* (1949)

CHURCHILL, Randolph, *They Serve the Queen* (1953)

CHURCHILL, Randolph, *Lord Derby, 'King of Lancashire'* (1960)

CHURCHILL, Winston S., *Lord Randolph Churchill* (1906)

CHURCHILL, Winston S., *My Early Life* (1930)

CLARENDON, Edward, Earl of, *The History of the Rebellion and Civil Wars in England* (1888)

CLYNES, J. R., *Memoirs* (1937)

COBBIN, Ingram, *Georgiana* (1820)

COLCHESTER, Charles, Lord (Ed.), *The Diary and Correspondence of Charles Abbot, Lord Colchester* (1861)

CONNELL, Neville, *Queen Anne* (1937)

COOPER, Diana, *The Light of Common Day* (1959)

CORBITT, F. J., *Fit for a King* (1956)

COULTON, G. G., *Medieval Panorama* (1947)

COUNTY HISTORY: P. H. Ditchfield and William Page (Eds.), *The Victoria History of the Counties of Britain*, Vol. 3 (1923)

COWLES, Virginia, *Edward VII and His Circle* (1956)

CRAWFORD, Raymond, *The Last Days of Charles II* (1909)

CREEVEY, John Gore (Ed.), *Creevey* (John Murray, 1948)

CREIGHTON, Mandell, *Queen Elizabeth* (1896)

CROKER: Louis J. Jennings (Ed.), *The Croker Papers* (1885)

CURZON, The Marchioness Curzon of Kedleston, *Reminiscences* (1955)

CUST, Sir Lionel, *King Edward VII and his Court* (1930)

DELANY: Lady Llanover (Ed.), *The Autobiography and Correspondence of Mary Granville, Mrs Delany* (1862)

DORAN, John, *Court Fools* (1858)

DRINKWATER, John, *Mr Charles, King of England* (1926)

DUFF, David, *The Shy Princess* (1958)

DUTTON, Ralph, *English Court Life* (1963)

ECKARDSTEIN, Baron von, *Ten Years at the Court of St James's* (1921)

EDINGER, George, *Rupert of the Rhine* (1936)

EDWARD VII: *The Private Life of the King. By One of His Majesty's Servants* (1901)

ELDON: Horace Twiss, *The Public and Private Life of Lord Chancellor Eldon* (1844)

ELPHINSTONE: M. H. MacClintock, *The Queen Thanks Sir Howard* (1945)

ERSKINE, Mrs Steuart (Ed.), *Twenty Years at Court: From the Correspondence of the Hon. Eleanor Stanley* (1916)

ESHER: Maurice V. Brett (Ed.), *The Journals and Letters of Reginald, Viscount Esher* (1934)

ESHER, Reginald, Viscount, *Cloud Capp'd Towers* (1927)

EVELYN: *The Diary of John Evelyn* (Everyman's Library, 1945)

EYTON, R. W., *Court, Household and Itinerary of Henry II* (1878)

FELLOWES, Edmund H., *The Knights of the Garter, 1348–1939* (n.d.)

FIENNES: Christopher Morris (Ed.), *The Journeys of Celia Fiennes* (1949)

FITZGERALD, Percy, *The Life and Times of William IV* (1884)

FRAMPTON, *The Journal of Mary Frampton* (1885)

FREEMAN, Edward A., *The History of the Norman Conquest of England* (1876)

FRERE, J. A., *The British Monarchy at Home* (1963)

FULFORD, Roger, *The Prince Consort* (1949)

FULFORD, Roger, *The Royal Dukes* (1933)

FULFORD, Roger, *George IV* (1949)

FULFORD, Roger, *Hanover to Windsor* (1960)

FULFORD, Roger (Ed.), *The Autobiography of Miss Knight, Lady Companion to Princess Charlotte* (1960)

FULFORD, Roger, *Queen Victoria* (1951)

FULLER, Thomas, *Church-History of Britain* (1655)

FURNIVALL, F. J. (Ed.), *Manners and Meals in Olden Times* (1867)

GALWAY, Margaret, 'Joan of Kent and the Order of the Garter' (*University of Birmingham Historical Journal*, i, 1947, 13–51)

GARDINER, S. R., *History of England 1603–1642* (1883–4)

GASH, Norman, *Mr Secretary Peel* (1961)

GEORGE III: The Hon. Sir John Fortescue (Ed.), *The Correspondence of George III* (1928)

GEORGE IV: Arthur Aspinall (Ed.), *The Correspondence of King George IV* (1938)

GIBB, M. A., *Buckingham 1592–1628* (1939)

GODDARD, Arthur, *Windsor: The Castle of Our Kings* (1911)

GOODMAN, Dr Godfrey, *The Court of King James I* (1839)

GORE, John, *King George V: A Personal Memoir* (1941)

GRAMMONT: Anthony Hamilton, *Memoirs of the Court of Charles II by Count Grammont* (1846)

GREEN, Mrs J. R., *Henry II* (1888)

GREVILLE: Lytton Strachey and Roger Fulford (Eds.), *The Greville Memoirs, 1814–1860* (1938)

GREVILLE, Fulke: F. McKno Bladon (Ed.), *The Diaries of Colonel the Hon. Fulke Greville* (1930)

GREY, General Charles, *The Early Years of the Prince Consort* (1867)

HALDANE, Richard Burdon, *An Autobiography* (1929)

HALL, Hubert, *Court Life Under the Plantagenets* (1890)

HAMILTON, Lady Anne, *Secret History of the Court of England* (1903)

HARDINGE, Helen, *The Path of Kings* (1952)

HARE, Augustus, *The Story of My Life* (1896–1900)

HARINGTON: Thomas Park (Ed.), *Sir John Harington's Nugae Antiquae* (1804)

HARVEY, John, *The Plantagenets* (1948)

HARWOOD, T. Eustace, *Windsor Old and New* (1929)

HASSALL, W. O., *How They Lived* (1962)

HEDLEY, Olwen, 'Court and Chapel, 1760–1873', *Report of the Society of the Friends of St George* (1960)

HENRY, *Letters and Diaries of Philip Henry* (1882)

HENTZNER, Paul, *A Journey into England in the Year 1598* (1759)

HERVEY, Lord, *Some Materials for the Memoirs of the Reign of George II*, Ed. Romney Sedgwick (1931)

HEYLIN, Peter, *Cosmographie and Historie of the Whole World* (1652)

HILL, B. J. W., *Windsor and Eton* (1957)

HODDER, Edwin (Ed.), *The Life and Work of the 7th Earl of Shaftesbury* (1886)

HOLT, Edward, *The Public and Domestic Life of George III* (1820)

HOPE, W. H. St John, *Windsor Castle* (1913)

HOPKINSON, M. R., *Anne of England* (1934)

HOPKIRK, Mary, *Queen Adelaide* (1950)

HUGHES, G. M., *A History of Windsor Forest, Sunninghill and the Great Park* (1890)

HUISH, Robert, *Memoirs of George III* (1821)

HUISH, Robert, *Memoirs of George IV* (1830)

HUTCHINSON, Lucy, *Memoir of the Life of Colonel Hutchinson*, Ed. C. H. Firth (1896)

IREMONGER, Lucille, *Love and the Princess* (1958)

JENKINS, Elizabeth, *Elizabeth the Great* (1958)

JENKINS, Roy, *Sir Charles Dilke* (1958)

JERNINGHAM LETTERS: Egerton Castle (Ed.), *The Jerningham Letters* (1896)

JERROLD, Clare, *The Married Life of Queen Victoria* (1913)

JERROLD, Clare, *The Widowhood of Queen Victoria* (1916)

JESSE, J. H., *Memoirs of the Court of England during the Reign of the Stuarts* (1901)

JESSE, J. H., *Continuation of Memoirs of the Court of England from the Revolution in 1688 to the Death of George II* (1901)

JESSE, J. H., *Memoirs of the Life and Reign of King George III* (1901)

JOHN, Evan, *King Charles I* (1933)

KENDALL, Paul Murray, *The Yorkist Age* (1962)

KENYON, J. P., *The Stuarts* (1958)

KINGSFORD, R. L., *English Historical Literature* (1913)

KNIGHT, Charles, *A Volume of Varieties* (1844)

KNIGHT, Charles, *Passages of a Working Life* (1864)

LAIRD, Dorothy, *How the Queen Reigns* (1959)

LEE, Sir Sidney, *King Edward VII* (1925)

LEGGE, Edward, *King Edward in His True Colours* (1912)

LEGGE, Edward, *More About King Edward* (1913)

LESLIE, Sir Shane, *George IV* (1926)

LEWINSOHN, Richard, *A History of Sexual Customs* (1958)

LIEVEN: Peter Quennell (Ed.), *The Private Letters of Princess Lieven to Prince Metternich 1820–1826* (1948)

LONGFORD, Elizabeth, *Victoria R. I.* (1964)

LONGMAN, William, *The History of the Life and Times of Edward III* (1869)

LYTTELTON: The Hon. Mrs Hugh Wyndham (Ed.), *The Correspondence of Sarah Spencer, Lady Lyttelton* (1912)

LYTTON: Mary Lutyens (Ed.), *Lady Lytton's Court Diary* (1961)

MACAULAY, Lord, *The History of England* (1914)

MACKINNON, James, *The History of Edward III* (1900)

MADDEN, Frederick, *Privy Purse Expenses of the Princess Mary* (1831)

MAGNUS, Philip, *King Edward the Seventh* (1964)

MALMESBURY, 3rd Earl of (Ed.), *The Diary and Correspondence of James Harris, 1st Earl of Malmesbury* (1844)

MANCHESTER: Duke of (Ed.), *Court and Society from Elizabeth to Anne: from the Papers at Kimbolton* (1864)

MANCHESTER: A. L. Kennedy (Ed.), *'My Dear Duchess': Social and Political Letters to the Duchess of Manchester* (1956)

MARIE LOUISE, Princess, *My Memoirs of Six Reigns* (1956)

MARLBOROUGH, *An Account of the Conduct of the Duchess of Marlborough* (1742)

MARTIN, Kingsley, *The Crown and the Establishment* (1963)

MARTIN, Theodore, *The Life of H.R.H. The Prince Consort* (1875–80)

MARTIN, Theodore, *Queen Victoria as I Knew Her* (1908)

MASSEY, William, *History of England during the Reign of George III* (1855–63)

MATHEWS, David, *The Age of Charles I* (1951)

MCELWEE, William, *The Wisest Fool in Christendom* (1958)

MCKISACK, G. May, *The Fourteenth Century* (1959)

MELVILLE, Lewis, *Farmer George* (1907)

MERSEY, Viscount, *A Picture of Life 1872–1940* (1941)

MOLLOY, J. Fitzgerald, *Court Life Below Stairs or London under the First George, 1714–1760* (1882) *and under the Last Georges, 1760–1830* (1883)

MORE, *Hannah More's Memoirs* (1834)

MORGAN, E. B. (Ed.), *Readings in English Social History* (1923)

MORRAH, Dermot, *The Work of the Queen* (1958)

MORRIS, Christopher, *The Tudors* (1955)

MORSHEAD, Sir Owen, *Windsor Castle* (1957)

MURRAY, Margaret, *The Divine King in England* (1954)

MURRAY, Margaret, *The God of the Witches* (1952)

MYERS, A. R., *The Household of Edward IV* (1959)

NEALE, J. E., *Queen Elizabeth I* (1934)

NICHOLS, J. G., *The Literary Remains of Edward VI* (1859)

NICHOLS, John, *A Collection of Ordinances . . . from Edward III to William and Mary* (1790)

NICHOLS, John, *The Progresses and Public Travels of Queen Elizabeth* (1788)

NICHOLS, John, *Recollections and Reflections* (1822)

NICOLAS, Sir Harris, *History of the Orders of Knighthood* (1841–2)

NICOLSON, Sir Harold, *King George V: His Life and Reign* (1952)

NORGATE, Kate, *England Under the Angevin Kings* (1887)

OGG, David, *William III* (1956)

OGLANDER, *A Royalist's Notebook: The Commonplace Book of Sir John Oglander* (1936)

OMAN, Sir Charles, *The Great Revolt* (1906)

ORMANTHWAITE, Lord, *When I was at Court* (1937)

OSBORNE, Francis, *Historical Memoirs* (1658)

OXFORD: Margot Asquith, *More Memoirs* (1933)

PAINTER, Sidney, *The Reign of King John* (1949)

PAPENDIEK: Mrs Vernon Delves Broughton (Ed.), *Court and Private Life in the Time of Queen Charlotte: The Journals of Mrs Papendiek* (1887)

PARKER, Charles Stuart, *Sir Robert Peel* (1899)

PEPYS, *Diary of Samuel Pepys* (Everyman's Library, 1923)

PETRIE, Sir Charles, *The Stuarts* (1958)

PICKERING, Anna Maria Wilhelmina, *Memoirs* (1903)

PLUMB, J. H., *The First Four Georges* (1956)

PONSONBY, Arthur, *Henry Ponsonby: His Life from His Letters* (1942)

PONSONBY, Sir Frederick, *Recollections of Three Reigns* (1957)

PONSONBY, Sir Frederick, *Sidelights on Queen Victoria* (1930)

POOLE, Austin Lane (Ed.), *Medieval England* (1958)

POPE HENNESSY, James, *Queen Mary 1867–1953* (1959)

PORTLAND, Duke of, *Men, Women and Things* (1937)

POTE, Joseph, *The History and Antiquities of Windsor Castle* (1749)

POWICKE, Sir Maurice, *The 13th Century* (1962)

POYNTER, Ambrose, 'An Essay on the History and Antiquities of Windsor Castle' in *Illustrations of Windsor Castle* by Sir Jeffrey Wyatville (1841)

PRESCOTT, H. F. M., *Mary Tudor* (1953)

PRINCE PHILIP: Her Majesty Queen Alexandra of Yugoslavia, *Prince Philip: A Family Portrait* (1960)

PRINCESS CHARLOTTE: Arthur Aspinall (Ed.), *Letters of Princess Charlotte* (1949)

PYNE, W. H., *The History of the Royal Residences* (1819)

RERESBY: Andrew Browning (Ed.), *Memoirs of Sir John Reresby* (1936)

RIBBLESDALE, Lord, *Impressions and Memoirs* (1927)

RICHARDSON, Joanna, *The Disastrous Marriage* (1960)

ROOSEVELT, Eleanor, *On My Own* (1959)

ROOSEVELT, James and Sidney Shalett, *Affectionately F.D.R.* (1960)

ROPER, Lanning, *The Gardens in the Royal Park at Windsor* (1959)

ROSE, George, *Diaries and Correspondence* (1860)

ROSE, J. H., *Life of Pitt* (1923)

ROSEBERY: The Marquess of Crewe, *Lord Rosebery* (1931)

ROWSE, A. L., *The Early Churchills* (1956)

ROWSE, A. L., *The England of Elizabeth* (1950)

SALTER, E. G., *Tudor England Through Venetian Eyes* (1930)

SANDERS, I. J., *Feudal Military Service in England* (1956)

SANDFORD, Francis, *Genealogical History* (1707)

SOMERVELL, D. C., *The Reign of King George V* (1935)

SOMNER, Dudley, *Haldane of Cloan: His Life and Times, 1856–1928* (1960)

STANLEY: The Dean of Windsor and Hector Bolitho (Eds.), *The Letters of Lady Augusta Stanley* (1927)

STOCKMAR, Baron E. von, *Memoirs of Baron Stockmar* (1872)

STRACHEY, Lytton, *Queen Victoria* (Zephyr Books, 1945)

STRUTT, Joseph, *The Sports and Pastimes of the People of England* (1845)

STRYPE, *Ecclesiastical Memorials* (1721)

STUART, D. M., *The Daughters of George III* (1939)

SWIFT, Jonathan, *Journal to Stella*, Ed. Harold Williams (1948)

SYKES, Christopher, *Four Studies in Loyalty* (1946)

TAYLOR, Sir Herbert, *The Taylor Papers: Being a Record of Certain Reminiscences, Letters and Journals* (1913)

TAYLOR, Joseph, *Relics of Royalty: Or Remarks, Anecdotes and Amusements of George III* (1820)

THACKERAY, W. M., *The Four Georges* (1861)

THOMS, William J., *The Book of the Court* (1838)

THORNLEY, Isobel D., *England Under the Yorkists* (1920)

TIGHE, Robert Richard, and Davis, James Edward, *Annals of Windsor, Being a History of the Castle and Town* (1858)

TOOLEY, Sarah A., *The Personal Life of Queen Victoria* (1901)

TRENCH, Charles Chevenix, *The Royal Malady* (1964)

TREVELYAN, Sir George Otto, *The Life and Letters of Lord Macaulay* (1908)

TRUMAN, Harry S., *Year of Decisions* (1955)

TURNER, E. S., *The Court of St James's* (1959)

TURNER, F. C., *James II* (1948)

VICKERS, Kenneth H., *England in the Later Middle Ages* (1926)

VICTORIA: *The Private Life of the Queen. By One of Her Majesty's Servants* (1897)

VICTORIA: *Queen Victoria: Leaves from a Journal* with an introduction by Raymond Mortimer (1961)

VICTORIA: A. C. Benson and Viscount Esher (Eds.), *The Letters of Queen Victoria* (1908)

VICTORIA OF PRUSSIA: James Pope-Hennessy (Ed.), *Queen Victoria at Windsor and Balmoral: Letters from her granddaughter* (1959)

VILLIERS, George, *A Vanished Victorian* (1938)

VULLIAMY, C. E., *Aspasia: The Life and Letters of Mary Granville, Mrs Delany, 1700–1788* (1937)

VULLIAMY, C. E., *Royal George* (1937)

WALDEGRAVE, James, Earl Waldegrave, *Memoirs from 1754–1758* (1821)

WALPOLE, Horace, *Memoirs of the Reign of George III* (1894)

WALPOLE: W. S. Lewis (Ed.), *Correspondence of Horace Walpole* (1937–)

WARREN, W. L., *King John* (1961)

WATSON, Vera, *The Queen at Home* (1952)

WEDGWOOD, C. V., *The King's Peace 1637–1641* (1955)

WELDON, Anthony, *The Court and Character of King James* (1651)

WHEELER BENNETT, Sir John, *King George VI* (1958)

WILKINSON, Clennell, *Prince Rupert* (1934)

WILLIAMS, Charles, *James I* (1951)

WILLSON, D. Harris, *King James VI and I* (1956)

WINANT, John, *A Letter from Grosvenor Square* (1947)

WINDSOR: *A King's Story: The Memoirs of H.R.H. The Duke of Windsor* (1951)

WINDSOR, The Duke of, *A Family Album* (1960)

WITHERS, Philip, *History of the Royal Malady: Variety of Entertaining Anecdotes. By a Page of the Presence* (1789)

WOODWARD, Kathleen, *Queen Mary* (1927)

WORTHAM, H. E., *Edward VII* (1933)

WOTTON: L. Pearsall Smith, *Life and Letters of Sir Henry Wotton* (1907)

WRAXALL: H. B. Wheatley (Ed.), *The Historical and Posthumous Memoirs of Sir Nathaniel William Wraxall, 1772–1784* (1884)

WYNN, A. Hayward (Ed.), *Diaries of a Lady of Quality* (1864)

Since this book was first published there have appeared several fresh royal biographies including those of William the Conqueror (David C. Douglas); Henry II (W.L. Warren); Edward IV (Charles Ross and Mary Clive); Henry VI (Bertram Wolfe); Henry VII (M. Van Cleave Alexander); Henry VIII (John Bowle, J.J. Scarisbrick, Neville Williams and Lacey Baldwin Smith); Anne Boleyn (Hester Chapman); Elizabeth I (Neville Williams and Paul Johnson); Mary Queen of Scots (Antonia Fraser); James I (David Mathew and Caroline Bingham); Charles I (John Bowle); Charles II (Maurice Ashley); James II (Jock Haswell); William and Mary (Nesta Robb, Henn and Barbara van der Zee and Elizabeth Hamilton); Anne (David Green and Edward Gregg); George I (Ragnheld Hatton); George II (Charles Chenevix-Trench); George III (Stanley Ayling and John Brooke); Queen Charlotte (Olwen Hedley); George IV (Joanna Richardson and Christopher Hibbert); Princess Charlotte (Thea Holme); William IV (Philip Ziegler); Victoria (Elizabeth Longford and Cecil Woodham-Smith); Edward VII (Philip Magnus, Gordon Brook-Shepherd, Christopher Hibbert and Giles St Aubyn); Queen Alexandra (Georgina Battiscombe); Edward VIII (Frances Donaldson). Messrs Eyre & Spottiswoode (Associated Book Publishers Ltd.) are publishing a series of biographies of English monarchs under the editorship of David C. Douglas; and Messrs Weidenfeld & Nicolson have published a series of shorter, illustrated biographies edited by Antonia Fraser.

LIST OF ILLUSTRATIONS

Black-and-white plates

Page 8. The earliest known drawing of the castle (Courtesy the Provost and Fellows of Eton. Photo: Courtauld Institute, London)

11. Probable arrangement of the Norman earthwork

14. Edward III and the first Knights of the Garter from Elias Ashmole, *Institutions of the Garter*, 1672 (Photo: R. Meredith)

19. Edward III c. 1378 (Dean and Chapter of Westminster)

21. The Regalia of the Garter from Elias Ashmole, *Institutions of the Garter*, 1672 (Photo: R. Meredith)

23. Pilgrims' badges (The British Museum)

24. The Gilbertus Door in St George's Chapel (Dean and Canons of Windsor)

28. Choir stall plate (Dean and Canons of Windsor)

31. Misericord (Dean and Canons of Windsor)

32. Grave of Edward IV (Society of Antiquaries of London. Photo: John Freeman & Co.)

35. Roof of St George's Chapel (Photo: A. F. Kersting)

37. Henry VIII and the Knights of the Garter, 1534 (Dean and Canons of Windsor)

39. Henry VIII (Mary Evans Picture Library)

44. Queen Elizabeth and her sword-bearer, 1578 (The British Museum)

47. Bird's-eye view of the castle, 1607 (The British Museum)

49. James I by Hoskins (Radio Times Hulton Picture Library)

53. George Villiers, 1st Duke of Buckingham, after Cornelius Janssen (Mary Evans Picture Library)

61. Charles II from Elias Ashmole, *Institutions of the Garter*, 1672 (Photo: R. Meredith)

63. The Knights of the Garter by Wenceslaus Hollar (Radio Times Hulton Picture Library)

65. Windsor Castle by Wenceslaus Hollar (National Trust, Anglesey Abbey)

65. Windsor Castle by Wenceslaus Hollar (The Mansell Collection)

67. Bird's-eye view and prospect of the castle by Wenceslaus Hollar, c. 1670 (Radio Times Hulton Picture Library)

68. The Upper and Lower Wards by Wenceslaus Hollar (Radio Times Hulton Picture Library)

69. The castle by John Wijck, c. 1680 (National Trust, Anglesey Abbey, Fairhaven Collection)

70–71. Ceilings in the State Apartments by Antonio Verrio (The British Museum and Her Majesty the Queen)

72. A carved surround by Grinling Gibbons (Her Majesty the Queen)

75. Nell Gwynn by Sir Peter Lely (National Portrait Gallery)

76. St George's Chapel from Elias Ashmole, *Institutions of the Garter*, 1672 (Photo: R. Meredith)

81. The castle by Leonard Knyff, c. 1708 (Her Majesty the Queen)

83. Queen Anne, after Godfrey Kneller (Mary Evans Picture Library)

84. Sarah, Duchess of Marlborough, after Kneller (Mary Evans Picture Library)

85. Burford House, Windsor, after Leonard Knyff (The Mansell Collection)

87. The North Terrace by Paul Sandby (Her Majesty the Queen)

88. View across the Park in the eighteenth century (Her Majesty the Queen)

91. Windsor Great Park by Benjamin West (Her Majesty the Queen)

92. Queen's Lodge, after George Robertson, 1783 (John Freeman & Co.)

94. Fanny Burney by E. F. Burney (National Portrait Gallery)

97. George III by Peter Edward Stroehling (Her Majesty the Queen)

101. The King's Presence Chamber (Her Majesty the Queen)

103. George III and the royal family (The Mansell Collection)

105. Mrs Delaney by John Opie, c. 1782 (Her Majesty the Queen)

107. North front of the castle by Paul Sandby (The Earl of Stair, National Galleries of Scotland. Photo: Tom Scott)

109. Queen Elizabeth's Gate by Paul Sandby (Her Majesty the Queen)

110. Henry VIII's Gateway by Paul Sandby (Her Majesty the Queen)

110. The South Entrance by Paul Sandby, 1777 (Her Majesty the Queen)

111. The Round Tower and Devil's Tower by Paul Sandby (National Gallery of Victoria, Australia; Felton Bequest, 1922)

111. The Norman Gate by Paul Sandby (Her Majesty the Queen)

115. The Oatlands Stakes, Ascot, by N. N. Sartorius, 1791 (Arthur Ackermann & Sons Ltd)

116. Queen Charlotte by Peter Edward Stroehling (Her Majesty the Queen)

119. George III by R. B. Davis, 1806 (The British Museum)

122. The Hundred Steps by Paul Sandby (Her Majesty the Queen)

125. George IV by John George Paul Fischer, 1820 (Her Majesty the Queen)

126. Memorial to Princess Charlotte by Matthew Cotes Wyatt (Dean and Canons of Windsor)

128. 'The Kettle calling the Pot Ugly Names' by John Marshall (Author's collection)

128. Mrs Fitzherbert by Richard Cosway (The Wallace Collection. Photo: The Mansell Collection)

129. The Royal Lodge (The Mansell Collection)

133. 'A Short Ride in the Long Walk or the Ponies Posed' by William Heath (Author's collection)

136. Design for the east front of the Upper Ward by Sir Robert Smirke (R.I.B.A.)

137. Design for a bridge over the Long Walk by John Nash (R.I.B.A.)

138. The Grand Corridor by Joseph Nash (Her Majesty the Queen)

139. Wyatville's proposals for the Great Drawing Room (Sotheby & Co.)

140. The Duke of Cumberland's 'Mandarine Yacht' (Her Majesty the Queen)

140. A design for a fishing pavilion by Frederick Crace (Cooper-Hewitt Museum of Decorative Arts and Design, Smithsonian Institution)

143. Classical ruins at Virginia Water (Photo: A. F. Kersting)

147. 'State of the Giraffe' by William Heath, 1829 (Author's collection)

147. 'Packing Up' by William Heath, 1830 (Author's collection)

149. St George's Hall by Charles Wild (Her Majesty the Queen)

151. The Old Gateway and Devil's Tower by Joshua Dolby (National Trust, Anglesey Abbey)

161. Detail of Prince Albert in a portrait of Queen Victoria by Herbert I. Smith (The Fishmongers' Company. Photo: C. M. Dixon)

163. Visit of King Louis Philippe to Windsor by Louis Haghe (Her Majesty the Queen)

164. The Riding School by Joseph Nash, 1846 (Her Majesty the Queen)

167. The Upper Ward in the mid-1840s by Joseph Nash (National Trust, Anglesey Abbey)

170. Performance of 'Macbeth' by Louis Haghe (Her Majesty the Queen)

173. Reception of the Emperor and Empress of the French (Her Majesty the Queen)

175. Interior of Prince Albert's Dairy (Eric de Maré)

177. The Blue Room (Her Majesty the Queen)

179. The Royal Mausoleum by H. Ward, 1871 (Her Majesty the Queen)

181. Wedding day photograph of the Prince and Princess of Wales (Her Majesty the Queen)

182. Queen Victoria (Her Majesty the Queen)

184. The Crimson Drawing Room in the 1860s (Her Majesty the Queen)

189. Queen Victoria, 1895 (Her Majesty the Queen)

193. Princess Beatrice and Queen Victoria, 1895 (Her Majesty the Queen)

195. The Queen's funeral procession, 1901 (Her Majesty the Queen)

197. The Prince of Wales, 1857 (Her Majesty the Queen)

199. The Prince and Princess of Wales, 1888 (Her Majesty the Queen)

203. Edward VII's sitting-room (Her Majesty the Queen)

204. Queen Alexandra's sitting-room (Her Majesty the Queen)

209. Edward VII's dog, Caesar (Her Majesty the Queen)

209. Edward VII's bathroom (Her Majesty the Queen)

211. A royal gathering, 1907 (Radio Times Hulton Picture Library)

214. King George V and Queen Mary digging potatoes, 1917 (Her Majesty the Queen)

217. King George V and Queen Mary at Ascot, 1931 (Radio Times Hulton Picture Library)

220. The Prince of Wales in the 1930s (Popperfoto)

223. The Duke of York (later George VI), 1920 (Press Association Ltd)

224. George VI and his family, 1946 (Radio Times Hulton Picture Library)

227. Elizabeth II, the Duke of Edinburgh, Prince Andrew and Prince Edward (Camera Press, London)

229. Windsor Castle by the Duke of Edinburgh (Royal Academy of Arts)

231. Windsor Castle today (Aerofilms Ltd)

Royal coats-of-arms, in chapter headings, reproduced by gracious permission of Her Majesty the Queen.

Colour plates

1. Edward IV. A painting on panel by an unknown artist, probably done from life when the King was about thirty years old (Her Majesty the Queen)

2. A choir stall with plates of the Knights of the Garter (The Dean and Chapter of Windsor)

3. The castle from the north in the reign of James I (National Trust, Anglesey Abbey)

4. The castle from the north in the reign of Charles II by Henry Danckerts (National Trust, Anglesey Abbey)

5. St George's Chapel from the altar by Charles Wild (The Royal Library, Windsor. Her Majesty The Queen)

6. The west end of St George's Chapel by Paul Sandby (The Royal Library, Windsor. Her Majesty The Queen)

7. The summer house by Paul Sandby (The Royal Library, Windsor. Her Majesty The Queen)

8. Roque's survey of Berkshire, 1752 (The British Museum. Photograph: Museum)

9. The castle from the Great Park in the late eighteenth century by Thomas Girton (The National Trust: Anglesey Abbey)

10. The Guard Room in the Round Tower in the early nineteenth century by James Stephanoff (The Royal Library, Windsor. Her Majesty The Queen)

11. The Thames at Windsor by J. M. W. Turner (The National Trust: Petworth House. Photograph: Jeremy Whitaker)

12. The east front of the Upper Ward in January 1824 (The Royal Library, Windsor. Her Majesty The Queen)

13. The proposed alterations to the east front of the Upper Ward (The Royal Library, Windsor. Her Majesty The Queen)

14. Wyatville's designs for the dining room (The Royal Library, Windsor. Her Majesty The Queen)

15. Queen Victoria in the early years of her marriage. A portrait by Herbert L. Smith (The Fishmongers' Company. Photograph: C. M. Dixon)

16. King Louis Philippe leading Queen Victoria into dinner in St George's Hall on 11 October 1844 (The Royal Library, Windsor. Her Majesty The Queen)

17. The interior of the mausoleum at Frogmore by W. Brewer (The Royal Library, Windsor. Her Majesty The Queen)

INDEX

Italicized page numbers refer to pages on which black-and-white photographs appear. Colour photographs are referred to by their plate number.

Aberdeen, Lord (1784–1860), 173
Adam of Hartington, 31
Adams, John (1735–1826), 117
Adelaide, Queen of William IV (1792–1849), appearance, 148; and Windsor Park, 152, 155; relations with William IV, 152, 154
Adolphus of Teck, Prince, 205
Aga Khan, (1877–1957), 192
Airlie, Lady, 215, 216
Albert of Saxe-Coburg-Gotha, Prince (1819–61), Consort of Victoria, *161, 167, 170, 173, 175*; and Victoria's proposal, 160; character, 160, 162, 167–8, 171; and Windsor, 162; gets rid of Baroness Lehzen, 165; organizes the Household, 165–7; his unpopularity, 167–8; as a husband, 171–2, 174–5; last illness and death, 176–8; mausoleum, *179*; and Napoleon III, 184–5; and the Prince of Wales, 196–7, 198
Alexandra, Princess (1844–1925), Queen of Edward VII, *181*, 199, 200; her marriage, 180–81, 201; as Queen, 205; character, 206, 207; and husband, 207; sitting-room, *204*
Alfonso, King (1886–1941), 212
Amelia, Princess (1783–1810), 107; her death, 122–3
Anne (1665–1714), 81, *83*; dislike of William III, 82; her children, 83–4, 86; character and appearance, 83, 84, 87; and her favourites, 84–5; love of hunting, 86; her Court, 86–7; Windsor Castle, 87–8; her death, 89
Anne Boleyn (1507–36), 2nd Queen of Henry VIII, 38
Anne, Queen of Bohemia (1366–94), Queen of Richard II, 26
Anne of Denmark (1574–1619), Queen of James I, 49, 50, 51, 53
Anson, George, 190
Arbuthnot, Charles (1767–1850), 130, 150
Arbuthnot, Mrs, 132, 146
Armstrong, Archie, 56
Arthur, King and the Round Table, 13–14, 17
Ascham, Roger (1515–68), 42
Ascot, 86, 117, 153, 159, 170; Oatlands Stakes, *115*
Ashley, Lord, 169
Ashmole, Elias (1617–92), 19–20, 68
Asquith, Herbert Henry, Earl of Oxford and Asquith (1852–1928), 206
Asquith, Margot (wife of above) (1865–1945), 207, 210

Bachelor, Thomas, 148

Baker, Sir George (1722–1809), and George III's insanity, 108, 112
Balmoral, 174
Baring, Hon. Susan, 190
Beatrice, Princess Henry of Battenberg (1857–1944), 178, 192, *193*
Bentinck, Hans Willem, Earl of Portland (1649–1709), 80, 84
Berkshire, survey, plate *8*
Birch, Henry, 197
Black Book of the Household, 27–8
Black Death, 26, 31
Boswell, James (1740–95), 96
Bradlaugh, Charles (1833–91), 183
Brett, Hon. Reginald (late Viscount Esher) (1852–1930), 201, 202, 203, 208
Brown, John (1826–83), and Victoria, 181–3, 187, 190
Bruce, Lady Augusta, 180
Brummel, Beau (George Bryan) (1778–1840), 129, 130
Buchanan, George (1506–82), 49
Buchanan, James, 169
Buckingham House (Palace), 92, 93, 224
Bulstrode, Sir Richard, 52
Burford, Earl of, and Duke of St Albans, (Charles Beauclerk) (1670–1726), 74 84, 141
Burford House, 74, 75, 84, *85*
Burke, Edmund (1729–97), 94
Burnet, Gilbert (1643–1715), Bishop of Salisbury, 64, 77, 81
Burney, Charles (1726–1814), 94, 105, 129
Burney, Fanny (Mme D'Arblay) (1752–1840), 94, life at Court, 94–7, 101, 104–7, 109, 118; encounters with George III, 105–7, 109, 112, 114, 115, 116, 118

Canning, George (1770–1827), 131, 132, 145, 147
Canterbury, Archbishop of, and Henry I's coronation, 12
Carlton House, 125, 130, 135, 141
Caroline of Brunswick (1768–1821), Queen of George IV, 125, 129, 145; relations with the King, 125, 127–9, 131; scandals concerning, 126, 127; cartoon of, *128*; death, 129
Carpenter, General Benjamin, 108
Carr, Robert, Earl of Somerset (d. 1645), 53
Carteret, Sir George (d. 1680), 60
Cassel, Sir Ernest (1852–1921), 204
Castiglione, Baldassare, Count (1478–1529), his *Book of the Courtier*, 49–50
Catherine Howard (d. 1542), 5th Queen of Henry VIII, 42
Catherine Parr (1512–48), 6th Queen of Henry VIII, 43
Catherine of Aragon (1485–1536), 1st Queen of Henry VIII, 34, 36, 38, 41
Catherine of Braganza (1638–1705), Queen of Charles II, 62, 64, 75
Chambers, Sir William (1726–96), 92, 120

Chaplin, Harry, Viscount (1840–1923), 207, 212
Charles I (1600–49), 22, 75; and Buckingham, 54; character and appearance, 55–6, 57; and his Court, 56, 57; at Windsor, 58; his execution, 59; burial at Windsor, 59
Charles II (1630–85), 22, 61, 83, 86; character and appearance 60–62, 64–6; court, 60, 62; women, 61–2, 74; influenced by France, 64–6; daily life, 64–6, 73–4; and the Feast of St George, 75; and Order of the Garter, 75; and Duke of York, 77
Charles, Prince of Castile, 35, 36
Charlotte Augusta, Princess (1796–1817), 123, 125; character, 125–6; marriage, 127; memorial to, *126*
Charlotte Sophia (1744–1818), Queen of George III, 92–3, *117*, 145; attendants, 94, 96, 103, 105, 118; daily life, 94–6; relations with King, 106, 108–118, 123; last years, 123
Chaucer, Geoffrey (1340?–1400), 20, 31
Chiffinch, William (1602?–88), 65
Chivalry, 15–17; and the Round Table, 17; Orders of, 20
Christian IV, King of Denmark (1577–1648), 50
Churchill, John, Duke of Marlborough (1650–1722), 84, 87, 88
Churchill, Lord Randolph (1849–94), 181
Churchill, Sarah, Duchess of Marlborough (1660–1744), *84*, 84–5, 86
Churchill, Sir Winston, 208, 222, 224
Clark, Sir James (1788–1870), 158, 176
Conroy, Sir John, 157–8
Constant, Benjamin (1845–1902), 199
Conyngham, Lady (d. 1861), George IV and, 132–4, 135, 142, 143, 148; leaves Windsor, 148; cartoon, *133, 147*
Conyngham, Lord (1766–1832), 132, 133, 143
Conyngham, Lord Francis, 155, 165
Cranfield, Sir Lionel, Earl of Middlesex (1575–1645), 51
Creevey, Thomas (1768–1838), 141, 154–6
Crofts, James, Duke of Monmouth (1649–1685), 78
Croker, John Wilson (1780–1857), 141
Crusades, 14, 19–20
Cumberland Lodge, 84
Cust, Sir Edward (1794–1878), 169

Dalton, John Neale, 213
Darnley, Lord (1545–67), 49
David II (1324–71), King of Scotland, 18
Davidson, Randall Thomas, Baron (1848–1930), Archbishop of Canterbury, 183
Davis, Moll, 74
De Grammont, Count, 62, 77, 82
Delany, Mary (1700–88), 105, *105*, 105–6
Desbrowe, Colonel, 96

Devereux, Robert Earl of Essex (1566–1601), 43
Dilke, Sir Charles Wentworth (1843–1911), 183, 212
Disraeli, Benjamin, Earl of Beaconsfield (1804–81), 180, 182, 187, 192
Dudley, Robert, Earl of Leicester (1532?–1588), 43, 47

Edward I (1239–1307), 14
Edward II (1234–1327), 14
Edward III (1312–77), 19; character, 15, 17; begins a Round Table, 16–17; and the Order of the Garter, 14, 18–25 passim; Court dress, 26
Edward IV (1442–83), plate 1, 23; and the Royal Household, 27–8; character, 29–30; Court life, 29–31; St George's Chapel, 31, 57; grave of, 32
Edward VI (1537–53), 40, 43; and the Order of the Garter, 75
Edward VII (1841–1910), 181, 197, 199; as Prince of Wales, 172, 176, 186, 187, 194, 196–200; marriage, 180–81, 200, 205, 207; upbringing, 196–8; character, 197, 198–9, 207–8, 213; insistence on regulations concerning dress, 198–9, 200, 205–6; sitting-room, 203; public reputation, 199–201; kingly duties, 201–2, 205–6; the aristocracy, 203; friends, 203–4, 210; bathroom, 209; members of his Household, 206; punctuality, 206; dog Caesar, 208, 209; ordinary life, 209–10; European reputation, 211–12; last days, 212; his children, 219–20; influence on Edward VIII, 220
Edward VIII (Duke of Windsor) (b. 1894), 220; and his father, 216–17, 218, 220, 222; early years, 219–20; character, 220–21, 222; and Mrs Simpson, 221; as King, 221; his abdication, 221–2
Edward, Prince of Wales (the Black Prince) (1330–76), 20
Eleanor of Aquitaine, Queen (1122?–1204), 10
Elizabeth I (1533–1603), 39, 40, 44; character and appearance, 42–6, 47; and her Court, 45–7, 49–50, 51
Elizabeth II (b. 1926), 227, early years, 225–6; character, 226; as Queen, 226–8; criticism, 228
Elizabeth (1596–1662), Queen of Bohemia, 53, 55
Elizabeth of York (1465–1503), Queen of Henry VII, 30, 34
Elizabeth Woodville (1437?–92), Queen of Edward IV, 29–30, 33
Elizabeth, Duchess of York (1900), Queen of George VI, 223, 224, 224; and her children, 226
Elizabeth, Princess (1770–1840), 105, 106, 117, 129
Elphinstone, Margaret Mercer, Vicountess Keith (1788–1867), 126
Emma, Queen of Sandwich Islands, 183
Engelard de Cicogné, 13–14

Ernest Augustus, Duke of Cumberland (1771–1851), 121, 135; scandal concerning, 146
Errol, Lord, 149–50
Esher, Lord, see Brett, Reginald
Esterhazy, Prince Paul, 131–2
Eton College, 57, 97, 156, 181, 195; Henry VI and, 27
Evelyn, John (1620–1706), 61, 67, 69, 71, 73, 76, 78

Fairfax, Thomas, Baron (1612–71), 58
Fiennes, Celia, 84
Finch, Lady Charlotte, 114
Fisher, John Arbuthnot, Baron (1841–1920), 203
FitzClarence, Lord Frederick (1794–1842), 149
FitzClarence, George Augustus, Earl of Munster, (1794–1842), 149
Fitzherbert, Maria Anne (1756–1837), wife of George IV, 124, 125, 128, 130, 143; William IV and, 150
Fitzroy, General, 122
Fort Belvedere, 221, 222
Franklin, Benjamin (1706–90), 118
Frederick, Prince of Wales (1707–51), 89
Frederick Augustus, Duke of York (1763–1827), 107, 121, 122, 130; his death and funeral, 144–5
Frogmore, 123, 174, 176, 179, 181, 219; interior of mausoleum, plate 17
Froissart, Jean (c. 1333–1405), 19, 20
Fulford, Roger, 164, 225

Garrick, David (1717–79), 94, 104
Garth, Captain Thomas, 145
Garth, General Thomas, 145
Gassiot, Mrs Sebastian, 168
George I (1660–1727), 89, 90
George II (1683–1760), 89, 90
George III (1738–1820), 119; character and attainments, 89–90, 98–9, 100; family relations, 93–4, 96, 106, 107, 111, 115, 119, 120, 130; Queen's Lodge and, 92; his Court life, 93, 94–7, 102–4; his Presence Chamber, 101; his interests, 97–100; in Windsor uniform, 97; and his servants, 99; and his family, 103; and religion, 100; meetings with Fanny Burney, 105–7, 109; his insanity, 108–12, 114–21, 122; treatment of, 108–17; at Kew, 114–15; at Weymouth, 117; and Amelia's death, 122–3; last years, 123–4
George IV (1762–1830), as Prince of Wales, 107, 124–8, 125; and father, 112, 117, 118, 130; relations with wife, 125, 127–8; cartoon of, 128, 133, 147; character, 124–5, 129–31, 134; and politicians, 131–2, 147, 153; Lady Conyngham, 132–4; and Knighton, his eccentricity, 134–5, 144, 146–7; Roman Catholic emancipation, 135, 146, 147; and rebuilding of Castle, 136–41, 143; Virginia Water, 141–2; daily life, 143; ex-

travagances, 143–4; last years, 146–8; death, 147–8
George V (1865–1936), 214, 217; and father's death, 213, 214; character, 213–15, 216–18; as King, 215, 218; daily life, 217–18; his children, 216–17, 219–20, 222–3, 229; during the War, 216; attitude to younger generation, 217; death, 218
George VI (1895–1952), 223, 224; and father, 217, 222–3; accession, 222; early years, 222–3; character, 223, 224, 225; resemblance to father, 223; marriage, 223; and the War, 224
George, Prince of Cambridge, 150
George, Prince of Denmark (1653–1708), Consort of Anne, 83, 84
Gibbons, Grinling (1648–1720), 73; surround by, 72
Gibbs, Mr (tutor), 197
Gladstone, William Ewart (1809–98), 162, 182
Goldsworthy, Colonel, 101–2
Goodman, Godfrey (1583–1656), Bishop of Gloucester, 53
Graves, Lord, 146
Greville, Charles (1794–1865), and Lady Conyngham, 143; and George IV, 144; and Windsor Castle, 141, 143; and the Duke of Cumberland, 145; and Queen Adelaide, 148, 152; and Victoria, 156, 157, 161, 171, 174, 185
Grey, Lady Jane (1537–54), 41
Gustavus Adolphus (1594–1632), King of Sweden, 57
Gwynn, Nell (1650–87), 74–5, 75, 84, 141

Haldane, Richard Burdon, Vicount (1856–1928), 199, 206
Halford, Sir Henry (1766–1844), 146
Hamilton, Lady Anne (1766–1846), 143
Hampton Court, 90, 92
Handel, George Frederick (1685–1759), 104, 116
Harcourt, Elizabeth Countess, 119
Harington, Sir John (1561–1612), 19, 50
Hartington, Lord (1833–1908), 188
Hastings, William, Baron (1430?–83), 30
Hastings, Lady Flora (1806–39), 158–9
Hatton, Sir Christopher (1540–91), 47
Hatzfeldt, Count, 190
Hay, James, 1st Baron (d. 1636), 51
Heberden, Dr William (1710–1801), 112
Heneage, Sir Thomas (d. 1595), 47
Henrietta Maria (1609–69), Queen of Charles I, 55, 56, 60
Henry I (1068–1135), 12; his marriage, 12
Henry II (1133–89), character and appearance, 9–10; his travelling Court, 10–11
Henry III (1207–72), 14, 22, 46
Henry IV (1367–1413), 27
Henry V (1387–1422), 27
Henry VI (1421–71), 23; Eton, 27, 31

Henry VII (1457–1509), 30, 33, n.; and the Archduke Philip, 34–7
Henry VIII (1491–1547), 22, 37, 57, 88; the Poor Knights, 25; funeral procession 33–4; character and appearance, 34, 37–40; Archduke Philip, 34–6; Court, 39–40, 46; lack of privacy, 40; and Knights of the Garter, 39
Herschel, Sir William (1792–1871), 98
Hervey, Lord, 93
Hill, Abigail (Lady Abigail Masham), 84, 85
Hollar, Wenceslaus (1607–77), 56, 68; preparatory drawings by, 65
Howard, John (1726?–90), 98
Hudson, Jeffrey (1619–82), 56
Hyde, Anne (1637–71), Duchess of York, 79, 82
Hyde, Edward, Earl of Clarendon (1609–1674), 62

Ibach, Josias, 73
Ingestre, Lady Flora, 159

James I (1566–1625), 49, 89; character and appearance, 48–9, 51–5; his Court, 49–51; love of hunting, 52, 54; and young men, 52–3; and his children, 53–4
James II (1633–1701), his character, 77–8; and the Papal Envoy, 78–9
Jane Seymour (1509?–37), 3rd Queen of Henry VIII, 34, 38
Jenner, Dr (later Sir) William (1815–98), 176, 178
Jersey, Lady, 125
Joane, Countess of Salisbury, 18, 20
John (1167–1216), 10; at Windsor, 13; signs Magna Carta, 13
Johnson, Samuel (1709–84), 94, 96, 117
Jonson, Ben, (1573?–1637), 50
Jordan, Mrs Dorothea (1762–1816), 148
Juana, Queen of Castile, 34–5

Kensington Palace, 90, 153, 157
Kent, Victoria Mary, Duchess of (1786–1861), 153–4, 156; and Victoria, 157–8, 164; her death, 176
Keppel, Arnoud van, Earl of Albemarle (1669–1718), 80
Keppel, Mrs George, 205, 207
Kéroualle, Louise Renée de, Duchess of Portsmouth (1649–1734), 74, 75
Kew, 114–15
Knight, Charles (1791–1873), 110
Knights of the Garter, choir stall, plate 2
Knighton, Sir William (1776–1836), George IV and, 141, 146, 147; and Lady Conyngham, 143
Labouchère, Henry (1831–1912), 206
Laud, William (1573–1645), Archbishop of Canterbury, 56
Lee, Sir Sidney (1859–1926), 202, 210
Lehzen, Baroness, 157–8, 162–4
Lennox, Charles, Duke of Richmond, 98
Lennox, Lady Sarah, 93
Leopold of Saxe-Coburg, Prince, King of

the Belgians (1790–1865), 127, 152, 154, 157, 181
Letellier, Mme, 207
Lieven, Dorothea, Princess (1784–1857), 130, 132, 134
Lipton, Sir Marcus, 204
Liverpool, Lord, 133
Loubet, President (1838–1929), 212
Louis de la Gruthuyse, Governor of Holland, at Windsor with Edward IV, 30–31
Louis Philippe (1773–1850), King, at Windsor, 163, 184, 185, 186; and Queen Victoria, plate 16
Lyttelton, Lady, 171, 172

Macaulay, Thomas Babington, Lord (1800–1859), 169
Margaret, Princess (b. 1930), 226
Martino, Eduardo de, 204
Mary I (1516–58), character and appearance, 41–2, 43
Mary II (1662–94), 79, 80, 81–2
Mary, Princess of Orange (1631–60), 80
Mary (formerly Princess of Teck) (1867–1953), Queen of George V, 214, 215, 217, 218, 226; her interest in objects of art, 215; character, 215–16; and her husband, 218; attitude to Mrs Simpson and her son, 221
Mary of France (1496–1533), 35, 36
Mary of Modena (1658–1718), Queen of James II, 78
Mary Queen of Scots (1542–87), 49
Mary, Princess, Duchess of Gloucester, (1776–1857), 123, 142, 147
May, Hugh (1622–84), 69
May, Princess, see Mary, Queen of George V
Mazarin, Duchesse, 74
Melbourne, William Lamb, Viscount (1779–1848), 153; and Victoria, 155, 156, 157, 158, 159, 164
Mersey, Lord, 208
Montgomery, Earl of, 53
Montrose, Duchess of, 159
Moore, Sir John (1761–1809), 121
Morland, Sir Samuel (1625–95), 73
Mount Charles, Lord, 135, 143
Muckle, John, 56
Murray, Dr Margaret, 20

Napoleon III (1808–73), at Windsor, 173, 184, 185–6
Nash, John (1752–1835), and Windsor, 128, 130; design for a bridge, 137
Nicholas I, Tsar (1796–1855), at Windsor, 167, 172, 184, 185
Nicolas, Sir Harris, and the Order of the Garter, 20
Nicolson, Sir Harold, 213
Norden, John (1548–1625?), 73
North, Lord (1732–92), 113

O'Connell, Daniel (1775–1847), 137
O'Reilly, Surgeon, 143, 146
Oglander, Sir John (1585–1655), 52
Order of the Garter, 57, 68, 114; stories of its origin, 18–20; first members,

20; robes, 21–2; patrons, 22; regalia of, 21; installation fees, 22; St George's Chapel, 23, 57; Feast of St George, 75, 120; restored to splendour by Charles II, 75–6; George III and, 120–21
Orléans, Duchess of, 80
Orléans, Duke of (1747–93), 129
Ormathwaite, Lord, 205
Osborne, 174, 178, 182
Overbury, Sir Thomas (1581–1613), 53

Paget family, 165
Palmer, Barbara, Countess of Castlemaine and Duchess of Cleveland (1641–1709), 60, 62, 74
Palmerston, Lady, 161
Palmerston, Lord (1784–1865), 190
Papendiek, Christopher, 145
Peel, Sir Robert (1788–1850), 131, 145, 147, 153; Victoria and, 159, 173
Penn, William (1644–1718), 64
Pepys, Sir Lucas (1742–1830), 112
Pepys, Samuel (1633–1703), 61, 62, 69, 74, 76
Perrers, Alice (d. 1400), 25
Persia, Shah of, Victoria and, 186–7
Peter of Blois (fl. 1160–1204), 10
Philip, HRH Prince, Duke of Edinburgh, (b. 1921), 227, 228–9, 230; character, 228–30
Philip II (1527–98), King of Spain, 41
Philip the Handsome, Archduke of Austria, at Windsor, 34–7, 41
Pitt, William (1759–1806), 104, 118
Ponsonby, Sir Frederick, 191, 192, 207
Ponsonby, Sir Henry (1825–95), 186, 191
Probyn, General Sir Dighton, 206

Radcliffe, Dr John (1650–1714), 82
Raikes, Robert (1735–1811), 98
Raincliffe, Gracie, Countess of Londesborough, 207
Raleigh, Sir Walter (1552?–1618), 43, 51
Reid, Sir James, 190, 191
Reith, Sir John (later Lord), 221
Reresby, Sir John (1634–89), 62, 73
Reynolds, Sir Joshua (1723–92), 94, 104
Ribblesdale, Lord, 178, 188
Richard I (1157–99), 19, 20, 23; character, 13
Richard II (1367–1400), 26; Court dress, 26; Court meals and customs, 26–7
Richard III (1452–85), 34
Richbell, Richard and Jeffrey, 54
River Thames at Windsor, plate 11
Rosebery, Lord, 199
Royal Household, under Henry II, 10–11; in fourteenth century, 26–7; fifteenth-century reforms, 27–8; rules and manners, 28–9; attendants on the King, 28–9; under Edward IV, 29–30; under Henry VII and VIII, 37–8; the Monarch's lack of privacy, 40; forced to move for sanitary reasons, 46; under Elizabeth I, 45–6, 50–51; under James I, 49, 50, 51–2,

53; under Charles I, 56; under George III, 93ff., 99, 100ff; expenses of George IV, 143–4; William IV's economies, 151–2; Prince Albert's reorganization, 165–7; anomalies in its running, 165–6; servants' wages, 166; its formality under Victoria, 168–9, 192; its unpopularity, 183; Edward VII's advent, 201ff.

Royal Lodge, *129*

Rupert, Prince (1619–82), 67

St George's Chapel, 23, 25, 36, 230; roof, *12*; from the altar, plate 5; west end, plate 6; its Poor Knights, 22, 24–5, 76; relics, 23; pilgrimage badges, *23*; misappropriation of donations, 24–5; Gilbertus Door, *24*; choir stall plate, *28*; its rebuilding, 31; misericord in, *31*; during the Civil War, 57–8; and the Feast of St George, 75; restored by Charles II, 75–6, *76*; George III and, 94, 100, 101, 104, 121; Victoria and, 178, 179

St George's Hall, 63; at the time of the Regency, *149*

Salisbury, Bishop of, 12

Sandby, Paul (1725–1809) and Thomas (1721–98), 141

Sardinia, King of, 184, 185

Saxony, King of, 190

Schorne, John, 23

Schwellenberg, Mme, 94–5, 96

Sellis, Mr and Mrs, 121–2, 145

Semon, Sir Felix (1849–1921), 204

Seymour, Charles, Duke of Somerset (1662–1748), 76

Seymour, Thomas, Baron (1508?–49), 43

Shakespeare, William (1564–1616), 50, 104

Sheffield, Sir Charles, 92

Sheridan, Richard Brinsley (1751–1816), 61, 130

Shore, Jane (d. 1527?), 29

Siddons, Sarah (1755–1831), 104

Sigismund, Emperor (1368–1437), 23

Simpson, Mrs Wallis *see* Windsor, Duchess of

Sophia, Princess, scandal concerning, 145

Soveral, Marquis de, 204

Stockmar, Baron (1787–1863), 175, 197; character, 162; and the Household, 165–6

Stonor, Sir Harry, 206

Strachey, Lytton, 178, 185

Strathavon, Lord, 150, 156

Stubbs, John (1543?–91), 47

Sutherland, Duchess of (1806–68), 185

Swift, Jonathan (1667–1745), 86

Taylor, Colonel Sir Herbert (1775–1839), 145

Temple, William (1881–1944), Archbishop of Canterbury, 218

Thackeray, William Makepeace (1811–63), 130, 169

Thynne, Lady Caroline, 145

Topcliffe, Robert. 43

Trevelyan, Sir George (1838–1928), 183

Turkey, Sultan of, Victoria and, 186

Van Dyck, Sir Anthony (1599–1641), 56

Vanderbilt, Consuelo (Duchess of Marlborough), 190, 205, 242

Venn, Colonel John (1586–1650), 57, 58

Vere, Lady Susan, 53

Verrio, Antonio (c. 1640–1707), 71, 120; ceilings by, *70*, *71*

Victoria (1819–1901), plate *15*, *161*, *170*, *173*, *182*; George IV at Virginia Water, 142; William IV and, 153; manner and appearance, 155; character, 155–6; and Melbourne, 156–7, 159; and mother, 158–9; Flora Hastings, 158, 159; becomes unpopular 159; Bedchamber Plot, 159; marriage, 160, 161; relations with husband, 161–2, 171–2, 174; formalities of Court, 168–9, 170–71, 172–3, 187ff.; at breakfast, *189*; Louis Philippe, plate *16*; her children, 175, 176; husband's death, 176–9; son's marriage, 180–81; relations with John Brown, 181–3; attitude to servants, 182–3; criticisms of Household, 183–5; receptions of royalty, 185–7; emergence from seclusion 187–8; behaviour at meals, 188–90, 192; inflexible morality, 190; attitude to smoking, 190; her increasing cantankerousness, 191–2; as an institution, 192–3; last years, 194–6; funeral procession, *195*; and Prince of Wales, 196–7, 199–200, 202–3; *Highland Journals*, 187

Victoria, Princess Royal (1840–1901), 175

Victoria, Princess (1868–1935), 194, 205

Villiers, Elizabeth, Countess of Orkney (1657?–1733), 80, 82

Villiers, George, Duke of Buckingham (1592–1628), 53, 52–4, 55, 56

Villiers, George William, Earl of Clarendon (1800–70), 175

Virginia Water, *140*, 141–2, 143, 162

Walpole, Horace, Earl of Orford (1717–1797), 69, 80, 120

Warren, Richard (1731–97), 112

Weldon, Sir Anthony (d. 1649?), 51, 54

Wellington, Arthur Wellesley, Duke of (1769–1852), 130, 137, 145, 147, 150; and Mrs Arbuthnot, 132, 146; and Lady Conyngham, 132, 133; and George IV, 135, 146, 147; and Victoria, 159; his deafness, 172

West, Benjamin (1738–1820), 104, 180; view of Windsor Great Park, 90

Wheeler-Bennett, Sir John, 223, 235

Whitchcott, Colonel Christopher, 58

Wigram, Lord, 221

Wilberforce, Samuel (1805–73), Bishop, 180

Whitelock, Bulstrode (1605–75), 66–7

William I (1027–87), 11, 12

William II (d. 1100), 12

William III (1650–1702), 79–82, 87

William II (1859–1942), Emperor of Germany, 181, 184, 212

William IV (1765–1837), as Duke of Clarence, 107, 117; his illegitimate children, 148–50; behaviour on accession, 150, 151; his tactlessness, 150; character, 150; daily life, 152; and his Ministers, 152–3; and the Duchess of Kent, 153, 157; death, 154

William Augustus, Duke of Cumberland (1721–65), 141, 219

William of Mulsho, 31

William of Wykeham (1324–1404), 31

Willis, Dr Francis (and sons), 113–15

Windsor, Duchess of (Mrs Wallis Simpson), (b. 1896), character, 221; Edward VIII and, 221

Windsor Castle, *8*, *229*, *231*; site, 11–12; Normans and, *12*; new buildings, *13*, *14*, 31; earthworks, *11*; building materials, 13, 17, 47; besieged, 13–14, 57; centre of Court life, 13, 15, 39; in 1607, 46; stabling of horses, 46; Elizabeth I and, 47, 50; James I and, 52, 54, plate 3; Civil War, 57–8, 66; Charles II and, 60, 64, plate 4, 66, 68, 73; drawing by Hollar, 65; duties of Constable, 66–7; bird's eye view, *1670*, 67; drawing by Hollar, *68*; in 1680, 69; May and, 69–70; Morland's water device, 73; Anne and, 83, 84–8, 89; in *1705*, 81; north terrace, *87*; and early Hanoverians, 89, 90; George III and, 90, 92–3, 98, 99, 104, 117, 118–20; view of north front, *107*; uniform for, 98; view through Queen Elizabeth's Gate, *109*; summer house, plate *7*; from Great Park, plate 9; Guard Room, plate *10*; views by Paul Sandby, *110*, *111*; Wyatt and, 120; The Hundred Steps, *122*; George IV and, 128, 134, 135–42; rebuilding by Wyatville, 135–42, plate *14*; design by Sir Robert Smirke, *136*; design for Grand Corridor, *138*; William IV and, 148–9, 150–52; rebuilding, 151; east front, 1824, plate *12*; alterations to east front, plate *13*; Victoria and, 155–6, 159–60; Albert and, 162, 163, 166; The Riding School, *164*; servants' wages, 166; Upper Ward, *167*; Reubens Room, *170*; lack of drainage, 176; Blue Room, *177*; criticisms of expenditure on, 183; Crimson Drawing Room, *184*; view across park, *188*; Edward VII and, 202, 203, 205–207, 208, 210, 212; royal gathering, 1907, 211; Edward VIII and, 214, 221; during War, 225–6; Elizabeth II and, 225–6; historical memories, 230

Wren, Sir Christopher (1632–1723), 69, 88

Wyatt, James (1746–1813), 120

Wyatt (Wyatville), Sir Jeffrey (1766–1840), Windsor Castle, 135–42, 152; Great Drawing Room by, *139*, 219

Yugoslavia, Queen of, 229